The Global Crisis and Korea's International Financial Policies

Thomas D. Willett

With contributions by
Nancy N. Auerbach
Kenneth S. Kim
Yoonmin Kim
Alice Ouyang
Orawan Permpoon
Thana Sompornserm
Lalana Srisorn
Ozan Sula

Korea Economic Institute • 1800 K Street NW, Suite 1010 • Washington, DC 20006
Telephone 202/464-1982 • Facsimile 202/464-1987 • Web address www.keia.org

Library of Congress Cataloging-in-Publication Data

Willett, Thomas D.
   The global crisis and Korea's international financial policies / Thomas D.
Willett ; with contributions by Nancy N. Auerbach ... [et al.].
      p. cm.
   Includes bibliographical references.
   ISBN 978-0-9747141-9-6
   1. Finance--Korea (South) 2. Monetary policy--Korea (South) 3.
Global Financial Crisis, 2008-2009. I. Title.
   HG187.K6W55 2009
   332'.042095195--dc22

                                          2009042680

Contents

	Foreword	iv
	Preface	v
1	Introduction and Overview	1
2	Korea's Exchange Rate Policies between the Crises	11
3	Dangers of Pegged Exchange Rates and Advantages of Inflation Targeting	39
4	International Reserve Adequacy	48
5	Financial Liberalization and International Capital Flows	58
6	International Aspects of Korea's Monetary Policies	76
7	Creating a Common Asian Currency Is the Wrong Approach to Asian Monetary and Exchange Rate Cooperation	89
8	Geopolitical Considerations and Lessons from Europe for Monetary and Financial Cooperation in Asia	109
9	Similarities and Differences between the 1997–98 Crisis and the Current One	118
10	Crisis Hits Korea	125
11	Conclusions and Policy Recommendations	137
	Appendix A: Econometric Estimates of Sterilization and Offset Coefficients for Korea	147
	Appendix B: Tables in Support of Appendix A	153
	List of References	157

Foreword

The Korea Economic Institute (KEI) is pleased to issue the fifth volume of its "Special Studies" series. This series affords individual authors an opportunity to explore in depth a particular topic of current interest relating to Korea.

Completion of this study is timely. Its planning commenced well before the bankruptcy of Lehman Brothers and ensuing broadening of the turbulence in U.S. financial markets into a global financial crisis and then a severe economic slowdown. However, its comprehensive assessment of Korea's international financial policies, with a foray into the feasibility of an Asian common currency, takes on greater relevance in light of these events and the early recovery of Korea's economy and financial markets. Dr. Thomas D. Willett, assisted by a number of coauthors of individual chapters and sections, provides not only a comprehensive assessment of Korea's policies but also considerable insight into issues such as the adequacy of foreign exchange reserves that are part of the debate on reform of the international financial architecture.

KEI is dedicated to objective, informative analysis. We welcome comments on this and our other publications. We seek to expand contacts with academic and research organizations across the country and would be pleased to entertain proposals for other "Special Studies."

Charles L. (Jack) Pritchard
President
October 2009

Preface

I have accumulated many debts in the preparation of this study. Chapter 2 draws heavily on a paper with Kim Yongbok, "Assessing Korea's Post Crisis Managed Float," that was prepared for a Bank of Korea workshop in 2004. A shortened version of that paper written with Kim Yongbok was published by the Korea Economic Institute in *Korea's Economy 2006,* with the title "Korea's Postcrisis Exchange Rate Policy." Chapter 2 has been substantially revised and updated with the assistance of coauthor Kenneth S. Kim, current Claremont Graduate University dissertation student. After completing his dissertation at Claremont, Kim Yongbok returned to the Bank of Korea, and neither he nor the Bank has responsibility for the policy views expressed. Chapter 2 as well as portions of Chapters 9 and 10 benefited from helpful comments by participants in the 2009 annual meetings of the Asia-Pacific Economic Association and Western Economic Association International.

Chapter 4 on the subject of demand for international reserves was cowritten with recent Claremont graduate Ozan Sula and draws on earlier research of Jung Sik Kim et al. (2004) for the Claremont-KIEP Conference on *Monetary and Exchange Rate Arrangements in East Asia.* Chapter 5 on financial liberalization and international capital flows is coauthored with current Claremont doctoral students Yoonmin Kim and Thana Sompornserm. Professor Nancy N. Auerbach of Scripps College is coauthor of the first section of Chapter 5, which draws heavily on our joint paper, "The Political Economy of Perverse Financial Liberalization," presented at a conference on the Korean economy at the University of Washington. Yoonmin Kim is also coauthor of section 2 of Chapter 10. Chapter 6 on international dimensions of Korean monetary policy was cowritten with recent Claremont graduate Alice Ouyang, who is now on the faculty at the Central University of Finance and Economics in Beijing. She is the primary author of Appendix A and Appendix B on the estimation of sterilization and offset coefficients. Chapters 7 and 8 draw heavily on the research for my joint paper, entitled "Asian Monetary Cooperation: Perspectives from the European Experience and Optimum Currency Area Analysis," written with recent Claremont graduate Orawan Permpoon, now with the Thai Ministry of Foreign Affairs, and current Claremont dissertation student Lalana Srisorn. This was first presented in November 2007 at a joint Claremont-KEI-KIEP workshop on the subject of Asian monetary cooperation at which many highly useful comments were received. Orawan is coauthor of Chapter 7 of this study, and Lalana is coauthor of Chapter 8.

This study draws more broadly on the ongoing research projects of the Claremont Institute for Economic Policy Studies on Asian economic cooperation, on currency and financial crises, and on reform of the international financial architecture. Financial support for this underlying research from the Freeman Foundation, KEI, and the National Science Foundation is gratefully acknowledged, as are the skills of the Institute's able administrator, Lynda Marquez, and my assistant, Lalana Srisorn. Extremely valuable comments by M. K. Kang, James Lister, Kwanho Shin, and Ted Truman on the entire manuscript and by Helen Popper on Chapter 2 are also gratefully acknowledged.

Thomas D. Willett
Director, Claremont Institute for Economic Policy Studies
and Horton Professor of Economics
Claremont Graduate University and Claremont McKenna College

1

Introduction and Overview

The global crisis that was ignited by the meltdown in the U.S. subprime mortgage market is a dramatic illustration of just how interdependent our economic and financial systems have become. The spread of the crisis from a downturn in a major real sector of the U.S. economy to the financial market most connected to it was to be expected. What caught many people, including experts, by surprise was how the crisis kept spreading to a much wider set of financial and credit markets in the United States and other industrial countries, then to a much broader set of countries around the globe—and then from the financial to the real sectors. The resulting recessions in the industrial countries spread the damage to many developing and emerging-market countries that had little direct financial connection with the fancy derivatives products that contributed so much to the initial spread of the crisis. In this process, Korea was in an intermediate position. It had little direct exposure to securities based on the U.S. subprime market, but its high level of financial interdependence made it the Asian country hardest hit when global financial markets seized up.

While less dramatic, economic and financial interdependence is also important in more ordinary times. International developments frequently have an important impact on an economy as open as Korea's. Witness the large international capital flows, both into and out of the Korean economy, in the years between the Asian crisis of 1997–98 and this one. These capital flows were strongly affected by policies in Korea as well as external developments, and, in turn, these flows had substantial effects on the exchange rate of the *won*. Such flows can have important implications for a wide range of domestic and international policies such as domestic monetary policies and the management of international reserves; and the flows have fueled debates about such issues as whether Korea has lost much of its control over its domestic monetary policy, whether Korea should rethink its strategy of progressive financial liberalization, and whether Korea should revise its exchange-rate policies. For many of these issues the best policy choices depend on the policies that are being adopted by one's trading and financial partners. Thus, concern with the broad scope of Korea's international financial policies involves issues such as the debates over Asian monetary and financial cooperation, the pros and cons of trying to establish a common currency in Asia, and reform of the International Monetary Fund (IMF) and the global financial system. In the midst of the crisis, some of these issues have become more urgent and others have been put on the back burner, but all of them remain important over the medium term.

Most of these issues are too complex to evaluate adequately on the basis of one's economic philosophy alone. The debate over fixed versus flexible exchange rates, for example, cuts across traditional ideological divides. Indeed, modern international monetary analysis concludes that there is simply no one best type of exchange rate regime for all countries. Fixed rates are better for some countries; flexible rates for others. Thus, to discuss such issues sensibly, we need to know a good deal of international monetary analysis—and a lot about the specific conditions facing a country. Likewise, how much international financial interdependence affects a country's ability to conduct national monetary policies effectively requires careful empirical research. The answer will vary greatly from one country to another. Thus, this overview of the key issues facing Korea's international financial policies has required a lengthy effort. Indeed, in some cases it has even been necessary to assess substantial debates about what Korea's policies are. Some experts have argued, for example, that Korea's exchange rate policy has been a free float, while others have gone to almost the opposite extreme and argued that Korea is still on a soft-dollar standard.

For those primarily concerned with the global crisis and how it has affected middle-income countries like Korea, this issue is not of major importance, but for economists and officials concerned with Korea's exchange rate policy it is crucial. Because of the wide range of likely interests of potential readers, we have paid considerable attention to presenting our analysis in a way that can be used for a number of different purposes. For example, those interested only in a broad overview of the crisis and how it has affected Korea need read only this introduction and the last three chapters, while a specialist interested in only a particular aspect of Korea's international financial policy can read only the chapter that covers that aspect. Although some of the chapters include rather technical original research, we have included sections in each chapter that can be read by those without strong expertise in economics and finance. In Chapter 2, for example, someone interested only in the broad issues involving Korean exchange rate policy should be able to read the first and last sections while skipping the more technical analysis in the middle.

The following section offers a broad overview of today's global crisis and highlights key similarities and differences between it and the Asia crisis of 1997–98 and their effects on the Korean economy. The final section offers a brief chapter-by-chapter overview of the study.

Korea in Crisis

The summer of 2007 saw the appearance of the first public signs that the downturn in the U.S. housing market might have broader ramifications in financial markets. This was exactly 10 years after the crisis in Thailand set off the Asian currency and financial crises. Psychologists tell us that we are much more likely to learn from our own tragedies than from those of others, and that certainly appears to be the case with the current crisis. As the Thai crisis went regional and resulted in economic devastation throughout much of Asia, the U.S. crisis has gone global. Compared with the situation in 1997, most Asian economies, including Korea's, were in far stronger positions today to deal with the present financial debacle, but this didn't mean they could fully escape its impact.

Careful diagnosis of the Asian crisis of a decade ago suggests that it was due less to the bad exchange rate policies and irrational contagion than was originally thought and more to a wide range of financial excesses.[1] While many of the specifics of the causes of the current global crisis differ considerably from those of the Asian crisis, a central thesis of this study is that the fundamental causes are actually quite similar. They lie in perverse incentive structures and a lack of sound prudential supervision combined with a degree of laziness in doing due diligence, herd behavior by investors, and overconfidence in sophisticated but fundamentally flawed risk management systems (which led banks and financial-market participants to take on far more risk than they realized). The result of such widespread excesses in both investment and borrowing decisions was that, when a crisis hit in one country, it served as a wake-up call that led to much broader reevaluations of risk positions and a repricing of risks. The result both a decade ago in the Asian crisis and today was a spread of crisis conditions far beyond those implied by direct economic interdependence. In other words, much of the spread of both crises was due to belated recognition of widespread financial excesses. And, as occurs in

---

1. See the analysis and references in Agenor et al. (1999); Desai (2003), Dooley and Frankel (2004), Edwards and Frankel (2002, 11–30), Eichengreen (1999, 2002), Furman and Stiglitz (1998), Goldstein (2002), Haggard (2000), Horowitz and Heo (2001), Mishkin (2006), Noble and Ravenhill (2000), Pempel (1999), Radelet and Sachs (1998), Rakshit (2002), and Willett et al. (2005).

such situations, the huge increase in risk aversion causes collateral damage to many who had not themselves engaged in the excesses.

The Asian crisis hit Korea so hard because Korea had been subject to many of the same kinds of bad investments and financial excesses that contributed to Thailand's problems. Thailand's overvalued pegged exchange rate was another major cause of its crisis. Korea's exchange rate was not similarly obviously overvalued before the crisis hit, but, as with Thailand and the other crisis countries, widespread beliefs that there was little risk of substantial depreciation contributed to massive unhedged foreign borrowing. When the Thai depreciation exploded this assumption, there was a quite rational rush for the exits, and efforts to cover open positions led in turn to a worsening of the crisis in a downward spiral quite similar to what we are seeing today on a global scale.[2] Since the AAA ratings on mortgage-backed securities became suspect and the short-term credit markets began to dry up, a wide range of overleveraged institutions have had to scramble for cash and sell assets, which in turn drives down prices further. Although such responses are often rational at the individual level, the macro implications can be devastating.

This fundamental difference between individual or micro and macro level incentives and effects is at the heart of one of the most fundamental problems with standard private sector risk management systems and national and international prudent regulatory schemes such as Basel I and Basel II. These all fail to recognize sufficiently that financial markets and credit relationships often operate quite differently during crisis than during normal periods.

Although these problems with risk management systems became clearly evident during the Asian crisis, they made little impact on investors and regulators in the industrial countries. Private investors did not repeat their specific mistake of overinvestment in Asia, but the period of extreme risk aversion that followed the Asian and Russian crises and the fall of Long-Term Capital Management (LTCM) soon gave way to new overenthusiasms for a wide range of so-called new investment opportunities, including the rapid spread of a wide range of mortgage and other types of asset-backed securities. The global economy became awash with liquidity, and leverage soared. And, while the development of new derivatives markets such as credit default swaps offered many beneficial opportunities for firms and individuals to hedge risks, they also offered opportunities for others to take on greater speculative risks.

---

2. Some financial institutions and other investors had anticipated the crisis and moved funds or covered positions before the depreciation of the baht, but the depreciation came as an unanticipated shock to a large portion of the market. The Mexican peso crisis in 1994 was similar.

Those Asian countries that had borne the brunt of the crisis in 1997–98 generally followed much more prudent policies. It seems to be one of the attributes of the human condition that we have to learn mainly from our own mistakes. Learning from the mistakes of others appears to be much more difficult. While in the industrial countries many financial-market participants deluded themselves that they had conquered risk through the marvels of financial engineering, Korea and other Asian countries rightly strengthened their domestic financial systems substantially. A recent summary in the IMF Survey by the IMF's Asia and Pacific Department (2008, 10) of the 2007 annual review of Korea says:

> Korea has done a lot in recent years to strengthen its financial sector. The payoff has been increased asset quality, profitability, and capital adequacy (that is, banks' capital is adequate to protect depositors and counterparties from balance sheet risks). At the same time, risk assessment practices and credit information have improved.

Substandard loans of the commercial banking sector fell from 3.3 percent in 2001 to less than 1 percent in 2006, while the corporate debt-equity ratio fell from more than 200 percent in 2000 to a much safer level of a little below 100 percent in 2006. Unlike in Europe, the exposure of the Korean banking system to mortgage-backed securities in the United States was quite low. And, instead of the deteriorating quality of mortgage lending that occurred in the United States, the structure of financing for the Korean housing market has improved, with a decline in the proportion of balloon payments or bullet-type mortgages in which the repayment of principal takes place in a lump sum at the end of the loan term.

This is not to say that Korea has completely avoided financial excesses since the 1997–98 crisis. Poor quality bank lending to firms before the crisis was replaced with an excessive expansion of credit card debt after the crisis. This binge was brought under control, albeit not before a minor crisis was generated. But the delinquency rate on credit card debt that had risen from 7.5 percent in 2000 to almost 12 percent in 2002 fell to below 3 percent by 2006.

Financial institutions in Korea have also carried out some highly questionable practices, perhaps the most bilateral being the so-called KIKO scandal, in which several banks took advantage of small- and medium-sized Korean exporters that were seeking to hedge their future export proceeds against the continuing appreciation of the *won*. As explained in Chapter 10, instead of offering these firms standard forward contracts, several banks took advantage of the lack of financial expertise of many of these small firms to sell them complicated options contracts that protected them against only a limited range of appreciation of the *won* and exposed them to unlimited potential losses if the *won* began to depreciate. When the *won* unexpectedly reversed course, the large resulting losses threatened many of these firms with bankruptcy. These contracts were so blatantly biased that they were declared illegal by the courts.

A major source of concern to many observers was the explosion of bank borrowing from abroad that began in 2006. Although this was monitored by the authorities and judged to be safe because the borrowing was undertaken mainly by Korean branches of international banks or was "covered" by future export receipts, such borrowing was viewed as a source of concern by many market participants after the crisis began. Analysts also focused on the withdrawal of foreign funds from the Korean stock market and the recently developed dependence of the Korean banking system on wholesale financing from the capital markets, not just customer deposits. Concerns have also been expressed about speculation in the market for forward exchange.

As a result of such factors, Korea was hit by the financial fallout from the crisis much harder than any other Asian economy. Thanks in part to the strong international reserve position that had been developed, Korea has pulled through that phase of the crisis rather successfully. It has shared with the other export-oriented Asian economies the next phase of the global crisis, the substantial slowdown in international trade. Unlike in 1997–98, however, Korea was in a position to adopt strong monetary and financial stimulus and thus has been able to cushion the effects of the world trade downturn to a substantial degree. Thus, the effects of the crisis on Korea, while certainly negative, have been far less disastrous than many had feared.

Outline and Overview of the Study

In the wake of the 1997–98 crisis, Korea initiated a number of important changes in policy. These included the adoption of a managed float for the *won*, inflation targeting as the primary objective of monetary policy, substantial additional domestic and international financial liberalization and strengthening of prudential regulation and supervision, and the accumulation of a strong international reserve position. These developments are analyzed in Chapters 2 through 6.

Chapter 2 reviews Korea's post–Asian crisis exchange rate policies. While Korea's policy is often described by officials—and some independent studies have concurred—as a freely floating rate, it is shown that it has in fact been a managed float as evidenced by Korea's large accumulation of reserves. It is argued that this is indeed a very appropriate type of policy strategy for a medium-sized economy, such as Korea's, that is heavily engaged in international trade and investment. Although one can always second-guess exactly how a regime is managed, in general Korean exchange rate management receives good marks. During the long period of upward pressure on the *won*, too much emphasis likely was placed on limiting appreciation, resulting in reserve accumulations that were excessive by many standards of reserve adequacy; but the high levels of reserve accumulation that resulted from this policy look much more desirable in light of the strains of the current crisis.

In Chapter 3, it is argued that the combination of a managed float and inflation targeting that Korea adopted after the crisis is a much superior approach to monetary stability than the strategy of exchange rate pegging advocated by some. It is more robust to a wide range of shocks and is better at dealing with the problems of time inconsistency, where policies that bring short-run benefits lead to longer-run costs.

In Chapter 4 we review new developments in the analysis of international reserve adequacy in a world of substantial international capital mobility and apply these to Korea. We make the somewhat controversial argument that, despite the large inflows of foreign capital into the Korean stock market, Korea had reached quite adequate international reserve levels by the first year or two of this decade, and the continued large reserve accumulations were not justified on these grounds. The large capital outflows during the current crisis have fallen within the range we projected for a future crisis and are consistent with our argument that Korea had accumulated more than adequate reserve levels.

In Chapter 5 we look more closely at the post-1997 financial liberalization and the behavior of international financial flows. In Chapter 6 we evaluate the argument that such capital mobility has undermined the ability of the Bank of Korea (BOK) to carry out domestic monetary policy effectively. We conclude that large capital flows do complicate the task of monetary officials, but that they have not undercut the ability of the BOK to implement its inflation targeting.

A major thesis of this study is that, although it is quite important for Korea to play a strong role in pursuing increased Asian monetary and financial cooperation, it is also important that substantive progress not be sidetracked by excessive focus on grandiose schemes such as creation of a common Asian currency to mimic the creation of the euro in Europe.

Chapter 7 argues that a number of recent research studies have focused on too narrow a range of economic criteria and as a result have tended to overemphasize the prospective benefits relative to the costs of creating a common Asian currency in the near future. It argues that monetary integration is fundamentally different from trade and financial integration. All countries should be able to have net gains from the latter types of integration. However, monetary union implied by a common currency provides rules for the conduct of monetary policy that would not necessarily always be in the interests of all the members.

The major factors that influence the costs and benefits of adopting a common currency are delineated in the literature on the theory of optimal currency areas. From this perspective, some countries would likely gain in aggregate from a common Asian currency, but Korea is highly unlikely to be one of these any time in the near future.

Chapter 8 turns to geopolitical concerns and the lessons to be drawn from the European integration process. It is argued that much can be learned from the European experience about ways to build up mutually beneficial cooperation over time, especially with respect to the need to build up strong regional institutions. The European experience can easily be misread, however. Contrary to the superficial interpretation that functional linkages cause trade integration to inevitably generate spillovers that lead eventually to monetary integration, the process toward European monetary union was due largely to a particular set of geopolitical conditions and beliefs that are absent in Asia. Indeed, if the euro did not already exist, it probably could not be negotiated today under current European political conditions. In our interpretation, the most important geopolitical lesson from Europe is not that monetary union is inevitable but that economic integration played a powerful role in creating a peaceful Germany and healing the wounds from World War II. There is of course a strong analogy today with the prospective benefits from encouraging the peaceful integration of China into the Asian and global economies. Korea is in a strong position to help with this process.

A careful look at the European experience also calls into question two other beliefs that are popular in some quarters. One is that the development of endogenous optimal currency area analysis shows that the traditional path of the sequencing of regional integration from trade to financial to monetary integration can be bypassed and that trade and financial integration will automatically be stimulated by formation of a monetary union.

A second questionable interpretation is that a regime of adjustable exchange rate parities such as was incorporated into the European Monetary System (EMS) that preceded the creation of the euro is a desirable way to provide both exchange rate stability and monetary cooperation and should be a blueprint for the evolution of Asian monetary cooperation. It is frequently argued that this exchange rate–based approach led to substantial coordination of monetary policy in Europe. In some cases this was true, but in many others it was not. The result was serious currency crisis in 1992 and 1993.

The attractiveness of such exchange rate–based approaches is that in the short run close coordination between exchange rate and monetary policies is generally not needed. Sterilized intervention allows a degree of short-run independence between these two policy instruments. Thus, governments can get the short-run benefits of establishing exchange rate stability with little cost. The cost comes later when policies must be adjusted or the risk of currency crisis mounts. There are many advantages of international coordination of monetary and exchange rate policies among highly interdependent economies. To date, however, Asian countries have shown little willingness to engage in monetary policy coordination. Hopes that this can be brought about indirectly by the need to deepen exchange rate commitments are understandable, and this strategy has sometimes worked. History shows, however, that it also often fails and is thus a high-risk strategy. Although there is no strong presumption from pure economic theory about the optimal sequencing of exchange rate and monetary policy coordination, there are strong political-economy arguments for requiring that significant progress be made on monetary policy coordination before strong commitments on exchange rate policy are made.

Chapters 9 and 10 deal with crises. Chapter 9 discusses the major similarities and differences between the current crisis and the Asian crisis of 1997–98. This provides background for Chapter 10, which analyzes the effects of the crisis on Korea and the policy responses that have been taken. It is argued that Korea's strong international reserve position has allowed the government to take strong actions that have substantially reduced the potential negative impact of the crisis on Korea.

Chapter 11 summarizes the major conclusions of the discussion and discusses strategies for global financial reforms to make future crises less likely. As this study goes to press at the end of October 2009, it appears that the worst of the crisis is past, although the pain is far from over. It is crucial that fundamental reforms be undertaken. We will likely never be able to completely eliminate financial crises, but there is much that can be done to make them less frequent and less costly. Chapter 11 does not attempt to lay out a full blueprint for reform, but it does draw a number of lessons that should help guide reform. Fortunately the general tenor of the reform proposals coming from the U.S. government and its G-20 partners is consistent with this analysis. While there is considerable room to dispute specific features of any of the blueprints for reform that have been offered, it is important that reformers not become so caught up in the search for perfection that we play into the hands of the strong political forces that would like to maintain as much of the status quo as possible. Let us hope that this crisis will lead to as productive domestic financial reforms in the advanced economies as the Asian crisis of 1997–98 did for Asia and that this time we will do a better job of dealing with the international dimensions of financial system supervision. With its chairmanship of the G-20 for the coming year, Korea is in a strong position to help this come about.

2

Korea's Exchange Rate Policies between the Crises

This section is coauthored by Kenneth S. Kim.

Debate has been vigorous about how best to characterize countries' exchange rate policies; it has been stimulated in part by the high correlation between pegged exchange rates and currency crises in Europe in the early 1990s and in emerging-market countries since. These developments have generated great interest in propositions such as the unstable middle hypothesis that argues that adjustably pegged exchange rates are inherently unstable in a world of substantial international capital mobility as well as the stronger and more controversial two-corners or bipolar hypothesis that argues that countries must move all the way to one end of the spectrum of flexibility of exchange rate regimes, that is, to hard fixes or floating rates. Critics of this latter view argue that neither of these extreme options is desirable for many countries because a hard fix requires giving up national monetary independence and floating rates can be highly volatile and disruptive. From this perspective, less extreme options like crawling bands or managed floats can provide a more effective solution. These issues are discussed in Chapter 3.

It is perhaps a surprise that the boundary lines between different types of exchange rate regimes are sometimes far from clear-cut. Considerable evidence shows that substantial differences often exist between the exchange rate regimes countries announce they are following and their actual behavior in practice. Furthermore, despite several major research projects that develop classification based on measures of actual practice, leading researchers have come to substantially different judgments about the policies being followed by particular countries. The concept of "fear of floating" popularized by Calvo and Reinhart (2002) is based on the observation that many countries with official floating rates in practice manage these rates quite a bit. Although some have argued for going all the way to fixed exchange rates, as will be discussed in Chapter 7, this conclusion does not logically follow, and for many countries the theory of optimum currency areas (OCA) suggests that the economic costs of hard fixes would substantially exceed the benefits.

More common are soft pegs that can be adjusted to avoid imposing costly inflation or recession on domestic economies. Most of the countries hardest hit by the Asian crisis initially floated their exchange rates, but fear-of-floating behavior was soon observed for many countries. This led McKinnon and Schnabl (2004) to argue that Asia had returned to a soft dollar standard or peg. This was certainly true for China for a number of years after the crisis (as well as before), and Malaysia did adopt a peg for several years; but for countries like Korea this is not a correct description of exchange rate policy.

Officials frequently describe Korea's policy as free floating. As this chapter will show, this description goes too far in the opposite direction because Korea has intervened heavily at times in the foreign exchange market. Officials argue that this is a free float because there is no set exchange rate target. This statement is an accurate description of Korea's exchange rate policy, but, according to the standard economic definition, such behavior is described as a managed float rather than a free float.

In the following section, we review the debate about what kind of exchange rate policy Korea has actually been following since the 1997 crisis and conclude that it is definitely most appropriately described as a managed float. This leaves open, however, how best to characterize how the float has been managed. Drawing on the concept that the degree of a country's exchange rate policy is best measured by how heavily it intervenes in the foreign exchange market to limit exchange rate movements, we analyze the behavior of Korea's exchange rate and intervention actions (as proxied by changes in international reserves) and show that such policy has gone through a number of distinct phases corresponding in considerable part to changes in the direction and strength of pressures in the foreign exchange market. In the last section of this chapter, we discuss various principles that have been offered for the management of flexible exchange rates and conclude that, on the whole, the *won* has been well managed.

Debate over Characterizing Korea's Exchange Rate Policies

The question of how we should characterize Korea's exchange rate policy might seem quite easy, but this is not the case. Korean officials have often referred to post–Asian crisis policy as a freely floating exchange rate, and this characterization meets the definitions that have been offered by some classifiers of exchange rate regimes (Reinhart and Rogoff 2004).[3] In contrast, some experts such as Dooley, Dornbusch, and Park (2002) have characterized Korea, even post crisis, as having an "intermediate" exchange rate regime.

This was clearly the case prior to the Asian crisis, when a de facto slowly crawling band against the dollar had characterized Korea's exchange rate policy. Although some have argued that such limited flexibility of the *won* was a major contributor to the 1997–98 crisis, the *won* had not become as clearly overvalued prior to the crisis as had the Thai baht. Indeed, some even argued that it was a little undervalued. The sharply limited flexibility had encouraged excessive unhedged foreign currency borrowing, however, and increased the Korean economic vulnerability after the crisis had begun. As the crisis worsened, efforts to maintain the crawling band became increasingly futile and were soon abandoned. During a crisis, a temporary move to a floating rate is standard operating procedure. Malaysia returned to a pegged rate after the crisis, but Korea and most of the other crisis countries stayed with a flexible rate.

Within this broad category are many varieties of regimes, however, and where within this range Korean policy should be placed has been the subject of some controversy. Recent research on exchange rate regimes has taught us that official classifications can often be misleading. China argued, for example, that it had a managed float even though its currency had remained pegged to the dollar within a narrow range from the mid-1990s until 2005. Calvo and Reinhart (2002) have labeled such heavy management of officially flexible rates as "fear of floating" and argue convincingly that the shifts in recent years in official classifications of floating rates have greatly overstated the true increase in flexibility. Indeed, some experts such as McKinnon and Schnabl (2004) have argued that Asia showed little real increase in flexibility after the crisis and that most of Asia can be best described as still being on a de facto dollar standard. This contention is overstated.

Korea officially maintains that it is practicing a free float but notes that official intervention is sometimes used. This terminology is not consistent with the standard textbook definition of freely floating. As Jeffrey Frankel (2004, 5) puts it, "With a free float, the central bank does not intervene in the foreign-exchange market." Ito and Park (2004) refer to this "nonexistence of official intervention" as the "fundamentalist" definition of free floating.

---

3. Although Reinhart and Rogoff (2004) categorize the Korean exchange rate regime as freely floating (July 1998–December 2001), the updated survey, Ilzetzki, Reinhart, and Rogoff (2008), lists the regime as managed floating (July 1998–November 2004) and the regime during the subsequent period as de facto crawling band (December 2004–December 2007).

Seldom is such a pure free float followed in practice. As Reinhart and Rogoff (2004) argue, "In reality, 'pure' floating exchange rates are an artifact of economics textbooks. Even in countries where the exchange rate is not an explicit target of policy, there are typically occasional (relatively rare) instances where there is unilateral or coordinated intervention in the foreign exchange market." The United States, Canada, and, in recent periods, Mexico would be examples of countries practicing only occasional foreign exchange market intervention. For years, New Zealand has been an exception and has practiced a complete free float although the central bank reserved the right to intervene if foreign exchange markets should become disorderly.

The Reinhart and Rogoff study makes valuable contributions to the literature on the classifications and analyses of exchange rate regimes, but its treatment of freely floating rates is open to the serious criticism that it is based solely on the behavior of exchange rates. Analytically, however, the degree of flexibility of an exchange rate regime should depend on the degree of exchange market pressure that it takes in the form of changes in reserves versus changes in exchange rates. In a pure float all change comes in the exchange rate, and in a pure fix all of it is taken as a change in reserves. (Of course, other policies such as monetary policy and controls can also be varied to deal with exchange market pressure and, as will be discussed below, this needs to be taken into account in the full description of a country's monetary policy–cum–exchange rate regime.) Where exchange market pressure is strong, there can be both a lot of exchange rate movement and a lot of intervention. Failure to take this into account led Reinhart and Rogoff to erroneously classify Japan as a free-floating regime despite the record amount of intervention that was undertaken.

In their original study, Reinhart and Rogoff similarly classify Korea's post-crisis regime as freely floating. However, the huge increase in Korea's international reserves indicates that it, like Japan, while clearly following a floating as opposed to a pegged-rate regime, is practicing substantially heavier management of its exchange rate than countries such as Canada, Mexico, New Zealand, and the United States. Of course, changes in reserves are far from a perfect proxy for official intervention, but, with reserve accumulations so large, this seems like a safe conclusion.

It is something of a surprise that the new behavioral IMF classifications of exchange rate regimes based on the judgments of IMF staff place Korea in its most flexible category, which they label "independent" floating. Such independent floating is described as follows (Bubula and Ötker-Robe 2003, 15): "The exchange rate is market determined; any foreign exchange intervention aims at moderating the rate of change and preventing undue fluctuations that are not justified by the fundamentals, rather than establishing a level for the exchange rate." This they contrast with "tightly or other managed floating" where (Bubula and Ötker-Robe 2003, 15): "The authorities influence exchange rate movements through interventions to counter the long-term trend of the exchange rate, without specifying a predetermined exchange rate path, or without having a specific exchange rate target ('dirty floating')." Their distinction between "tightly" and "other managed floating" is not entirely clear, but for the latter "the exchange rate is influenced in a more ad hoc manner." Even the distinction between independent and managed floating does not seem clear, however, since "moderating the rate of change" and "countering the long-term trend" can both be forms of "leaning against the wind" intervention.

In other words, under both of the IMF's categories of managed and independent floating, heavy or light exchange rate management could take place. This distinction (albeit subject to a fuzzy dividing line) is more relevant for policy analysis. Likewise, Reinhart and Rogoff's distinction between managed and free floating is based purely on the amount of exchange rate movement using a measure based on the mean absolute monthly percentage change in the exchange rate over a rolling five-year period. For some purposes such classifications based on the variability of the exchange rate alone may be useful, but, for issues of the stability of exchange rate regimes and questions of possible exchange rate manipulation and beggar-thy-neighbor policies, the amount of official intervention is of crucial importance. The latter considerations emphasize that exchange rate policy needs to be evaluated from the standpoint of both the country in question and also its trading partners.

The most blatant forms of beggar-thy-neighbor policies involve government-induced devaluations when a country is running a balance of payments surplus. The development of international monetary cooperation in the post–World War II period has virtually eliminated such blatant practices as were implemented by some countries, including the United States, during the 1930s. Today, manipulation usually is more passive and acts merely to reduce or halt appreciations, not actively force major depreciations. Such policies can still generate substantial disequilibrium, however, and thus may have an important influence on the international distribution of adjustment pressures. With the substantial increase in exchange rate flexibility since the 1970s, such issues have become considerably less contentious than during the days of the Bretton Woods adjustable peg system. They are not entirely eliminated, however, and the large reserve accumulations in Asia in recent years have become the subject of a great deal of commentary.

It is certainly wrong to suggest that the heavy exchange market intervention by Asia in the years after the crisis has been the only major cause of the huge

U.S. current account deficits.[4] In the case of both China and Korea, a substantial increase in reserves in the postcrisis period was extremely sensible from both national and international points of view. Recent crises have highlighted the strong contributions of inadequate reserve holdings to increased risk of crisis.[5] As will be discussed in Chapter 4, however, Korea's reserve accumulations substantially exceeded most estimates of its reserve needs although the absolute size of such calculations of excess is relatively small compared with that of China.

Like most countries Korea does not publish data on its intervention activities. Thus, an outsider cannot be sure just how effective the government's and central bank's strategies for intervention are. Changes in international reserves are far from a perfect proxy for intervention, but the substantial increases in reserve levels strongly suggest that direct and indirect intervention were substantial and went far beyond smoothing short-run fluctuations in the exchange rate. Park, Chung, and Wang (2001) argue that they also find strong evidence of intervention from the empirical relationships between stock prices and exchange rates.

Note that, where surrender requirements for foreign currency proceeds are in place, reserves could be accumulated by the central bank without taking any active measures in the foreign exchange market. Much of Korea's initial reserve accumulation after the Asian crisis came through this mechanism. In this sense, the central bank could say that it was not directly intervening in the foreign exchange market and thus had a free float. From an analytical point of view, however, the benchmark of no substantive intervention would require the government or central bank to place the surrendered foreign exchange in the market rather than use it to accumulate reserves. The accumulated reserves would place the same depressing influence on the value of the currency whether the reserves were acquired actively through direct intervention or passively through surrender requirements.

Other channels of indirect official influence on the exchange rate are also possible. For example, Dooley, Dornbusch, and Park (2002) suggest:

> The Korean authorities, it appears, have not resorted to the use of reserves to moderate the movements of the nominal exchange rate. Instead, they have relied on a few state-owned banks to intervene in the market, using their own holdings of foreign exchange, which are not counted as part of the central bank foreign reserves.

---

4. For evidence on this point, see McKibbin, Lee, and Park (2004).
5. For empirical studies of these relationships, see the analyses and references in Willett et al. (2005) and Li, Sula, and Willett (2008).

Authorities can also intervene in the forward rather than the spot market. This approach was used heavily by the Thai central bank in the run-up to the 1997 crisis. The forward interventions were used in part to disguise the extent of pressure against the currency in the foreign exchange market. By the time the Thai authorities decided that allowing the baht to depreciate was necessary, the level of reported reserves was still at roughly $30 billion, but forward sales had been so substantial that net reserves were almost zero.

In Korea, in recent years, the Ministry of Finance and Economy (currently known as the Ministry of Strategy and Finance) decided to intervene in the forward market to try to hold down the appreciation of the *won*. Most exchange market intervention in Korea and other countries is undertaken by the central bank, but authority for the Finance Ministry to also intervene on its own account is not unusual. This is the case in the United States, for example. The substantial losses believed to have been made on the Ministry of Finance and Economy's forward intervention have made its actions a major subject of controversy, however; and this will be discussed later in this chapter.

In discussing government intervention, we have been following the standard convention of assuming sterilized intervention or its equivalent. How effective such intervention can be in influencing the exchange rate is a subject of considerable debate. Where capital mobility is perfect, such intervention could work only through signaling effects. There is substantial capital mobility for countries such as Korea, but it is far from perfect, and it is usually argued that the foreign exchange market for the *won* is relatively thin.[6] Thus, sterilized intervention has at least some scope to be effective.

Where intervention is unsterilized, it in effect implies monetary policy actions, which without question can have powerful effects on exchange rates (although there is a debate about the possible existence of a Laffer curve with respect to the effects of interest rate increases). The question of how much weight should be given to exchange rate movements in setting national monetary policy is largely separate from issues of strategies for unsterilized intervention. The literature on optimal or, more realistically, sensible strategies with respect to both will be discussed below.

As Rhee and Lee (2005) note in gauging potential instability in the foreign exchange market, the BOK looks at a number of factors, including the degree of exchange rate volatility, volume of transactions, and the width of the bid-ask spread. Rhee and Lee (2005, 198) describe the intervention objectives of the BOK as "not to target a certain level but to smooth radical changes in the

---

6. On estimates of capital mobility for Korea, see the analyses and references in Keil et al. (2004), Keil, Rajan, and Willett (2009), Willett, Keil, and Ahn (2002), and the appendices to this study.

exchange rate when there is transient external shock or bid-offer gaps due to one-sided exchange rate expectations." Kim and Yang (2008) in their econometric work find evidence that the BOK has been rather successful in limiting the short-run effects of fluctuations in capital flows on the *won*. Korea certainly has allowed substantial longer-run movements in the exchange rate, and in this sense the evidence certainly supports Rhee and Lee's judgment (2005, 198) that "the authorities in Korea have maintained the principle that the exchange rate should be determined by the interaction of the demand for and supply of foreign exchange." Given the substantial magnitudes of Korean intervention, however, and its strongly asymmetric nature until recently, it appears that the authorities have rather consistently underestimated the extent to which the upward pressures on the *won* were due to fundamentals rather than erratic fluctuations.

Statistical Description of Korea's Postcrisis Exchange Rate Policy

It has become widely recognized that in analyzing exchange rate regimes we should not look at the behavior of the exchange rate alone. The variability of an exchange rate could be low because of heavy official intervention or because few shocks have taken place. Thus, at a minimum, we need to look at the relationship between exchange rate changes and intervention. In the absence of publicly available information on actual intervention, the imperfect proxy of changes in reserves is often used. Some studies go further and also examine relationships with monetary policy, usually measured by changes in interest rates.

These recent studies are all based directly or indirectly on the concept of exchange market pressure, and they consider how it is reflected in the behavior of its various components. Thus, such measures control for the size of shocks and focus on the extent to which such shocks are allowed to fall on various policy instruments. Although the degree of response of monetary or interest rate policy is crucial for descriptions of a country's overall monetary–cum–exchange rate policy regime, we focus here only on the exchange rate–intervention dimension. Because Korea and most other countries do not publish data on their intervention, we follow the standard approach in the literature and use the changes in the reported levels of international reserves as a proxy. This is far from a perfect measure, but it does give a rough picture of actual intervention policies. Note that, where there is an upward trend in reserves, interest earnings could lead the increases in reserves to overstate the amount of intervention. Given the rapid growth in Korea's reserves through 2007, however, such earnings can account for only a small fraction of the increase.

Several studies have implemented this approach by looking at the ratio of variances. This has two serious problems, however. As discussed in Willett and Kim (2006) and Willett, Nitithanprapas, and Kim (2008), where trends are important, simple standard deviations and variances can give misleading results. Other important issues concern the time periods and exchange rate measures to be used. For purposes such as looking at effects on growth rates over long periods of time, Reinhart and Rogoff's (2004) method of using five-year averages has much to commend it. In studying the details of strategy under a managed float, however, frequent changes in policy could occur. Rather than basing calculations on arbitrary time periods, we look for changes in relationships and thus identify a number of subperiods. We begin our analysis of postcrisis behavior in January of 1999 after the *won* had substantially completed its rebound from its overdepreciation.

A problem for many countries is that more than one foreign currency is important for their international trade and financial relations. This had led to many proposals for pegging to baskets of currencies and surely indicates that under managed exchange rate regimes focusing on just one currency can be less than optimal and in some cases quite dangerous. Although we present our main analysis with respect to the won-dollar exchange rates, we will discuss also the behavior of other important bilateral rates and the weighted average of exchange rates, termed the effective exchange rate.

In the framework in Willett and Kim (2006), the propensity to intervene indicates the degree to which authorities allow pressures in the currency market to move the exchange rate versus intervening to damp down its movement.[7] This approach gives us a crude method of attempting to distinguish between reserve buildup and exchange rate smoothing motivations for intervention. Dooley, Dornbusch, and Park (2002) describe an early version of Hernández and Montiel (2003) as finding that Korea was not using reserves for smoothing operations but was instead showing a systematic tendency to accumulate reserves over time. A country can be doing both, however, and our investigation shows that this has been the case for Korea.[8]

Our analysis supports the findings of Hernández and Montiel (2003) against those of McKinnon and Schnabl (2004) that Korea had adopted a soft dollar peg. The *won* has indeed been more flexible since the crisis than before. Korea has displayed considerable evidence of fear of completely free floating, but such fear appears to be much less strong than would be implied by

---

7. An updated version of the framework and critical analysis of alternative approaches is presented in Willett, Nitithanprapas, and Kim (2008).
8. The published version of Hernández and Montiel (2003) makes only the milder argument that the behaviors of Korea's reserves are not consistent with smoothing operations only. Thus, their analysis and ours are in qualitative agreement.

a return to a de facto dollar standard. This can clearly be seen by the large movements in the exchange rate.[9] This qualitative conclusion is robust with respect to different measures of the exchange rate and of calculating the intervention coefficient.

Not all government intervention shows up immediately in changes in reserves. During the six-month period starting in February 2003, the Ministry of Finance and Economy traded approximately $40 billion of nondeliverable forwards (NDFs) in Hong Kong and Singapore. According to the Korean National Assembly Finance and Economics Committee and the Ministry of Finance and Economy, during September 2006, the Korean government is estimated to have lost around nine trillion *won* by investing the Foreign Exchange Equalization Fund[10] in speculative derivatives to defend the exchange rate (Lee S. K. 2006). Such transactions take pressure off the spot market in the short run and would reduce the amount of appreciation without this showing up immediately as increases in reserves. During the policy audit hearing in the Korean National Assembly on 17 October 2007, Lee Sang-kyung, a member of the National Assembly, estimated that during 2004 more than two trillion *won* was lost from the NDF transactions alone (Chung 2007). Lee Sang-kyung argued that the policy intervention had led to such large losses that the exchange rate defense should be considered a "failure" overall. With the turnaround of the *won*, however, the expected losses in 2007 turned into a positive net profit.

In November 2008 it was reported (*Chosun Ilbo* 2008) that an official of the Ministry of Strategy and Finance announced that "unless there is an exceptional case of the exchange rate extremely sharply rising or falling, they have stopped intervening in the market." This was soon followed, however, by the plunge in the *won*, and heavy intervention was resumed; intervention was now being used to hold up the *won*, not keep it down.

---

9. In defense of McKinnon and Schnabl, it should be noted that their analysis was based on a much shorter span of data so that there was more room for differing interpretations. Subsequent behavior has made it much easier to draw a clear-cut conclusion. We note that another well-known classification exercise by Levy-Yeyati and Sturzenegger (2005) also classifies Korea as having a fixed rate for the years after the crisis. We view this as an indication of serious problems with the complicated methodology used in that study.
10. The Foreign Exchange Equalization Fund was established by the Foreign Exchange Transaction Act, which was instituted after the 1997–98 Asian financial crisis, that allowed the Ministry of Finance and Economy to manage the fund to mitigate the smooth operations of the foreign exchange market functioning. For details of the Foreign Exchange Equalization Fund, refer to the Foreign Exchange Transaction Act, Chap. 3, Art. 13: Foreign Exchange Equalization Fund.

Overview of the Behavior of the Won

Figure 2-1 plots changes in Korea's foreign currency reserves against the *won*-dollar exchange rates from 1990 into June 2009. Higher values of the exchange rate imply depreciation of the *won*. Note that prior to the 1997 crisis there was a mild trend toward depreciation of the *won*. Although months of reserve increases are more frequent than those of declines, intervention in the foreign exchange market as proxied by changes in reserves is much less asymmetric than during the postcrisis period in which months of declining reserves were quite rare up to 2008. We see the sharp drop in reserves and depreciation of the *won* associated with the 1997 crisis followed by the strong rebound of the *won* consistent with the hypothesis that there was a substantial overshooting of depreciation during the crisis. Korea sensibly made use of this postcrisis strengthening of the *won* to restock its depleted reserve position by slowing the appreciation of the *won* by buying dollars. After a dip in the early part of this decade, the *won* began to appreciate again in 2002. This appreciation trend picked up speed in 2004 and continued into late 2007, by which time the *won* was almost back to its precrisis level.

Notice in Figure 2-1 a peak change of $14.2 billion in foreign currency reserves in November 2004. This coincides with a sharp appreciation of the *won*. It appears the BOK tried to defend the exchange rate from sharply appreciating during the month by selling Korean *won* and accumulating foreign reserves aggressively. During 2005, efforts to reduce the rate of appreciation of the *won* appear to have been reduced and the rate of reserve accumulation slowed. Although we see evidence of substantial official management of the exchange rate, this was done in a way that also allowed substantial movement of the exchange rate. A reversal of the appreciation trend occurs in November 2007, and then a sharp depreciation began in March 2008. This latter period will be discussed in Chapter 10.

Figure 2-1 shows a definite change in the pattern of intervention before and after the Asian crisis. Although limits on allowable exchange rate movements were much tighter before the crisis, the pattern of intervention was much more balanced, with a sizable number of months of both reserve increases and decreases. In the post–Asian crisis period, there were much larger exchange rate changes, but intervention was much more one-sided, with very few months of reserve declines being recorded before the turnaround of the *won* in 2008.

Korean officials (for example, Ahn 2008, 305–20) often describe their policies as exchange rate smoothing, but this is only partly accurate, as the smoothing was strongly in one direction. Smoothing intervention is supposedly aimed at countering erratic movements in the exchange rate caused by such failures as temporarily disorderly or thin markets and destabilizing speculation. There is no reason that such episodes should exactly balance on the up or down side, but neither would they be expected to be predominantly in one direction over a long period of time. Thus, smoothing motivations appear to have been clearly complemented by leaning-against-the-wind behavior, and the latter behavior has clearly dominated the data on a monthly basis. Publicly available information does not allow us to determine how much intramonth smoothing takes place.

Figure 2-1: **Changes in Foreign Currency Reserves Compared with Won-Dollar Exchange Rates in Korea, January 1990–June 2009**

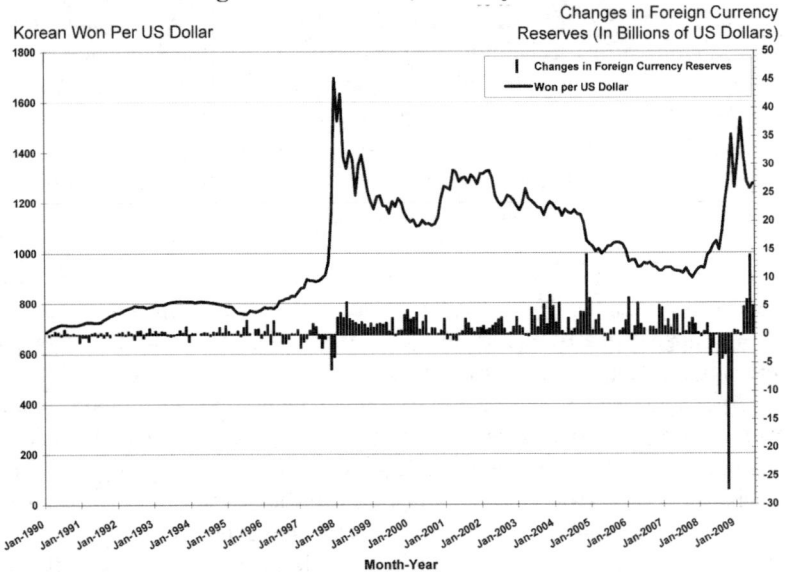

Source: International Financial Statistics database of the International Monetary Fund; author's calculations.

When the wind keeps blowing in the same direction for a long period of time, economists' traditional assumption has been that this is strong evidence that the pressures are due primarily to fundamentals rather than questionable speculation. The lengths of some of the stock market bubbles of recent decades suggest that there may not be as strong a basis for such a presumption as many economists once thought, but still there are good reasons to believe that the strength of the *won* during the 1999–2007 period had a strong basis in the fundamentals, however inconvenient this was for export interests. As discussed in Chapter 4, there were initially also strong reasons to rebuild reserve levels after the crisis and to add additional precautionary reserves in the face of substantial inflows of financial capital. And the strength of the *won* made it easy for increased reserve levels to be accumulated. As is also discussed in Chapter 4, however, large reserve accumulations continued well

Figure 2-2: **Changes in Foreign Currency Reserves Compared with Won-Dollar Exchange Rates in Korea, January 1999–June 2009**

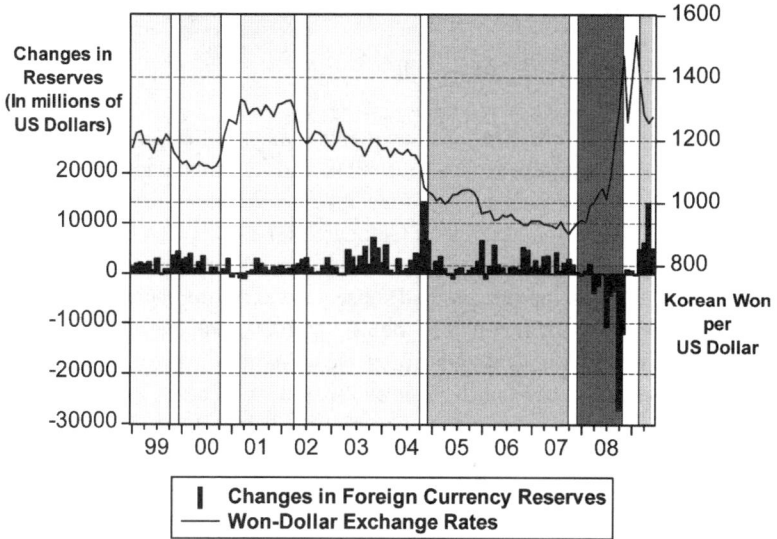

Sources: International Financial Statistics database of the International Monetary Fund; author's calculations.

Figure 2-3: **Changes in Foreign Currency Reserves Compared with Won-Dollar Exchange Rates, with Trend Lines for Subperiods, in Korea, January 1999—June 2009**

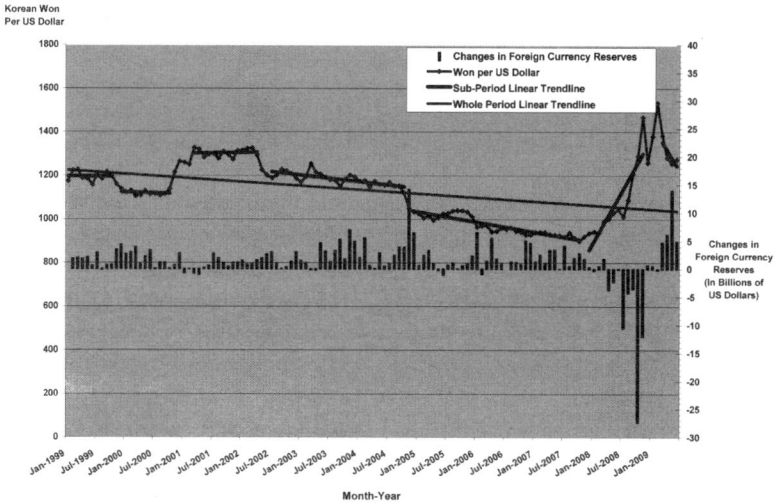

Sources: International Financial Statistics database of the International Monetary Fund; author's calculations.

after most calculations suggested that quite adequate levels of reserves had been obtained. This suggests that concerns over competitiveness were also an important motivation.

Structural Breaks: Seven Subperiods

In their earlier study of Korea's exchange rate policy, Willett and Kim (2006) divided the postcrisis period into four subperiods. In this study, we extend and update the time periods through June 2009, adding three new subperiods. We extend the fourth subperiod until October 2004 and divide the subsequent data into three additional subperiods, the first of continued gradual appreciation, the second of the turnaround and subsequent sharp depreciation, and the third beginning with the rebound of the *won* in 2009, a recovery period from the turbulent period of up and down after the extreme period of depreciation. These changes are illustrated in *Figures 2-2* and *2-3* (Figure 2-3 adds trend lines for the whole period and the subperiods). *Tables 2-1* and *2-2* provide a statistical summary of the changes in exchange rates and reserves and the annualized level changes for the seven subperiods

Figures 2-2 and 2-3 and Tables 2-1 and 2-2 show the quite substantial changes over time in both the size of exchange rate movements and the changes in international reserves used to slow down these movements. To get a better idea of the varying degrees of official management of the exchange rate, *Table 2-3* and *Figure 2-4* present estimates of the authorities' propensities to intervene over the various time periods. This is proxied by the ratio of the change in reserves to the total of the change in reserves plus change in the exchange rate. Thus, a completely fixed rate has a coefficient of one and a pure float is zero.[11]

The rapid accumulation of the reserves during the period implies that an intervention of a given size would yield a much lower percentage change in reserves toward the end of the period than at the beginning. To correct for this, we calculate reserve changes as a percentage of the previous month's M2.[12] Without knowing the relevant elasticities of excess demand and supply in the Korean foreign exchange market, we cannot say at what level of the ratio more of the exchange market pressure is taken on the exchange rate or by intervention. As long as these elasticities do not change greatly from one

---

11. Because we have broken down the float into various subperiods based on changes in the behavior of the exchange rate, we do not here estimate separate propensities that account for trends versus movements around trends; instead we focus on the combined propensity to intervene. This is constructed by taking the ratio of the proxy for intervention, the change in reserves, to total exchange market pressure, the sum of changes in reserves and the exchange rate. Absolute values of percentage changes are used.
12. Note that other scale variables such as GDP could be used, but the results would not vary a great deal.

Table 2-1: **Changes in Exchange Rates during Seven Subperiods in Korea, January 1999–June 2009**

Sub-periods	Exchange rates		Changes in exchange rates	
	Beginning	Ending	Whole period	Annual change
Period 1: January 1999–October 1999	1175.0	1200.0	25.0	30.0
Period 2: December 1999–October 2000	1138.0	1139.0	1.0	1.1
Period 3: March 2001–April 2002	1327.5	1294.0	−33.5	−28.7
Period 4: July 2002–October 2004	1188.0	1119.6	−68.4	−29.3
Period 5: December 2004–October 2007	1035.1	900.7	−134.4	−46.1
Period 6: December 2007–November 2008	936.1	1469.0	532.9	532.9
Period 7: March 2009–June 2009	1383.5	1273.9	−109.6	−328.8

Sources: Bank of Korea data; author's calculations.

Note: Exchange rates and changes in exchange rates are in Korean *won* per U.S. dollar, so a negative change implies appreciation of the *won*.

Table 2-2: **Changes in Foreign Currency Reserves during Seven Subperiods in Korea, January 1999–June 2009**

Sub-periods	Foreign currency reserves		Changes in foreign currency reserves	
	Beginning	Ending	Whole period	Annual change
Period 1: January 1999–October 1999	53.24	65.84	12.60	15.12
Period 2: December 1999–October 2000	73.70	92.28	18.58	20.27
Period 3: March 2001–April 2002	94.11	107.29	13.18	11.30
Period 4: July 2002–October 2004	114.99	177.53	62.54	26.80
Period 5: December 2004–October 2007	198.18	259.69	61.51	21.09
Period 6: December 2007–November 2008	261.77	199.79	−61.98	−61.98
Period 7: March 2009–June 2009	205.62	230.73	25.11	75.33

Sources: Bank of Korea data; author's calculations.

Note: Foreign currency reserves and changes in foreign currency reserves are in billions of U.S. dollars.

period to another, we can use differences in the ratios to tell us whether the propensity to intervene has been higher in one period than another.

During the second period there was a substantial increase in reserves although there was little overall change in the exchange rate, suggesting that building up adequate levels of international reserves was still a major objective. In the third period, the rate of accumulation of reserves fell despite substantial appreciation, suggesting that reasonable reserve levels had been reached and the extent of leaning against the wind had been reduced. In period four, somewhat heavier intervention was resumed, consistent with a more mercantilist interpretation that the major motivation was to limit the loss of export competitiveness owing to the substantial appreciation of the *won*. During the fifth period, the propensity to intervene fell to its lowest level to that point, perhaps reflecting recognition that the continuing pressure for appreciation of the *won* was caused primarily by fundamentals.

Table 2-3: **Combined Propensities to Intervene (CPI) and Components of CPI during Seven Subperiods in Korea, January 1999–June 2009**

Time period[†]	CPI for the sub-periods	Sum of the monthly changes in reserves, as a percentage of one-month lag of M2, for the sub-periods	Sum of monthly log changes in exchange rates (Δe) for the sub-periods
Whole period: January 1999–June 2009	0.746	23.75%	8.08%
Period 1: January 1999–October 1999	0.543	2.50%	2.11%
Period 2: December 1999–October 2000	0.977	3.77%	0.09%
Period 3: March 2001–April 2002	0.449	2.08%	−2.56%
Period 4: July 2002–October 2004	0.593	8.65%	−5.93%
Period 5: December 2004–October 2007	0.305	6.11%	−13.91%
Period 6: December 2007–November 2008	0.109	−5.52%	45.06%
Period 7: March 2009–June 2009	0.239	2.60%	−8.25%

Sources: Bank of Korea data; author's calculations.

Note: Components of CPI = Changes in reserves as percentage of one-month lag of M2 and changes in exchange rates, respectively.

† First month changes in reserves and exchange rates, not counted.

During the sixth period, from December 2007 to November 2008, these appreciation pressures were sharply reversed, and the *won* depreciated from 936.1 to 1,469 to the dollar. The value of the Korean *won* depreciated by more than 36 percent against the dollar during that period. This was the largest one-year drop in the value of Korean *won* since the 1997 Asian currency crisis. Although the initial fall was engineered by the government, it got out of hand, and the government switched policies. This was followed by the large capital outflows associated with the global crisis. Although the absolute magnitude of intervention was quite large during this period, the propensity to intervene was quite low, raising the issue of whether intervention should have been much stronger during this period. This question will be discussed in Chapter 10. Period seven reflects the turnaround again of the *won* as the financial pressure from the crisis eased. The BOK began to recoup some of the reserve losses but quite sensibly allowed most of the exchange market pressure to be felt in the rebound of the *won*.

Effective and Other Bilateral Exchange Rates

The *won*'s exchange rate against the dollar is not the only one that is important for the Korean economy and financial institutions. As shown in ***Figure 2-5,*** however, the broad outlines of the *won*'s movements against various weighted averages of the currencies of its major trading partners have been quite similar to those of its movements with respect to the dollar.

Figure 2-4: **Combined Propensities to Intervene (CPI) for Seven Subperiods, for Korea**

CPI index

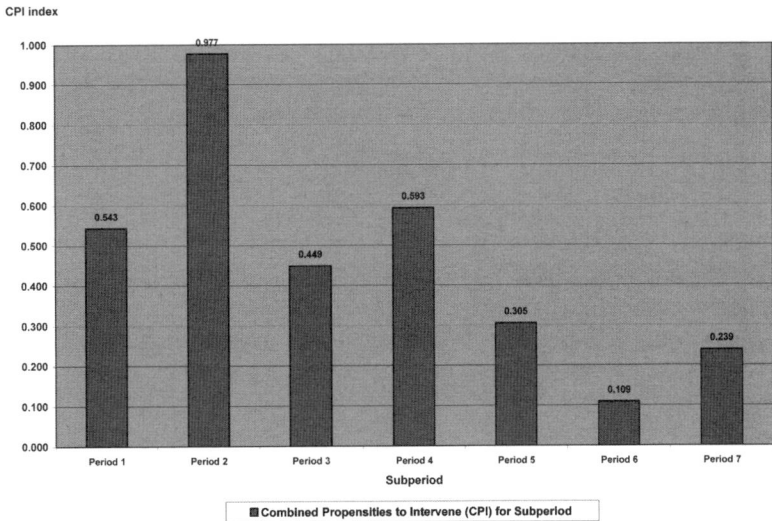

Combined Propensities to Intervene (CPI) for Subperiod

Sources: International Financial Statistics database of the International Monetary Fund; author's calculations.

Notes: CPI = |ΔReserve/(-1)M2|/(|Δe|+|ΔReserve/Lag(-1)M2|); not counting first month changes. The subperiods are defined as follows: Period 1: January 1999–October 1999; Period 2: December 1999–October 2000; Period 3: March 2001–April 2002; Period 4: July 2002–October 2004; Period 5: December 2004–October 2007; Period 6: December 2007–November 2008; Period 7: March 2009–June 2009.

At a more fine-grained level, however, many economists would argue that, in deciding on the possible desirability of short-run intervention policy, Korean officials should also pay attention to developments in the *won*'s exchange rate against other currencies (*Figure 2-6*). In commentaries, the *won-yen* exchange rate is often a particular focus of attention because of Japanese-Korean competition in many export markets. Since the unpegging of the Chinese renminbi from the dollar in 2005, the behavior of the *won-renminbi* exchange rate has taken on independent importance. The substantial fluctuations among the dollar, euro, and *yen* in recent years have further increased the need to look beyond just the dollar in considering Korean exchange rate policy. A good deal of discussion has taken place about the possible creation of a commonly agreed weighting scheme for a basket of Asian currencies to be used as a focal point for exchange rate policy and perhaps eventually a common Asian currency. These issues will be discussed in Chapters 7 and 8.

Figure 2-5: **Bilateral Nominal Exchange Rate (BNER; Won-Dollar), Nominal Effective Exchange Rate (NEER), and Real Effective Exchange Rate (REER) for Broad and Narrow Indices for South Korea, January 1994–June 2009**

Exchange Rate Indices
(2005 index = 100)

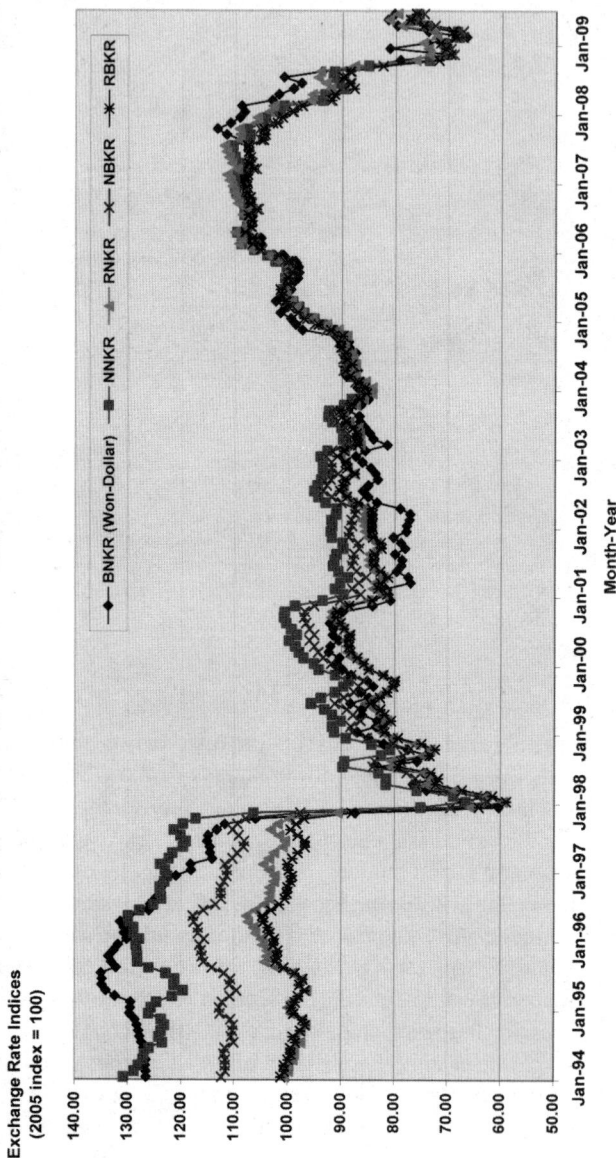

Sources: Bank for International Settlements (for effective exchange rates); author's calculations based on Bank of Korea data (for BNER).

Definitions: BNER: Bilateral Nominal Exchange Rates; NNKR: Nominal Narrow Effective Exchange Rates; RNKR: Real Narrow Effective Exchange Rates; NBKR: Nominal Broad Effective Exchange Rates; RBKR: Real Broad Effective Exchange Rates

Figure 2-6: **Monthly Foreign Exchange Rates of Korean Won against the U.S. Dollar, the Japanese Yen, and the Euro January 1995–June 2009**

Won/Foreign Currency

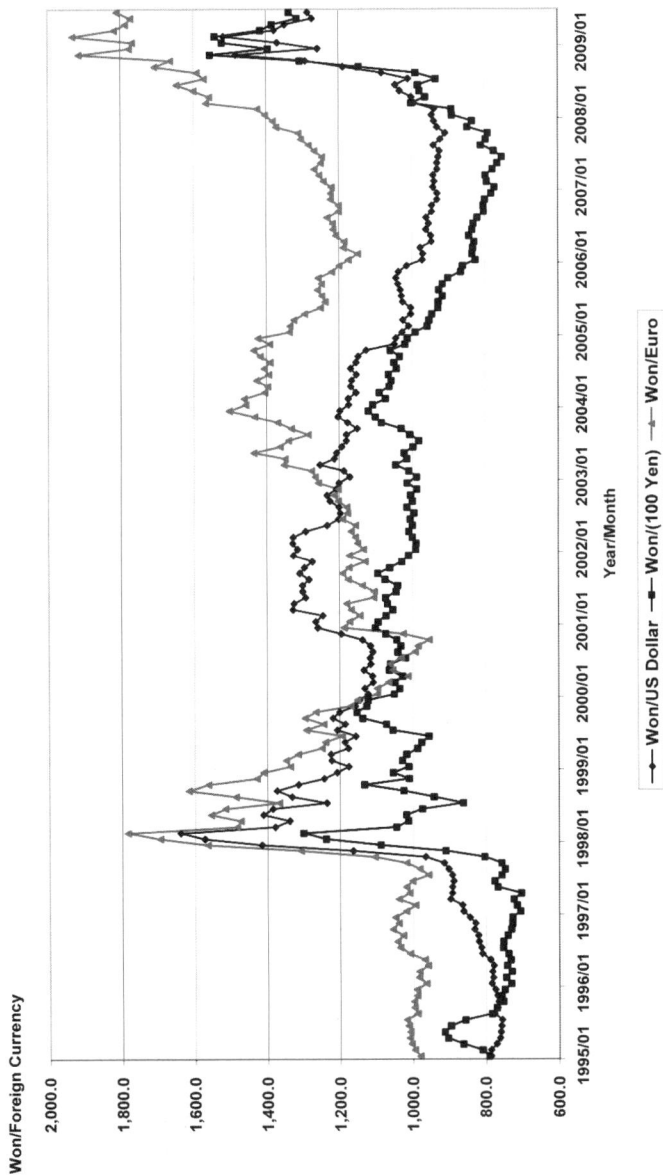

Year/Month

→ Won/US Dollar ■ Won/(100 Yen) ▲ Won/Euro

Source: Bank of Korea.

Figure 2-7: **Normalized Korean Foreign Exchange Rates against the U.S. Dollar, the Chinese Yuan, the Thai Baht, and the Indonesian Rupiah, January 1998–June 2009**

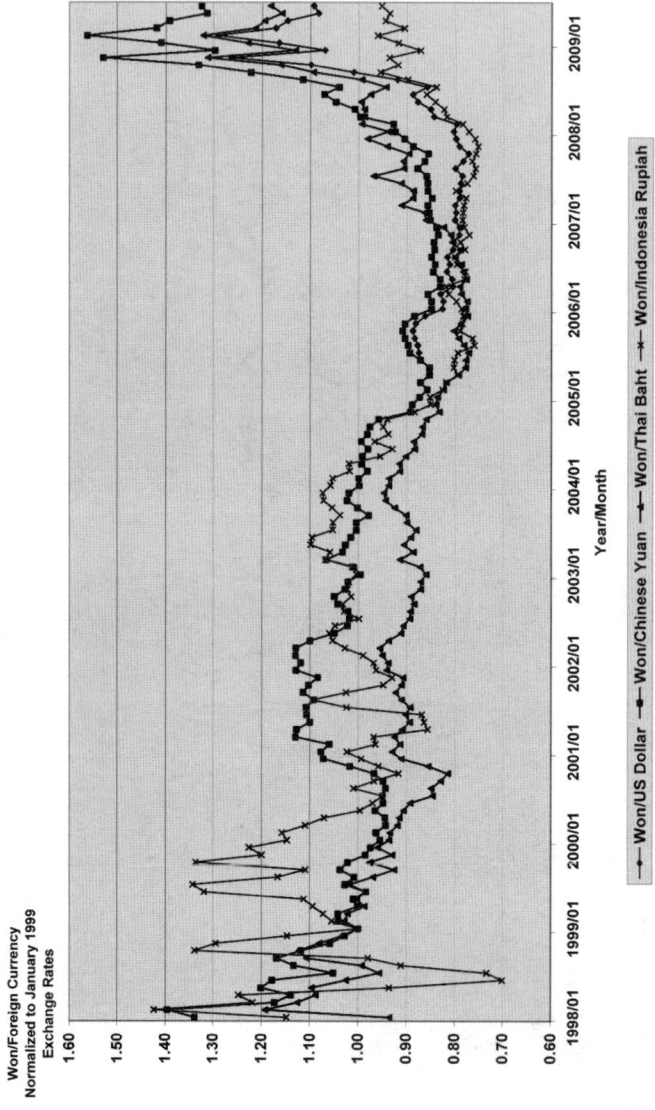

Won/Foreign Currency
Normalized to January 1999
Exchange Rates

— Won/US Dollar — Won/Chinese Yuan — Won/Thai Baht — Won/Indonesia Rupiah

Source: Bank of Korea.
Note: Prior to 2005 the Chinese Yuan was fixed to the U.S. dollar, so the *Won*/U.S. dollar rate and the *Won*/Chinese Yuan rate moved together.

Figure 2-8: **Normalized Foreign Exchange Rates of the Korean *Won* against the Singapore Dollar, the Malaysian Ringgit, the Thai Baht, and the Indonesian Rupiah, January 1998–June 2009**

Won/Foreign Currency
Normalized to January 1999
Exchange Rates

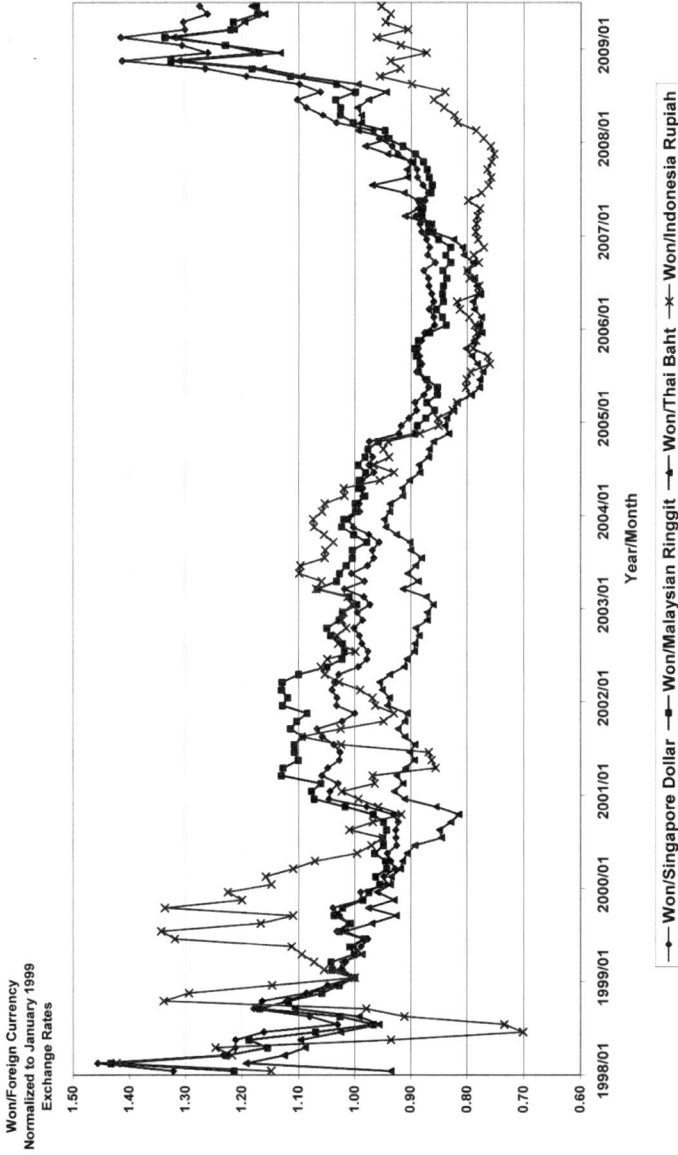

Source: Bank of Korea.

The similarity of the broad movements in the *won*-dollar effective exchange rates reflects broadly similar swings in the *won* against the dollar, euro, and *yen* despite the considerable fluctuations that have occurred in the euro-dollar and *yen*-dollar rates. Figure 2-6 shows these rates from 1995 through June of 2009. The *won* began its turnaround against the euro considerably before it did versus the *yen*, which in turn led the turnaround against the dollar.

Figure 2-7 shows movements of the *won* against the dollar, the Chinese yuan, the Indonesian rupiah, and the Thai baht from the beginning of 1998 through June of 2009. (The yuan was pegged to the dollar until 2005.) Again we see a broad similarity of movements. Some differences in behavior are observable, reflecting developments such as the volatility of the Thai baht from late 2006 through 2007 owing to political instability and controversial economic policies, but overall the fluctuations of the *won* against other major Asian currencies were not a great deal less than those against the dollar. From March of 2006 up until September 2008, the *won-rupiah* rates move very closely to the *won*-dollar rates. Then, starting in October 2008, the Indonesian rupiah began to move independently from other currencies.

Figure 2-8 shows the movements of the *won* against the currencies of four selected ASEAN countries, namely, the Singapore dollar, Malaysian ringgit, the Thai baht, and the Indonesian rupiah, from the beginning of 1998 through June of 2009. We can see that the exchange rate movements against these currencies seem to be highly synchronized throughout much of the current decade. Notice in Figures 2-7 and 2-8 the considerable similarity in the behavior of the Chinese yuan and Malaysian ringgit, particularly until 2005. The Singapore dollar also moved very closely with these two currencies throughout this period. These figures show that Malaysia and China were basically pegging their currencies to the U.S. dollar until 2005. Since July of 2005, when Malaysia's official stance became a managed float against some basket of currencies, its exchange rate regime in fact seems to be more accurately described as a band around the U.S. dollar. China's official managed float during this period was in fact a narrow band peg to the dollar. For Singapore, which claimed to have a band adjusted on the basis of a basket of currencies, the actual behavior seems to be a de facto band around the U.S. dollar. If these countries are truly basing their policies on a basket of currencies, their baskets seem to be predominantly filled with the U.S. dollar.

How Should Flexible Rates Be Managed?

Recent research (Willett 2003a) has suggested that the theory of optimal currency areas, which will be discussed in Chapter 7, can be reinterpreted more broadly in terms of the weight given to exchange market developments in the setting of monetary policy. Genuinely fixed rates imply 100 percent weight is given to the exchange rate, while a completely freely floating rate implies a zero weight. We can carefully classify monetary–cum–exchange rate regimes from this perspective as well as in terms of exchange rate behavior and the amount of sterilized interventions. From this perspective, a small, fairly open economy should certainly give greater attention to exchange market developments than a large, relatively closed one. Thus, Canada, Mexico, and New Zealand should all give more weight to the exchange rate in setting monetary policy than should the United States.[13]

This would occur automatically for countries following inflation targeting. For some economies, it may be optimal to go beyond this and give direct weight to the exchange rate over and above its influence on domestic prices. Up to a point this could be consistent with flexible inflation targeting that allows for some concern with short-run employment and output effects as long as this does not compromise longer-term inflation goals.

In contrast, countries such as Canada, Mexico, New Zealand, and Singapore have all chosen not to give 100 percent to the exchange market (balance of payments) as would be necessary for a fixed-rate regime. (Of course, even with completely fixed rates, there could be some scope for independent monetary policy in the short run if capital mobility were not high.) Thus, some types of intermediate regimes as defined in terms of the weight given to exchange market considerations in setting domestic monetary policy are quite consistent with a floating regime in the sense of no official intervention in the foreign exchange market.

It is not always recognized that it is this issue of the orientation of monetary policy to which most of the OCA literature is addressed. This is largely different from the criteria for the desirability of sterilized intervention. These criteria, which will be discussed in the following section, focus on the behavior of speculation and types of shocks.

There is a vast literature on criteria for exchange market intervention. The least controversial analytically is sterilized intervention to offset imperfections in private speculation. The easiest of such possible deficiencies of private speculation to identify in practice is when markets become disorderly. Although complete agreement does not exist about precise criteria, one can usually identify a disorderly market when one encounters it: usually some event has generated great uncertainty, and the market has become temporarily much more risk averse than normal (that is, risk tolerance has declined while perceptions of risk have increased). In consequence, relatively small transactions can often lead to large movements in the market price. Such market disorder, in the classic sense, generally does not last long.

---

13. Just how much weight these countries have given is an issue of some dispute.

More difficult to classify are episodes of high risk aversion that may last for a considerable period, such as occurred in Asia in 1997–98 and globally after the Russian default and LTCM crisis in 1998. Such market conditions are often described as being the result of destabilizing speculation based on herd behavior. In these crises, however, there was much less activity destabilizing speculation than is often assumed. More important was a sudden drying up of stabilizing speculation combined with capital outflows induced by borrowers attempting to cover their foreign currency exposure. Remember that the analytic distinction between stabilizing versus destabilizing speculation rests on whether speculative actions tend to move price (in this one case the exchange rate) toward or away from its equilibrium value. Judgments about equilibrium values often differ widely among experts, of course, so even where we have agreement about objectives there still may be considerable disagreement about what should be done in particular situations. Still, it is useful to keep these analytic distinctions in mind.

Where speculation is actively destabilizing, it would normally be optimal to offset it with sterilized official intervention. With very high capital mobility, however, such sterilized intervention would be largely ineffective. Thus, such destabilizing speculation could force a serious dilemma on domestic monetary policy—whether to adjust policy to reduce destabilizing movements of the exchange rate, or keep it aimed at domestic objectives and suffer large exchange rate changes.

Where the incipient exchange rate movements are instead due to a temporary increase in risk aversion that leads primarily not to destabilizing speculation but to insufficient stabilizing speculation, capital mobility in effect temporarily falls, and sterilized intervention can become effective. This in turn could substantially lessen the dilemma forced on domestic monetary policy.

For a number of the Asian crisis countries, of which Korea is a prime example, the substantial overshooting of exchange rates during the Asian crisis was due in considerable part not just to capital outflows but to a drop in capital inflows against the background of substantial current account deficits.[14] To the extent that this occurred, an increase in the amount of sterilized intervention during the crisis could have substantially reduced exchange rate overshooting. Unfortunately, data problems make it difficult for us to judge just how well this story fits Korea. The large current account deficit part certainly fits. For 1996, Korea's current account deficit was approximately $23 billion. It is the size of capital outflows that is more difficult to measure, however.

Contrary to the common view that puts most of the blame for capital account instability on international portfolio investors, they were far from the major

---

14. See Willett (2000) and Willett et al. (2005).

source of capital outflows from Korea. The dollar value of foreign holdings in Korean stock did fall dramatically, from more than $17 billion at the end of the third quarter of 1996 to barely more than $5 billion one year later. However, most of this drop was due to falls in stock prices and the depreciation of the *won* against the dollar, not capital outflows. Quarterly data on the dollar value of capital flows show actual portfolio equity outflows in only two quarters, almost $2 billion in the fourth quarter of 1997 and less than $0.5 billion in the third quarter of 1998. Total portfolio flows including debt were negative in the fourth quarter of 1997, turned positive for the first half of 1998, and then turned negative again from the third quarter of 1998 through the end of the year. During the year from mid-1997 to mid-1998, total portfolio flows were $9 billion.

In contrast, during this period short-term international bank debt fell by $40 billion, from approximately $72 to $32 billion, with the majority of the drop coming in the first half of 1998. Overall, the financial account in the balance of payments ran a negative $25 billion for this period and $29 billion for the period through the end of 1998. Although one should not have confidence in any precise estimate, overall the data suggest that a large but manageable scale of official intervention (had reserves been available) could have substantially reduced the amount of the huge overdepreciation of the *won*.

Note that such sterilized intervention would not have been able to save the precrisis peg. There is disagreement among experts over whether prior to the crisis the *won* was a little overvalued or a little undervalued or just right, but there is no question that the recognition of substantial problems in Korea's financial sector implied a sizable fall in the equilibrium value of the *won*. There can be little question that a major depreciation was needed. We have seen no convincing analysis, however, that argues that the *won* needed to fall all the way from 849.88 in January 1997 to 1,701.53 in January 1998. The amount of exchange rate overshooting could have been substantially reduced through greater sterilized intervention.

Despite former IMF deputy managing director Stan Fischer's call for the IMF to seriously consider substantially increasing its capacity to operate as a quasi lender of last resort during capital account crises, there was no indication of support for a major movement in this direction by either the IMF or its principal shareholders until the current crisis erupted. Thus, Korea's policy of substantial reserve accumulation to make it better prepared to handle possible future crises has been quite wise.[15] We show in Chapter 4, however, that reserves reached levels that are more than adequate.

---

15. See the discussions and references in Eichengreen (2004) and Willett (2003a).

Other criteria for intervention focus on effects on the domestic economy. Even with strict inflation targeting, in open economies, central banks need to pay attention to the implications of exchange market developments for future inflation. It is now well understood that because of adjustment lags monetary policy should respond more to expected future inflation than to past inflation, otherwise dynamic instability may result. In this context, exchange rate developments are likely to be a component of central banks' operating strategies, although this need not involve direct intervention in the foreign exchange market. Beyond strict inflation targeting, central banks and governments may want to give consideration to the economic benefits of price level versus exchange rate stability where there is a conflict between the two. As Keynes once put it: What is the relative importance of internal versus external price stability? Obviously the more open the economy, the greater is the weight that should be given to the latter, but beyond this qualitative judgment we are far from a professional consensus on how these should be weighted or even how inflation targeting is best implemented in open economies. These are important areas for further research.

Concluding Remarks

This review of Korea's postcrisis exchange rate policy suggests that Korea's broad strategy of a managed float combined with an inflation target—what Morris Goldstein (2002) labeled managed floating plus—is the right one. Within this strategy, however, there appears to have been excessive reserve accumulation. In the wake of the almost complete depletion of reserves during the 1997 crisis, a substantial rebuilding of reserves was certainly called for. It would make a major contribution to international financial stability if more countries outside of Asia would follow Korea's example on this score. There is no one exact scientific way to judge reserve adequacy in today's world of substantial capital mobility, but a review of a number of benchmarks suggests that these accumulations substantially exceeded prudent levels (Kim, Kim, and Wang 2004) and raises concerns that the continued increases were motivated more by mercantilist concerns, or by short-run stabilization policy objectives, or both, than by prudent reserve rebuilding and short-run smoothing intervention.

In their recent paper proposing a framework for Korean exchange rate policy, Dooley, Dornbusch, and Park (2002) advocate the combination of inflation targeting with managed floating and suggest specific guidelines for management. Dooley, Dornbusch, and Park (2002, 497) are skeptical of John Williamson's BBC proposal (basket, band, and crawl) largely on the grounds that "We do not believe that it will be possible to identify an equilibrium exchange rate. . . ." We concur in that judgment.

Dooley, Dornbusch, and Park (2002, 495) specifically propose that sterilized intervention be used to moderate fluctuations in excess of 3 percent a day and 6 percent a week against a basket of the dollar, euro, and *yen*. They note, however, that "there is no scientific basis to determine a good band width." The same applies with respect to setting daily or weekly limits. No clear theoretical rationale can determine what such limits should be, but Korea appears to have followed a policy of greater short-run smoothing than recommended by Dooley, Dornbusch, and Park (2002, 511) perhaps because, as they suggest, "in . . . Korea where hedging facilities are expensive and limited to a few firms in the trade sector, the authorities have been under constant pressure to moderate fluctuations in the *won*-dollar exchange rate."

A major part of the justification for heavy short-run management of the Korean exchange rate has been that the foreign exchange market was thin and underdeveloped. In recent years, however, the size of Korea's foreign exchange market has expanded rapidly. From 2002 to 2007, the average daily turnover in the spot foreign exchange market rose more than threefold, from $5.0 billion to $18.8 billion, and the forward market and swaps increased even more from $3.2 billion to $19.4 billion (Ahn 2008). Furthermore, as Dooley, Dornbusch, and Park (2002) note, some degree of variability is needed to make private speculation profitable.[16] Thus, to the extent that the problem is insufficiently stabilizing speculation rather than actively destabilizing speculation, it might be wise to allow some degree of excessive variability in the short run to help facilitate the development of a broader and better-functioning private market for the longer term. Furthermore, artificially suppressing the market signals of underlying risk can lead to too little hedging of international transactions. Large, unhedged positions were, of course, a major cause of the severity of the Asian crisis.

Dooley, Dornbusch, and Park (2002) indicate concerns about the possibility of excessive intervention and argue for strong rules in this area. They propose that a specific target for net reserves be set and that, if reserves deviate from this by more than 25 percent, the imbalance should be corrected over a six-month period. As Kim Jun-il (2002) notes in his comments on Dooley, Dornbusch, and Park, this specific formulation may be too rigid and could generate wide swings in the exchange rate.

Such issues were investigated in the discussion of the Committee of 20 on possible reforms of the international monetary system following the breakdown of the Bretton Woods exchange rate mechanism (ERM) in the early 1970s. There was considerable interest in the development of a reserve indicator system to limit payments imbalances by both surplus and deficit countries. A general conclusion is that, if officials do not begin to make adjust-

---

16. See also the comments by Krueger (2002).

ments until stock limits are hit, this is likely to generate dynamic instability in flows much as strict backward-looking inflation targeting could lead to greater variability in future inflation.[17]

---

17. On the Committee of 20 discussions, see Willett (1977) and Williamson (2000).

3

Dangers of Pegged Exchange Rates and Advantages of Inflation Targeting

Given the substantial level of openness of many Asian economies, developments in their international sectors are of considerable importance to the overall economy. This makes national monetary and fiscal policymaking more complicated. Deciding on the best combination of monetary, fiscal, and exchange rate policies can often be quite difficult. It is much easier to adopt simple policy rates such as a fixed exchange rate. But, while this may make life easier for officials, it will often be worse for the economy.

Political Economy of Time Inconsistency Issues

Many economists over the years have argued the superiority of rules over discretion in setting domestic monetary policy. The problem is that they have usually supported their proposals with analysis in which one major type of shock predominates and for which their proposed policy rule implies an optimal or at least a good response.[18] In the old debate between monetarists and Keynesians about whether monetary policy should focus more on interest rates or monetary aggregates, Keynesians tended to talk about shifts in the demand for money, and in this case focusing on interest rates is indeed better. Monetarists, on the other hand, tended to focus on shifts in aggregate spending and inflationary expectations for which focus on the monetary aggregates is superior. This tendency carried over to the external sector as well. Thus, global monetarists such as Ron McKinnon (1982) focused on international currency substitution where his policy rule of fixed exchange rates and no sterilization would be optimal, while national monetarists such as Milton Friedman (1953) tended to focus on monetary disturbances abroad or spend-

---

18. On these issues see the analysis and references in Willett (1988).

ing shocks at home under which a domestic monetary growth rule with flexible exchange rates would be a good policy regime.

The problem is that economies can be subjected to all of these various types of shocks. In such a world, ideal discretionary policy is clearly the best option. However, time asymmetries, that is, different time profiles of the positive and negative effects of policies, generate time inconsistencies that can lead policymakers subject to short-run political pressures to adopt policies that promote long-run instability. To be more concrete, where wages and prices are sticky in the short run, changes in monetary and fiscal policies have their primary initial effects on quantities and their longer-run effects primarily on prices. This means that expansionary effects have their good effects first and their bad effects later, while for tightening of macroeconomic policies it is just the opposite. As a result, short-run maximization generates a bias toward too much expansion relative to tightening and leads to higher inflation and greater instability in the longer run. As a consequence, unconstrained discretionary policy can turn out to be bad for the economy. What is needed is some type of institutional arrangements to offset such biases.

One way of dealing with the problem is to adopt automatic rules, among which Friedman's money growth rate and fixed exchange rates were initially the most popular. Financial innovation undermined the fairly stable relationship between money growth and spending that Friedman had found for earlier periods; thus, support for pure money growth rates has virtually disappeared today.

For much of the 1980s and 1990s, fixing the exchange rate became the most popular policy rule for promoting monetary discipline. Often described as using the exchange rate as a nominal anchor or as exchange-rate-based stabilization, this approach was strongly supported by officials from many of the members of the EMS for their own political reasons as well as many economists and some of the top officials from the IMF, and it was adopted by a number of countries. Subsequent experience and theoretical and empirical analyses showed that this approach had been greatly oversold. One of the basic problems was that the theoretical analysis supporting this approach was mostly based on the adoption of genuinely fixed exchange rates while in practice the type of fixed rates most frequently adopted was of the adjustable variety. It was frequently inappropriately assumed that the credibility benefits that would accrue from the adoption of a genuine fixed rate would carry over to more adjustable versions, but this would occur only if market participants were fooled into thinking that the soft pegs were in fact hard ones. This did indeed occur surprisingly often in the short run but often was not maintained over the longer run.

Much of the attractiveness of this approach came because it often did provide a quick fix in the short run. Over the medium term such policies tended to work much less well. They did tend to reduce inflation rather rapidly, but usually by not enough to make a fixed rate sustainable. Currencies would often become gradually overvalued, and currency crises were the result. Converting an initial fix to a gradually depreciating crawling band often extended the life of such process, but over time the rate of depreciation tended to be too slow and crisis often eventually erupted, as in Brazil and Mexico. Not all such programs ended in failure, but enough did so that the initial support for this approach has waned substantially.[19]

The basic problem was that adjustably fixed rates were themselves subject to serious time asymmetries. With exchange rate changes, the time asymmetries in the effects on prices and quantities are just the reverse of those for monetary policy. With depreciation, the bad effects of higher prices tend to show up fairly quickly while the good effects on output expansion tend to show up with a lag. Thus, where short-run political pressures are strong, there is a tendency to delay needed deprecations for too long. This is one of the most important reasons why adjustably pegged exchange rate regimes tend to be crisis prone. Combined with substantial international capital mobility, the resulting one-way speculative option presented by adjustably pegged exchange rates provides the rationale for the unstable middle hypothesis—that soft pegs are highly crisis prone.[20]

Inflation Targeting

Given these limitations of exchange rate discipline, the majority view among monetary economists today favors central bank independence as the best way for most countries to overcome time inconsistency problems. What is desired, however, is to make central banks independent of the short-run political pressures to follow policies that will generate longer-run instability, not to be independent to follow whatever whims might enter their heads. Thus, many economists today support inflation targeting to be implemented by independent central banks. The central banks' range of discretion is limited by their obligations to meet agreed inflation targets, and accountability is thus provided. Such central bank independence must be real, not just nominal, and the conditions needed to make independence do not occur in all countries. In Korea it is important for the government to take a strong stand that it supports central bank independence.

---

19. On the issues, see the analysis and references in Willett (1988), Martin, Westbrook, and Willett (1999), and Westbrook and Willett (1999).
20. On these issues see the analyses and references in Angkinand, Chiu, and Willett (2009) and Willett (2007).

Monetary authorities control inflation only indirectly, of course, and this control is imprecise. Thus, targets need to focus on average rates of inflation over a reasonable time period and need to take the form of an acceptable range, not a precise number. In the face of some type of shocks, attempts to meet short-run inflation targets precisely could lead to the same types of instabilities as would money growth rate targets or exchange rate targets. A big advantage of using a medium inflation range as a target is that its desirability is robust to a much wider range of shocks than would be a comparable width of an exchange rate band or money growth range.

A natural question is: Does the adoption of inflation-targeting support a normative conservative anti-inflation agenda over more liberal concerns about unemployment and growth? The answer from a long-run perspective is no. Where wages and prices are sticky, there are short-run trade-offs among inflation and unemployment and growth—the Phillips curve. But over the medium and longer run both theory and mounting empirical evidence suggest that the relationships are just the reverse.[21] In the short run a little inflation can be good for growth, but, over the longer run, repeated efforts to maximize the short-run growth will lead to escalating inflation, which in turn will generate greater uncertainty and depress the economy. Thus, over the longer term higher inflation tends to retard rather than stimulate growth. This is another example of the basic time inconsistency problem.

Inflation targeting is a framework, not a simple rule.[22] Support for inflation targeting does not necessarily imply that the monetary authorities should have no concern with unemployment and growth. Frequently the economy may face shocks where expansionary policies can be followed without a serious risk of escalating inflation. Indeed, many countries find themselves in that situation today in the face of the global financial crisis. While some economists favor strict inflation targeting that would pay no attention to the real economy, many economists favor flexible inflation targeting that allows concern about the real economy as long as this does not lead to the type of continuously escalating inflation that will hurt longer-run growth.

Although it is not clear just how flexible Korea has been in its inflation targeting, it has certainly been quite successful in keeping inflation at modest levels. A look at the performance of the real economy during the inflation-targeting period could suggest that the strategy has been costly in terms of growth because even before the current crisis recent growth rates have

---

21. See the analysis and references in Burdekin et al. (2004).
22. For an overview of inflation targeting see Truman (2004). It is true as Choi (2007) argues that inflation targeting can be more difficult to implement in emerging-market economies, but Korea seems to have managed quite well. For more on these issues in emerging-market economies, see Genberg and He (2007) and Schaechter, Stone, and Zeimer (2000).

averaged well below precrisis levels. This is not an appropriate comparison, however, since there are numerous reasons to believe that precrisis growth rates were not sustainable. In part this was due to Korea's success in moving up to the technological frontier in many industries. Obviously growth can be much faster during catch-up periods. A second important factor is that, in the last years before the 1997 crisis, serious deficiencies in the financial system generated excessive investment in inefficient activities. In the short run this kept the growth rate high but led to the corporate and financial-sector problems that contributed so much to the 1997 crisis.

Indeed, a concern with growth and unemployment is embedded in most inflation targets that aim for low but positive rates of inflation. The empirical evidence suggests that low rates of inflation do not have a negative long-run effect on growth and employment. The results of our econometric estimates are not robust enough to allow us to pinpoint exact upper bounds for "safe" inflation in various economies, but average rates of up to 2 to 3 percent for most economies do seem to be quite safe. In contrast, where there is considerable wage and price stickiness, actual deflation tends to have strong negative effects on the economy, and the Japanese experience during the 1990s suggests that these negative effects continue beyond the short run. Thus, for negative inflation and perhaps even for quite low positive rates of inflation there do appear to be longer-run Phillips curve–type effects. As a result, it is quite consistent to argue that it is desirable to constrain political inflationary biases and at the same time favor keeping national monetary sovereignty to avoid the effects of deflation.

In the current crisis, the BOK has been quite active in reducing interest rates, and the Korean economy has slowed. Thus, there is little reason to think that excessive concern with inflation targets has seriously hindered the BOK's ability to engage in countercyclical policy. Note that inflation targeting automatically takes into account the openness of the economy as long as its focus is on an economy-wide index, not just prices of nontraded goods. Good inflation targeting requires careful study of the linkages between the exchange rate and domestic inflation. The more open the economy, the more important are exchange rate developments for forecasting future inflation; and it is on expected future—not past—inflation that the monetary authorities need to concentrate. Focusing only on past inflation could also create dynamic instability. As noted above, setting appropriate monetary policy in an open economy is not an easy task, and adopting an inflation-targeting approach does not really make it much easier. We cannot expect even the best monetary officials to get it optimal all the time. The more realistic goal is to avoid big mistakes.

It has been argued by some, for example Martin Wolf (2009), that the current crisis demonstrates the failure of inflation targeting. This is true of the view that if inflation is kept low the financial system will always take care of itself. But this was never a terribly sensible view. With a high degree of financial development, excessive credit creation can flow into bubbles in asset markets without a big pickup in inflation. Indeed, that was one of the lessons that should have been taken from the Asian crisis. Before the crisis there had been real estate and stock market bubbles combined with low inflation in a number of Asian economies. There is considerable debate whether monetary authorities should pay attention to asset prices in setting monetary policy and, if so, how much. There is no question that prudential regulators should pay great attention. Low inflation is likely a necessary but is certainly not a sufficient condition to avoid financial instability.

Exchange Rate Issues

There is little question that less variability of exchange rates would make economic policymaking much easier. The biggest danger here is another aspect of the time inconsistency problem. For many types of shocks the international coordination of policies is the optimal response. To date, however, both Asian governments and central banks have shown little willingness to give up their freedom of action to engage in such coordination. This is no different from nations in most regions and is unlikely to change drastically any time soon. As long as they did not have to coordinate monetary and fiscal policies first, governments have frequently agreed to coordinate their exchange rate policies through regimes of adjustably pegged or crawling exchange rates. The ERM of the EMS before the initiation of the euro is a prime example.

It has been recommended frequently that, just as for the euro, this would be a good way for Asia both to deal with the problem of short-run currency instability and to provide a path to eventual monetary union. Such an approach does have some attractive features. It is also highly dangerous, however; and the danger lies in its very attractiveness. It holds out the promise of something for nothing: exchange rate stability without serious infringement of national monetary policies.

The magic comes from sterilized intervention. While capital mobility has grown substantially for most Asian economies, it is generally not yet so high that sterilized intervention has lost all of its effectiveness.[23] Furthermore, many Asian countries are much more financially integrated with centers outside of Asia like the United States and the eurozone than they are with many of their fellow Asian countries. As a result, there is more scope for influenc-

---

23. See, for example, Willett, Keil, and Ahn (2002), Ouyang, Rajan, and Willett (2008), and the appendices to this study.

ing many of the bilateral exchange rates within Asia than for rates against the dollar and euro. (This holds much less for bilateral rates against the Japanese *yen* and Hong Kong dollar and Singapore dollar.) This scope for sterilized intervention allows exchange rate policy to be separated from domestic monetary policy in the short run. Sometimes making use of this scope for separation will be optimal policy. An example is the case of financial capital inflows that are expected to be temporary. Sterilized intervention would cushion the effects of this temporary disturbance on the economy. Of course, the problem here is the difficulty of determining which capital flows are temporary and which are longer term. As will be analyzed in Chapter 6, despite facing considerable international capital mobility, the BOK has been able and has chosen to engage in substantial sterilization. To a considerable degree these sterilization policies have been wise and are an appropriate part of operating a managed float regime.

When one moves from managed floating to a regime of adjustable pegs or target zones, the time inconsistency problems, which are not entirely absent under a float, are multiplied. The temptation is to wait too long to adjust either the exchange rate or monetary policy to restore the longer-run consistency between the two that is needed for stability. As Jeffrey Frankel (2004) has pointed out, there is no reason in economic logic why any type of intermediate exchange rate regime cannot be operated without generating frequent crisis. All that is needed is that exchange rate and monetary policy be kept mutually adjusted to each other, and this can be done by any combination of the amount of adjustment by one or the other. The problem that makes the adjustable peg regimes so unstable in the face of substantial capital mobility is a political economy, not a purely economic one (Willett 2007). Unless both policies are operated with a long time horizon in mind, there will be a tendency under many circumstances to delay this adjustment. There is a range of capital mobility, into which many Asian economies fall, where capital mobility is high enough to make a sticky adjustable peg unstable but low enough to allow sufficient effective sterilization to allow a prolonged but not infinitely long separation between monetary and exchange rate policy.

Because both depreciation and monetary tightening often have greater costs than benefits in the short run, the tendency of officials facing short-run political pressures is understandably to delay adjustment in hopes that the situation will reverse and adjustment will not become necessary after all. Market participants do not face this same political cost-benefit calculation so they are likely to decide that the situation is unsustainable before officials do. The results are speculative attacks and currency crises (Willett 2007).

Moving from adjustable pegs to crawling bands reduces but does not eliminate this problem. Again the European experience is instructive. After the

Bretton Woods exchange rate regime broke down in the early 1970s, it became widely accepted that a major cause had been the excessive stickiness of its adjustable pegs in a world where capital mobility had grown substantially and support for extensive capital controls had declined substantially. As a result, when the Europeans designed their new regional monetary system in the late 1970s, they were careful to not base it on the old narrow band adjustable peg regime of Bretton Woods. They adopted wider bands and called for more frequent parity adjustments so that the band could be moved up or down without necessarily affecting market rates. The idea was that, if an exchange rate was staying near the bottom of its band, the parity would be depreciated so that the market rate would be toward the top of a new lower rate. Initially this regime worked quite well, and parity adjustments were frequent. Over time, however, greater rigidity began to set in just as it had with the Bretton Woods regime. It is hard to believe today, but the designers of Bretton Woods, like John Maynard Keynes and Harry Dexter White, were primarily concerned that parity adjustments would be too frequent rather than too delayed. But this had been the problem during the 1930s.

One sometimes sees glorified accounts of how the exchange rate commitments of the EMS imposed substantial discipline and led to effective monetary policy coordination among the member nations. In the same way some writers have expressed optimism that, by creating an Asian currency unit and developing a system of currency bands based around it, monetary and currency policy coordination in Asia could be substantially increased. The problem is that the view of the European experience on which such proposals are frequently based is a romantic fiction. Some countries such as France did use the ERM effectively to promote domestic monetary discipline, but this was far from the general rule. The system did make it through the 1980s without major crises. This was much longer than many economists, including this author, expected. It led to a false sense of security among officials and many market participants, but this was shattered by a series of major crises in the early 1990s. In some cases, such as Italy, the cause was a lack of sufficient domestic monetary and fiscal discipline. But the deathblow to the regime came from the shock of German reunification, where the combination of the huge fiscal deficits that resulted and the Bundesbank's maintenance of tight monetary policies led to massive capital inflows into Germany.[24] Efforts at fiscal and monetary policy coordination were unsuccessful, and the huge capital flows soon overwhelmed the system's effective financing mechanisms.

The case against efforts to construct a looser target-zone approach in Asia with wide bands and soft edges is not as strong. Such a system might prove workable. It runs a risk, however, that it would follow the European example

---

24. Technically the regime did not die; the exchange rate bands were just widened to ±15 percent, making the parities effectively meaningless.

of hardening the exchange rate regime much more over time than the commitment to coordinating monetary policy. At a minimum we can say with some confidence that it is highly dangerous to make strong exchange rate commitments on the assumption that this will force monetary policy coordination. There is a high risk that the result would be crises rather than sufficient monetary policy coordination.

Although starting with exchange rate commitments has the short-run political advantage of starting the process on the cheap, it seems unlikely that this would actually prove to be the best way to get increased policy cooperation over the longer term. Much safer and more likely to provide long-run results is to begin with ad hoc efforts at coordination in the face of particular shocks where such coordination could be mutually beneficial. For example, when there is a substantial fall in the dollar, countries will worry about their currencies' appreciation not only against the dollar but also against their Asian competitors. Completely decentralized decision making might lead most Asian countries to intervene too heavily and limit appreciation against the dollar too much. Group discussion could well lead to more collective appreciation.

4

International Reserve Adequacy

This chapter is coauthored by Ozan Sula.

Korea has not been unusual among Asian countries in its large accumulation of international reserves since the Asian crisis of 1997–98. These huge area-wide accumulations have attracted considerable interest by researchers and policy officials and have been a major element in the debates about global imbalances. During such research and debate there has been a fundamental preconception of how we should think about appropriate levels of international reserves. (In most of the formal economics literature the focus is on determining optimal levels of reserves while in the policy community the focus is on adequate and excessive levels of reserves.)

New Views of Reserve Adequacy

Traditional rules of thumb about reserve adequacy focused primarily on how many months of imports could be financed with current reserve lends, with three months' worth being a popular figure. In a world of low international capital mobility, this was a sensible approach. Balance of payments difficulties tended to emerge gradually over time, and the primary functions of reserves were to allow countries to avoid unnecessary adjustments in the face of temporary deficits and to allow more time to undertake adjustments when they were necessary. Underlying these rationales were the ideas that adjustments would frequently take the form of tightening macroeconomic policies and that the total costs of such adjustments could be reduced if they could be spread over time rather than occurring all at once through what has come to be known as "shock therapy."

In this world there was also generally perceived to be a trade-off between the degree of exchange rate flexibility and the need for reserves because the greater use of exchange rate adjustments would reduce the need for macroeconomic adjustments. This led to predictions that, with shifts to flexible exchange rates, the demands for international reserves would fall drastically. In fact this did not occur, in large part because of the substantial increase in international capital mobility, which led to an offsetting increase in the demand for international reserves.

With substantial international financial interdependence, both the size of balance of payments crises and the speed with which they can emerge increased dramatically. Furthermore, substantial levels of reserves would not only help cushion the effects of the crisis when they occurred but could also reduce the probabilities of crises occurring in the first place. This possibility has been captured in what are called second-generation crisis models. If the fundamentals of a country are excellent, it will have a crisis only if there is a bad shock; but if the fundamentals are terrible, a crisis is virtually inevitable and higher initial reserves can only postpone the timing of the crisis. These conditions correspond with the concepts of fundamental and nonfundamental disequilibrium enshrined in the Bretton Woods agreement. The dividing line between these two states is not always clear-cut, however. Indeed, there is often a fairly broad range of intermediate conditions where the fundamentals are neither very strong nor very weak. In this vulnerable zone a crisis is possible but not inevitable. With good luck and an absence of bad shocks the situation will remain stable, but with bad luck of a wide variety of types a crisis may be sparked.

Increases in international financial interdependence have both considerably broadened the width of this intermediate or vulnerable zone and increased the importance of adequate reserve levels in avoiding crises. Under substantial capital mobility, we need to look at a country's international financial position, not just from its traditional balance of payments perspective but also from a banking perspective emphasizing liquidity risk. Even if it is highly solvent, a bank needs to keep on hand or have the ability to quickly borrow reserves to meet customers' demands for cash and to pay off maturing borrowings. Normally, the needed reserve ratios can be fairly low. If negative events raise doubts about the soundness of the bank, however, the demands to convert the banks' liabilities into cash can mount quickly, as we have seen in the current financial crisis. In such situations, much greater than normal reserves are needed. And the knowledge that reserves are high or can be borrowed quickly tends to make customers less likely to ask for their money.

Internationally, the closest analogy is to a country's international reserves relative to its short-term foreign debt. Of course, the size of a run on a country could substantially exceed its short-term foreign debt. Foreign investors in the country's stock market can flee, and, to the extent they are not effectively inhibited by capital controls, domestic residents can move their money abroad, in the process further draining the country's international reserves if efforts are made to keep the currency from depreciating.

As a result, the popular recommendation that countries facing substantial capital mobility should aim for reserves equal to three months' worth of imports plus 100 percent of short-term foreign debt may not provide adequate reserves. While the most appropriate ratio of reserves to short-term foreign debt is open to some question, empirical studies have found the ratio of reserves to short-term debt to be one of the more robust predictors of currency crises for emerging-market countries. To account for potential drains from internal funds, some studies have preferred to focus on ratios of reserves to countries' broad money supplies or even GDP.

Wijnholds and Kapteyn (2001), for example, recommend a reserve range equal to between 5 and 20 percent of M2. Another approach is to combine such ratio analysis with measures of vulnerability to crises. Thus, Bussiere (1999) recommends that countries should hold reserves equal to 100 percent of short-term foreign debt plus an additional 5 percent increase in reserves for each 1 percent of exchange rate overvaluation, and another 5 percent for each percentage point of the ratio of current account deficit to GDP.

Potential Capital Flow Reversal Approach

The literature on capital flow surges (what Reinhart and Reinhart [2008] have labeled capital flow bonanzas) and their reversals or sudden stops suggests another approach. In traditional analysis, large capital inflows were generally interpreted as a sign of strong fundamentals, which would imply that the need for international reserves would be less. Although economists are still debating the reasons, recent experience has clearly demonstrated that large surges in financial capital inflows to emerging-market countries are frequently dramatically reversed within a few years. As a result, it is wise for a country facing large capital inflows to channel a portion of these flows into increased reserves even when they take the form of purchases of stocks and long-term bonds rather than just short-term debt. Such considerations have led some researchers such as Ruiz-Arranz and Zavadjil (2008) to recommend that countries focus on increases in total external liabilities. This likely goes too far, however, because numerous empirical studies have found that some types of capital flows have displayed less reversibility than others. Foreign direct investment (FDI) displays the lowest variability. While the statistics understate the variability of capital flows associated with FDI because these flows can show up in other accounts, it seems doubtful that these would be sufficiently large to change the rankings. The relative sizes of the reversals of portfolio and bank flows have varied across different crises.[25]

A number of writers have put particular emphasis on the perceived fickleness of international stock market investors. In the Asian crisis of 1997–98, however, outflows from stock markets were quite modest, and by far the largest reversals were in bank loans.[26] One cause of the excessive concerns about vulnerability to reversals for foreign stock market investments may be conceptual misconceptions about some of the frequently used data. In the 1997–98 crisis the value of foreign holdings of Asian stocks fell drastically, but, as is documented in Kim, Kim, and Wang (2004), most of this was due to the fall in stock prices, not actual outflows. The same has occurred in the current crisis. According to data posted by the Bank of Korea as part of its Economic Statistics System (Ecos), the value of foreign holdings on the Korean stock market fell by $97 billion, from $230 billion to $133 billion. But during this period the stock market fell by 46 percent. Actual outflows were much smaller, $1.25 billion (from January to September 2008), a drop of 38 percent, from the same period in 2007.

Another misconception is that what is relevant for determining reserves needs is the volatility of capital flows as commonly measured by the standard deviation or coefficient of variations of the flows. Portfolio flows do often tend to be fairly volatile by these definitions. A recent study on reserve adequacy that was prepared by IMF researchers (Ruiz-Arranz and Zavadjil 2008, 7) states, "portfolio flows have proven to be the most volatile form of capital flow." As Sula and Willett (2009) have argued, however, the volatility of capital flows during inflow periods is of little policy relevance compared with the magnitudes of reversals during crises, and the former has little predictive power for explaining the latter. Much more relevant, we believe, is looking at the magnitude of capital flow reversals during crises. This approach was adopted in Kim, Kim, and Wang (2004). One serious problem is that during crises considerable capital outflows are often unrecorded. Thus, economists often treat large shifts in the errors and omission component of the balance of payments as reflecting primarily shifts in capital flows.

We consider several different methods of estimating the size of capital outflows during the Asian crisis (Kim, Kim, and Wang 2004). To be conservative we focused primarily on the measures that gave the largest numbers and then converted these to percentages of the most popular scale variables such as short-term foreign debt, broad money supply, and GDP. These are reproduced

---

25. On these issues, see the analysis and references in Levechenko and Mauro (2007) and Sula and Willett (2009).
26. In the Mexican crisis of 1994–95, however, portfolio outflows were much larger than bank outflows. On this issue, see Sula and Willett (2009).

in *Table 4-1* for the countries with the largest net outflows during the crisis: Indonesia, Korea, and Thailand. In *Table 4-2* we use these ratios to scale up through 2007 the sizes of the capital outflows that would be implied by repeats of the high and low values of the crisis.

Table 4-1: **Ratios of Net Capital Outflow during 1997–98 Asian Crisis percentage**

Country	Gross domestic product	M2	Short-term debt
Indonesia	7–10	13–19	41–59
Korea	7–10	19–25	60–78
Malaysia	(-2)–5	(-3)–5	(-22)–41
Philippines	1–4	2–7	13–43
Thailand	17–23	22–28	66–86

Source: S. Kim, S. H. Kim, and Y. Wang, "Macroeconomic Effects of Capital Account Liberalization: The Case of Korea," Review of Development Economics 8 (2004): 624–39.

Table 4-2: **Reserve Adequacy in Korea, 1993–2008, in billions of dollars**

Year	Foreign reserve	GDP	Ratio of reserve/ GDP	Short-term external debt	M2	Ratio of STD/ reserve
1993	20.3	362.1	0.0561	32.2	248.3	1.5862
1994	25.7	423.3	0.0607	44.1	300.7	1.7160
1995	32.7	517.3	0.0632	60.2	370.6	1.8410
1996	33.2	557.4	0.0596	74.8	432.3	2.2530
1997	20.4	516.4	0.0395	63.8	517.3	3.1275
1998	52.0	346.1	0.1502	39.6	639.7	0.7615
1999	74.1	445.2	0.1664	43.1	672.5	0.5816
2000	96.2	533.5	0.1803	49.7	707.7	0.5166
2001	102.8	504.6	0.2037	40.3	765.0	0.3920
2002	121.4	575.9	0.2108	48.2	872.1	0.3970
2003	155.4	643.6	0.2415	50.8	898.1	0.3269
2004	199.1	722.4	0.2756	56.3	954.7	0.2828
2005	210.4	844.7	0.2491	65.9	1,021.4	0.3132
2006	239.0	951.1	0.2513	113.8	1,149.3	0.4762
2007	262.2	1,049.3	0.2499	160.2	1,273.6	0.6110
2008	201.2	928.7	0.2166	151.1	1,425.9	0.7510

Source: Bank of Korea data; author's calculations.
Notes: GDP = gross domestic product; STD = short-term debt.

There is, of course, no presumption that future crises would follow the same pattern as past ones, and indeed the magnitude of outflows in the Asian crisis varied considerably from country to country. Our range of estimates of outflows as a percentage of GDP varied from as low as 0 to 5 percent for Malaysia and 1 to 4 percent for the Philippines, to 17 to 23 percent for Thailand. Korea and Indonesia fell in the middle, with estimates of 7 to 10 percent.

One would not want to have to run down one's reserves to zero to cushion the effects of capital outflows in a crisis since knowledge of such low levels of reserves would itself be likely to stimulate further capital outflows. Thus, countries with little or no access to emergency international borrowing should aim for a comfortable margin of reserves above generous estimates of maximum likely capital outflows for a high level of safety. Experiences with the IMF during the Asian crisis unfortunately have made it quite difficult politically for some countries, such as Korea, to undertake new IMF programs, and this in turn increases the demand for costly self-insurance.

The IMF certainly made some mistakes in its handling of the Asian crisis, but in our judgment its performance was not nearly as poor as is often charged, and there is considerable evidence that it has learned from this experience. Although it is legitimate to question whether this learning and resulting changes in policy strategies have been sufficient, it is quite unfortunate that attitudes toward future involvement with the IMF are generally so negative that substantive discussion of how IMF programs could be improved appears to be quite rare. This makes it difficult to evaluate which aspects of the IMF's policies during the Asian crisis were of most concern. It is thus difficult to probe beyond the widespread attitude that there should be no future involvement with IMF programs. It is symptomatic that in Korea the 1997 crisis is frequently referred to as the IMF crisis.

Several recent studies have emphasized that this precautionary motive for reserve accumulation in the wake of the crisis of the late 1990s was quite prudent, and that the large reserve increases by most Asian countries during the early part of this decade were quite justified. With the prominent exception of the recent study by IMF researchers Ruiz-Arranz and Zavadjil (2008) that will be critiqued below, almost all estimates of optimal reserve holdings have suggested that in recent years the reserve accumulations by Korea and a number of other Asian countries had begun to exceed levels justified by prudent concerns with reserve adequacy.

Reserve Accumulations to Promote Exports and Reduce Adjustment Costs

A popular alternative explanation offered for these continued accumulations was mercantilism. Countries wanting to maintain large export surpluses were holding down their currencies to enhance export competitiveness. In the minds of many commentators, mercantilism is a deeply embedded characteristic of many Asian countries, with Japan long having been the prime example. It is certainly true that the "Asian development model" has been outward oriented while for many years Latin American countries tended to follow more inward-looking strategies of import substitution rather than export promotion. Furthermore, all countries practice some degree of mercantilism in the form of protectionism with respect to some politically sensitive industries.

For export-led growth it is important that overvalued currencies be avoided, but undervalued currencies and large trade and current account surpluses are not required. Thus, it is quite important to distinguish between the sensible strategies of export-led growth that many Asian countries including Korea have followed and the traditional mercantilist objective of seeking large trade and current account surpluses. While Japan could be labeled mercantilist on these criteria for many decades, many Asian countries including Korea cannot. Indeed, one of the most common characteristics of the countries hardest hit by the Asian crisis was large current account deficits. As Aizenman and Lee (2007) have argued, it is hard to believe that there was a spontaneous outbreak of mercantilism across Asia following the 1997–98 crisis. Thus, in explaining the shift toward rapid reserve accumulation in this decade, a much more convincing explanation lies in precautionary motives based on the recognition, stimulated by the rash of crises, that in a world of increased financial interdependence the thresholds for reserve adequacy have increased substantially.

This explanation does not work as well for recent years, however, as substantial reserve accumulation continued for Korea and a number of other Asian economies, most notably China, well beyond sensible precautionary needs. Li, Sula, and Willett (2008) suggest that many of the continuing reserve increases until the current crisis were motivated by concerns with reducing adjustment costs that led to leaning-against-the-wind intervention in the foreign exchange market as documented in Chapter 2. In the face of pressures for appreciation, behavior based on this view and on old-fashioned mercantilism cannot be distinguished, but over the longer run they can differ considerably.

In our interpretation, Korea's reserve increases after 2002 or 2003, when reserve levels had risen to around 20 percent of GDP (see Table 4-2), were primarily the result of neither the precautionary motive nor of old-fashioned mercantilism but rather short-run considerations aimed at reducing the dislocation effects that can be caused by substantial short-run changes in exchange rates. This is a sensible strategy that is consistent with the interests of both Korea and the global economy as long as such efforts are combined with policy efforts to stimulate domestic demand to help offset the effects of less favorable conditions for exports.

As Eichengreen (2007a) has argued, while a strategy of export-led growth has served Korea and other Asian countries well in the past, as income levels have risen it is wise to begin to place more emphasis on domestic sources of growth. As Noland (2005, 2) argued, "the de-linking of domestic and international financial markets was an essential component of the country's state-led development strategy" and emphasized growth for firms rather than profitability. As Korea caught up to the technological frontier, the case for more decentralized allocation of resources increased, and with financial liberalization a new model for development with less focus on exports needed to be developed. At the same time, trade liberalization and general trends toward globalization led to increasing ratios of international trade to GDP.

The argument is not that increasing ratios of trade are harmful, but that special efforts should no longer be made to encourage production for export over that for domestic consumption. Thus, efforts to create and maintain a large trade surplus and a large current account surplus are not a desirable development strategy for Korea. Of course, avoiding large current account deficits is necessary. As domestic and international conditions shift, it is difficult to know what would be the optimal mix of short-run policy responses, but it seems clear that, for a country like Korea, initial responses should include substantial doses of both changes in exchange rates and changes in reserves through intervention that reduces the magnitudes of the exchange rate changes that would otherwise have occurred.

In this view, reserves are best viewed as a buffer stock with rather wide boundaries. Efforts to develop models of optimal reserve levels will never be definitive because full optimization involves a complex set of variables with relationships among them often being nonlinear and there being considerable uncertainty about the values of some of the most relevant parameters.[27] In this respect it is much like the estimation of equilibrium exchange rates. Such efforts can be quite useful, but we cannot expect full agreement among researchers.

A Look at Korean Reserve Adequacy

Thus, it should not be surprising that one recent study by Ruiz-Arranz and Zavadjil (2008) has challenged the widespread perception that reserve levels had grown too high in most emerging Asian countries. (They grant that China is well above their estimates of optimal levels.) By their calculations, before

---

27. For recent efforts and discussions of these issues see Jeanne and Ranciere (2006), Jadresic (2007), McCauley (2007), and Li, Sula, and Willett (2008).

the current crisis began Korea's reserves were only slightly above optimal. They present ratios relative to a number of the standard benchmarks. Perhaps most surprising is their conclusion that reserves should not just exceed short-term foreign debt but should do so by a factor of three. It is interesting to compare this with our estimates of capital outflows during the Asian crisis in J. S. Kim et al. (2004). Our maximum estimate of outflows as a proportion of short-term debt was 86 percent for Thailand. The high for Korea was 78 percent. Ruiz-Arranz and Zavadjil rightly note that in recent years short-term debt has become a declining proportion of emerging-market international finance and, as we discussed, that this is not the only potential source of outflows. Thus, holding reserves greater than 100 percent of short-term debt may be quite sensible. A 300 percent benchmark seems unreasonably high, however, unless short-term debt has fallen to dramatically low levels.

Just the opposite has occurred with Korea. After a drop of more than $30 billion or almost 50 percent between 1996 and 1998, short-term debt remained fairly stable at approximately $40 billion through 2002. Short-term debt then began a gradual increase up to almost $66 billion by the end of 2005. Changes in regulations, heavy demands for financing increased exports—especially in shipbuilding—and hedging activities, and changing interest differentials led to an explosion of short-term external debt in 2006, with year-end totals jumping to more than $113 billion in 2006 and almost $160 billion in 2007. Thus, while Korean reserves were continuing to increase as a percentage of GDP, exceeding 30 percent in 2006, the ratio of reserves to short-term debt peaked in 2004. By 2006, reserves, while still increasing, had fallen below 200 percent of short-term debt. It is interesting to note, however, that during 2008 short-term debt fell by less than $10 billion, less than one-third of the fall during the 1997–98 crisis, even though the precrisis level had been twice as high. In contrast, as will be discussed in Chapters 5 and 10, the outflow of portfolio investment during the current crisis was substantial. Overall, however, the total capital outflows during the crisis appear to have been well below 10 percent of GDP while initial reserve levels were more than twice that figure.

We conclude our discussion of the Ruiz-Arranz and Zavadjil estimates by considering their estimates of optimal reserves for Korea as a proportion of the broad money supply. Their estimate for Korea is slightly over 40 percent. This is less out of line with the ratios of outflows during the Asian crisis but is still considerably largely than our highest estimates, which were 28 percent for Thailand and 25 percent for Korea. Before the current crisis, Korea's ratio of reserves to broad money had risen to 33 percent, and total outflows during the current crisis appear to have been below 10 percent.

Furthermore, several improvements in access for Korea to official international borrowing reduce at least somewhat the need for owned reserves. As will be discussed in Chapter 8, the IMF has made important strides in improving access to short-term borrowing for countries such as Korea that are following generally sensible economic policies; and, in addition to the funds potentially available on a regional basis through the Chiang Mai Initiative, Korea now has large swap lines with the U.S. Federal Reserve and the central banks of China and Japan. As noted above, Korea is extremely reluctant to borrow from the IMF, and it is disappointing that all countries have shown a great hesitancy to make use of the Chiang Mai Initiative. Even without these, unlike the situation in 1997, Korea's reserve position was strong when the latest crisis hit.

5

Financial Liberalization and International Capital Flows

The first section of this chapter is coauthored by Nancy Auerbach. The rest of the chapter is coauthored by Yoonmin Kim and Thana Sompornserm.

It is interesting that domestic and international financial liberalization are among the most often cited causes of the 1997–98 crisis. Liberalization in the Asian crisis countries took place prior to the crisis as did large capital inflows, many of which reversed during the crisis in the classic pattern of capital flow bonanzas ending in sudden stops (Calvo, Izquierdo, and Mejía 2008; Reinhart and Reinhart 2008; Sula and Willett 2009). Furthermore, China and India, with much less general financial liberalization and a continuing array of capital controls, were little hit by the crisis. Malaysia's experiment with increasing capital controls during the crisis, while not the resounding success that some enthusiasts suggested, was certainly not the catastrophe that many critics predicted. As a result, in many quarters support for financial liberalization suffered a strong blow.

The free-market euphoria that followed the collapse of the former Soviet Union had burst. The massive reversal toward greater financial controls that was predicted with glee by some and with fear by others did not come to pass, however. The IMF became more circumspect in its preaching for liberalization.[28] Controls in some countries were increased, but in many others, such as Korea, the crisis spurred further and more balanced liberalization but combined with efforts to improve prudential regulation and financial supervision.

This was a wise response. A careful look at the previous financial liberalization in Korea and many other countries suggests that the major problems

---

28. In actuality, the IMF had generally been more nuanced in its advocacy of liberalization than many of its critics charged; see IEO (2005; 2007).

were not caused by financial liberalization per se, but by the perverse ways in which it was done. It was more their strong economic fundamentals than their capital controls that protected China and India from the 1997–98 crisis (Willett et al. 2005). Furthermore several studies have found positive rather than negative correlations between measures of capital controls and the frequency of currency crises (Potchamanawong et al. 2008). There are sufficient difficulties with the various quantitative measures of capital controls currently available (Potchamanawong et al. 2008)[29] to keep one from being confident that capital controls are a strong cause of crises, but the evidence certainly supports caution about the belief that capital controls provide strong protection against crises.

Perverse Liberalization before 1997

When we look at the Korean experience we see that the liberalization that preceded the 1997–98 crisis was quite partial and frequently violated standard economic advice about how liberalization should proceed. A large literature has been developed by economic theorists and practitioners alike about the necessary preconditions and sequencing needed for liberalization to work well. Not surprisingly considerable disagreement about optimal sequencing still exists, but experts have arrived at a considerable degree of consensus that some paths work much better than others. What has become much clearer from the rash of crises during the past decade is that not only do some paths work less well, but that they can be disastrous.

The total amount of domestic and international financial liberalization undertaken by Korea before the 1997–98 crisis was much less than is often assumed, and most of the qualitative measures of the level of international capital controls in Korea and several of the other Asian crisis countries were still fairly high (Willett et al. 2005). This may help explain the positive association that some studies have found between capital controls and crises. A nontrivial amount of financial liberalization did begin in Korea in the early 1990s and was accelerated by the program agreed to as part of Korea's entry into the Organization for Economic Cooperation and Development (OECD), but Marcus Noland (2005, 17) in his study of Korea's experience with liberalization and international capital flows concluded that, even with the completion of the OECD application plan, "the South Korean financial system would have remained among the most repressed in Asia."

---

29. Using a more detailed new measure of capital control developed by Potchamanawong (2007) that distinguishes between controls on inflows and outflows, Potchamanawong et al. (2008) find that crises are associated more strongly with controls on outflows than on inflows. An example of the problems with the quantitative measures of capital controls is that the widely used measure of Chinn and Ito (2006) shows an increase in controls for Korea before the 1997 crisis, while qualitative discussions indicate there was a reduction. The measures developed by Potchamanawong (2007) and Schindler (2009) do show a decrease.

The liberalization did not result primarily from a conversion of Korean policymakers to neoliberal ideas. As Noland (2005, 38) puts it, "the liberalization undertaken in the early 1990s was less a product of textbook economic analysis than of parochial politicking. . . . Neither South Korean government officials nor the intelligentsia evidenced much ideological commitment to the notion of freer financial markets. . . ." This helps explain why, from the standpoint of standard economic analysis, a number of basic mistakes were made.

The state of the Korean financial system was not strong as the liberalization process began. Noland (2005, 20) describes it as "bureaucratized, bloated, and backwards." Under the old system of government support and directed credit, there was little incentive for Korean financial institutions to invest substantial resources to develop strong capabilities in credit analysis and risk management. As Frederic Mishkin (2006, 87) comments in his analysis of Korea's precrisis financial system, "Because of the government safety net for the *chaebol*s [which were generally considered to be too big to fail], banks had little need to develop a credit culture."

These capabilities cannot be developed overnight, so strong regulatory oversight is particularly important in early stages of liberalization. And, as we have discovered from the U.S. subprime crisis, even in mature financial systems this is true with respect to the development of new types of financial arrangements. As has been true in many other countries, Korea's initial financial liberalization was not accompanied by a strong boost to regulatory oversight. Mishkin (2006, 87) offers a likely reason for this failure: "Just as in Mexico, lax banking regulation and supervision [in Korea] were no accidents. It was in the interests of both the banks and the firms that borrowed from them that they be allowed . . . to do their business . . . unfettered by bothersome regulations and inspections."

In Korea, lax prudential regulation allowed heavy concentration of lending and the disproportionate growth between Korean banks and nonbank industries. In the three-year period leading up to the crisis, merchant banks acquired $20 billion in foreign debt (Chang, Park, and Yoo 1998, 738). Regulation was especially lax for newly licensed merchant banks whose capital requirements in proportion to loans were woefully inadequate. The same can be said for Thailand. This fact alone significantly further increased the vulnerability of the banks to business failure. But the lack of prudential regulation, an act of omission, also interacted with the removal of various government restrictions on foreign borrowing, an act of commission, to exacerbate banking-sector weaknesses. Financial liberalization and tight money kept domestic interest rates above world rates, which encouraged domestic banks to rely on foreign credit. The pegged exchange rate also encouraged the perception that foreign capital was relatively cheap, contributing to the wave of excessive short-term foreign borrowing that was intensified by ineffective prudential supervision. And, because private actors considered the pegged exchange rate system quite credible, they made borrowing decisions under a false sense of security (Demetriades and Fattouh 1999, 788). But the concentration of bad loans leading up to the crisis may not have been due only to the government's encouragement to lend short term through the unintentional creation of perverse incentives. There is evidence that government officials supported lending to the *chaebol* by Korean banks even after *chaebol* profitability had fallen sharply (Krueger and Yoo 2002, 602).

One contributor to the financial weakness of the private banking sector has to do with the incentives behind bank ownership. Privatization of state-owned banks constitutes an important component of the financial reform process. Yet the privatization process itself can fall prey to perverse incentives. This can be viewed as an incompatibility between political motivations and economic incentives, or as political capture of the reform process. Privatization in theory should lead to greater overall efficiency as, for example, the private sector possesses some comparative advantage over government in making profit-maximizing economic decisions. Given the stakes involved, however, the privatization process is particularly susceptible to political capture and rent seeking, as with the charter of new merchant banks in Korea. The government converted 24 financially weak short-term financing companies into merchant banks in two separate rounds: 9 in 1994 and 15 in 1996. The merchant banks then proceeded to engage in risky foreign exchange transactions. Among the banks whose licenses were revoked in 1998, 5 were new entrants from 1994, and 10 were from 1996. Thus, government reforms seem to have encouraged greater debt exposure in an already overexposed financial system (Auerbach 2001, 208).

In Korea, moreover, as part of financial reform banks were allowed to open and expand operations overseas. As a result, banks expanded their foreign currency–denominated business as aggressively as they did their domestic loan portfolios. The net result was an increase in foreign currency liabilities of overseas branches that was almost as large as the external debts of domestic branches (Dooley and Shin 2000, 9). Nor did this happen only in Korea. The number of nonbank financial institutions expanded dramatically in Thailand as well prior to the crisis (Furman and Stiglitz 1998, 7). In fact, throughout East Asia in the 1980s and 1990s, there had been a proliferation of new banking and quasi-banking institutions with little equity capital and less experience, nearly all engaged directly or indirectly in intermediating foreign capital (Katz 1999, 428).

Obviously the buildup of short-term debt severely weakened the domestic banking sectors of crisis countries in Asia. And clearly the governments had a lot to do with encouraging short-term debt buildup (Fischer 1999). One way to understand why short-term debt skyrocketed with financial deregulation is to look at the incentive structures created by state regulation of the financial sector before liberalization and to understand that before liberalization those perverse incentives might have been held in check by government oversight. For example, continued government control over the long-term capital market, in the form of window guidance or direct controls over interest rates, created a shortage of long-term capital during the earlier rapid growth period in most Asian countries. This shortage encouraged the use of short-term credit to finance long-term investments. This perverse incentive ultimately led to a perverse outcome in the form of a mismatch of borrowing and lending terms, which is widely acknowledged to be one of the main ingredients of the Asian financial crisis (Katz 1999, 429). Under these conditions, reform may encourage market actors to take advantage of pre-existing incentives because oversight has diminished.

The starkest example of this kind of perverse incentive is the liberalization of the short-term loan market in the context of an already weakened banking sector (Demetriades and Fattouh 1999, 788). When governments in East Asia liberalized their banking sectors and capital markets, they began by opening up only the short-term maturity end of these markets. Unfortunately, this segment of the market tends to be characterized not only by short-term horizons on the part of investors but also by short-term rent seeking for quick profits by banks taking advantage of close ties with government (Katz 1999, 429). Some Korean banks actually had a negative net worth when the loan market was liberalized. The fact that banks with negative net worth could continue to operate obviously is more a function of inadequate prudential regulation in the preliberalization period than of liberalization per se. In this context of insolvency, however, liberalization may have actually exacerbated the problem because banks with negative net worth do face strong (perverse) incentives to load up on short-term debt as a means of gambling for redemption in a liberalized short-term loan market. That is, if the banking system is unsound owing to a large debt overhang or a large percentage of nonperforming loans that have not yet been written off, these banks have very little to lose by loading up on more risky but potentially highly profitable new loans made accessible as a result of liberalization. This is especially true when viewed in conjunction with the too-big-to-fail form of moral hazard. In both cases, the downside risks of taking on more short-term loan risk are considerably discounted in comparison with the upside of redeeming a failing business enterprise with the infusion of fresh capital.

Governments further encouraged the buildup of short-term debt by liberalizing the loan market while implicitly lowering the perceived costs of foreign borrowing through the pegged exchange rate (Demetriades and Fattouh 1999, 788; Dooley and Shin 2000, 5). Most of the crisis country governments sharply limited the size of exchange rate fluctuations and fostered the impression that the private sector need not worry about the possibility of a large depreciation. The substantial differential between high domestic interest rates in the crisis countries and low rates in Europe, Japan, and the United States was seen as a source of arbitrage profits or low borrowing costs rather than as an indicator of differentials in risk (Krueger and Yoo 2002, 603). As a consequence, much of the crisis country foreign borrowing went unhedged. Thus, financial-sector liberalization and exchange rate policies interacted perversely. In many countries, often with explicit government encouragement, the private sector came to believe that large exchange rate depreciations would not be allowed, or, if such changes did occur, nationals would be compensated by the government (Krueger and Yoo 2002, 603). This both encouraged foreign borrowing and discouraged the purchase of forward cover as an insurance against the risk of major exchange rate changes (Krueger and Yoo 2002, 606).

Korean state managers came under significant pressure by 1993 from the chaebol to liberalize short-term finance (Lee, Lee, and Lee 2000, 1). There is no question the move toward liberalized financial markets fit in with the Kim Young-sam government's globalization priority and therefore served a political function. But this does not explain why both short-term and long-term credit markets were not liberalized. Ironically, policymakers suggested that one of the strongest reasons for introducing competition in the market for bank loans was to mitigate the considerable economic power and influence of the *chaebol.* Indeed, controlling the excesses of big business throughout the liberalization process was an explicit goal for Korean policymakers (Auerbach 2001, 85–87).

The state first embarked upon financial liberalization in 1980 not with the idea of giving market forces free rein, but rather with the idea of building new institutions between the state and big business that would serve to ensure economic control over big business irregularities and to prevent its dominance in the market. Korean officials saw liberalization as redefining the rules in order to continue meeting prudential objectives and prevent the exercise of cartel-like private market power. Part of the long-term liberalization plan was to restrict the privileged access of big business to policy loans and these businesses' oligopolized production in the market (Rhee 1994, 154). Reform-oriented officials firmly believed that economic liberalization would not be successful without preventing further business concentration. State control over big business served not only the state's economic goals but also its political goals. The Chun government (1981–88) put an emphasis on the political goal of the welfare and justice society against the previous regime's collusive state–big business ruling coalition, thus pinning the new regime's legitimacy on its ability to control big business (Rhee 1994, 193).

Despite rather explicit state goals to avoid such outcomes, there is considerable evidence that the content and sequence of Korean liberalization ultimately allowed the *chaebol* to take advantage of perverse incentives. That is, the rather unbalanced form that financial opening took was partially a result of the unyielding pressure from the *chaebol,* which saw short-term borrowing as a way to get around government restrictions on borrowing and investment decisions as well as the capitalization restrictions. Some observers have described the government strategy of liberalizing short-term borrowing while leaving long-term borrowing regulated as government officials giving in where pressures were strong and holding back where it was not. Given the short-term nature of borrowing by nonbank financial institutions, the liberalization of the short-term market prior to the long-term market was an understandable outcome of interest politics. Between 1994 and 1996, foreign bank lending to Korea went from $52 to $108 billion. About $60 billion of debt outstanding in 1997 was used by the *chaebol* to finance direct investments abroad. Korean banks invested in foreign assets with funds borrowed from foreign banks in the range of $23 billion (Haggard and Mo 2000, 204). The reliance of the *chaebol* on bank borrowing—as opposed to equity or bond financing—increased leverage ratios and made the *chaebol* highly susceptible to bankruptcies when hit with shocks. In turn, the health of the banking sector became heavily dependent on the viability of the *chaebol* because such a high fraction of bank assets are in the form of lending to these enterprises (Dekle and Ubide 1998, 18). Korean financial institutions were overexposed to foreign exchange risk, and a high proportion of foreign liabilities had relatively short maturities. So, at the very least, deregulation of the financial sector in the early 1990s, together with ongoing features of the government-banking-*chaebol* relationship, increased Korea's vulnerability to outside capital flows by creating the incentive for short-term indebtedness (Haggard and Mo 2000, 215).

Finally, large business groups throughout Asia benefited from the process of bank privatization. As many scholars have pointed out, privatization because of the large stakes involved is particularly prone to rent seeking and capture. In countries like Korea, government relaxation of controls over entry and ownership has led to the largest business groups' domination of both the ownership of commercial banks and nonbank financial institutions (Tan and Schneider, forthcoming). One result in Korea was that credit became concentrated, with the largest 30 business groups receiving more than 70 percent of total short-term credit (Rhee 1994, 203). One potential sticking point for Korean officials was that, in order to strengthen banks, it was necessary to end the ban on *chaebol* ownership of them. But bank privatization only strengthened the already powerful *chaebol.* In short, the privatization process allowed big business groups to capture an ever-increasing proportion of the banking sector, thereby fortifying the large business groups' position in relation to government control.

Not all the pressures for liberalization were domestic. International pressures were also important. These can operate through a number of channels. One is through impersonal market forces; that is, the degree of international capital mobility can influence the costs and benefits of a wide array of financial strategies. Actions by other emerging-market governments may also have important effects through this channel. Liberalization of competitors raises the costs of continued restrictions in the home country.

A second is through influence on actors' mental models. Although the extent of influence is open to debate, there can be little question that attitudes toward financial liberalization had become much more favorable by the 1990s compared with the 1970s, and that the international transmission of ideas has a good deal to do with these changed attitudes.

A third channel is through direct pressure. This can come from the international financial institutions such as the IMF and World Bank and via direct lobbying on emerging-market governments by international financial interests, but such pressures are perhaps more commonly intermediated by national governments in the industrialized countries (Bhagwati's Wall Street–Treasury complex). Lobbying, persuasion, and arm-twisting by industrial-country governments and the international financial institutions can come of course from the sincere belief that liberalization is in the best interests of the emerging-market countries. The relative influence of interests and ideas or ideology in this context will often be difficult if not impossible to tease out. Assuming that bureaucrats throughout Asia have been reluctant to cede discretionary power to the private sector, one could interpret the decision to liberalize short-term finance as the result of market pressure. That is, international finance brought the most market pressure to bear in the short-term credit market in part because the volume of short-term financial flows was so much greater. In other words, bureaucrats failed to liberalize long-term finance because they possessed the capability to resist, whereas they could not resist the tide of market forces in the short-term financial market.

External pressure for financial-market opening can be extremely powerful. This is an area in which unintended consequences are of major importance. Sometimes the effects on emerging markets are the result of industrial-country policies. Fluctuations in credit conditions in the rich countries have been shown to have strong effects on the size of international financial flows to emerging markets. Less inevitably, the efforts of the industrial countries to develop better standards for risk management by the major international banks resulted in incentives for the banks to shift from longer-term to short-term lending (Goodman and Pauly 1993; Cohen 1996). The so-called Basel Accord on capital adequacy standards for banks reflected a substantial achievement of international cooperation, but few noticed at the time that this was followed quickly by a dramatic increase in the ratio of short-term to long-term bank loans going to emerging markets. This was the result of the much higher ratios of capital required to back bank loans of over one year.

The Czech Republic, Mexico, and Korea were hit by a double whammy. By achieving sufficient economic and political success to be allowed to join the industrial countries as members of the OECD, they automatically qualified under the Basel rules for a lower risk category with lower capital requirements on loans. While not all international banks were following these regulatory rules, enough were so that the admissions of these countries to the OECD were followed by surges of capital inflows (concentrated of course on the short-term end). We also cannot totally discount the more formal external pressures to liberalize. In Korea, President Kim Young-sam's desire to join the OECD, combined with pressure from the IMF and the U.S. government, may have led to the liberalization of domestic financial markets before existing weaknesses in the banking system, including poor regulatory and supervisory framework, could be addressed (Demetriades and Fattouh 1999, 791). So, although some liberalization would undoubtedly have taken place in the absence of foreign pressure, the nature and timing of liberalization may have been acutely affected.

Perhaps the strangest aspect of Korea's liberalization sequencing was the decision to liberalize short-term capital flows before long-term ones—the exact opposite of the normally recommended sequencing. As Mishkin (2006, 88, 29) explains, however, allowing an "unlimited short-term foreign borrowing by financial institutions while maintaining quantity restrictions on long-term borrowing . . . made no economic sense, . . . however [it] made complete political sense." ". . .[This] allowed the government to say that it was still redirecting foreign capital inflows, and to claim that it was opening up to foreign capital in a prudent manner." Just the opposite was the case, of course.

At least one minor contribution to the excessive short-term foreign borrowing that developed was due to the unconsidered consequences of the international efforts to improve financial systems' stability through the Basel I capital requirements. These crude risk control measures drew a sharp distinction between countries that were and were not members of the OECD, so when Korea was admitted the capital requirements for some loans to Korea were substantially lowered for banks in countries following Basel I, then leading to greater incentives for banks to lend to Korea. Although the revised declarations in the Basel II agreement appeared to be much more sophisticated, the current crisis has shown that much of this apparent sophistication was an illusion, as little if anything had been done to improve consideration of the possible effects on systemic risk that might be generated by following the regulations.

Perhaps the most serious weakness in financial system oversight came, however, not from issues with the behavior of the commercial banks but from the merchant-banking sector that Mishkin (2006, 89) describes as "virtually unregulated." In 1990 Korea had only six merchant banks, all affiliates of foreign banks. Wanting greater access to foreign borrowing, the *chaebol* launched a lobbying campaign that "persuaded government officials, often through bribery and kickbacks, to permit many finance companies which were not allowed to borrow abroad, to be converted into merchant banks, which could." The result was that by the time of the crisis the number of merchant banks in Korea had grown to 30, 16 of which were controlled by the *chaebol*.

The result was a domestic credit boom financed heavily by foreign borrowing. Not surprisingly, the rapid expansion of credit led to an increasing proportion of lending of a dubious nature. Regulators in Korea were no more successful in limiting this problem than were U.S. regulators in taking action to head off the subprime crisis. The major problem was not that the regulatory agencies could not pay enough to hire competent supervisors. The danger signs were not difficult to see if one was looking. Rather the biggest problem (Mishkin 2006, 93) was that "political pressure on bank supervision led to 'regulatory forbearance,' the supervisors were not forcing banking institutions to reveal these bad loans and were allowing insolvent institutions to stay in business."

Given these problems, it seems likely that a major financial crisis was inevitable. The financial system was in much too fragile a state to weather the spillover from the crisis that started in Thailand. The result was huge capital outflows, substantial overdepreciation of the *won*, and widespread financial distress and economic hardship.

Postcrisis Liberalization

Fortunately Korea drew the right lessons from the Asian crisis concerning the financial sector. Instead of pushing for re-regulation, the government saw that more and especially better liberalization was needed, accompanied by greatly strengthened prudential supervision in order to improve the soundness of the financial system (Kim, Kim, and Suh 2009; Kang 2009).

A number of regulations on the banking sector and stock market, particularly aimed at the foreign investors, were largely eased or eliminated. At the same time, incentives were created to induce foreign investors to return their investments or to attract new investors to Korea. In addition, after the Asian crisis, the Korean government nationalized many large domestic banks that were vulnerable to solvency risks, and Korean authorities also concurrently loosened some restrictions on the entry of foreign banks in order to attract foreign banks to purchase or merge those nationalized banks. In 1998, for example, the Emergency Economic Committee allowed foreigners to buy up to one-third of a company's shares without prior approval of the target firm's board of directors (Bekaert and Harvey 2004), foreign investors were allowed to directly participate in Korean banks through acquisition or through equity markets, and foreign banks were subject to the same restrictions as Korean banks. The Korean government also engaged in intensive financial reforms in order to strengthen its prudential regulation and supervision, increase its financial-market development, and improve corporate governance (Kim, Kim, and Suh 2009). An important aspect of this push was the creation of the Financial Supervisory Commission in 1999. The result has been a much sounder domestic financial system.

Korea has generally kept tighter restrictions on capital outflows than on capital inflows (*Figure 5-1*). During the crisis restrictions on inflows were reduced in order to moderate the downward pressure on the *won*; this was followed after the crisis by more liberalization of both capital inflows and outflows (*Table 5-1*). The regulations in several asset categories were lifted for both foreign and domestic investors; categories included securities, bonds, short-term money market instruments, derivatives, collective investments, and real estate. In 1998, for example, foreigners were freed to purchase domestic collective investment securities without restrictions; in 1998 domestic corporations were allowed to issue securities abroad with maturities of less than three years; in 1998 nonresidents were allowed to issue securities denominated in foreign currency (Bekaert and Harvey 2004); and in 2003 the government extended the range of foreign securities qualified for investment by residents (Ahn 2008). In 2007, restrictions on the investments by residents in overseas real estate were relaxed (Kim, Kim, and Suh 2009).

Recent empirical research by Sompornserm (2009) has found that domestic financial liberalization in emerging markets often plays an important role in attracting foreign investors over and above capital account liberalization. The process of liberalization not only affects prices and returns on assets directly, but it also leads to an improvement of investors' expectations about further economic policy reforms or acts as a signal of an improvement of economic policies, making foreign investors more confident about investing in the liberalized countries. In addition, financial liberalization has on average had

Figure 5-1: **Potchamanawong and Schindler Capital Control Indexes 1995–2004**

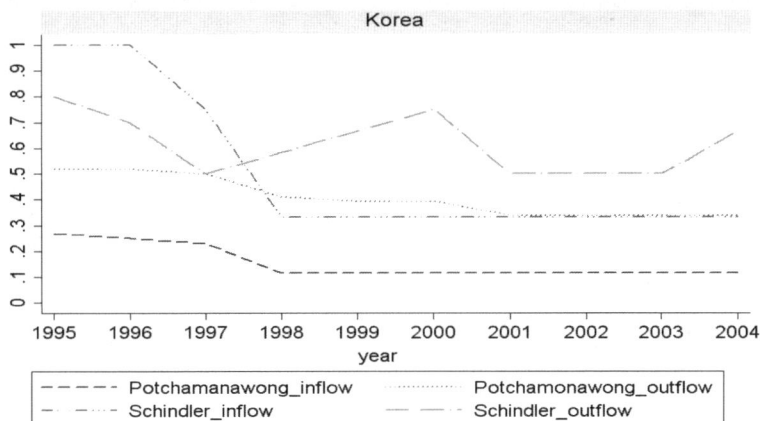

Graphs by country_code

Sources: P. Potchamanawong, "A New Measurement of Capital Controls and Its Relation to Currency Crises" (Ph.D. dissertation for Claremont Graduate University, 2007); M. Schindler, "Measuring Financial Integration: A New Data Set," IMF Staff Papers 56 (2009): 222–38.

Note: The Potchamanawong and Schindler capital control indexes range between 0 and 1. The higher value represents a higher degree of capital control.

Figure 5-2: **Patterns of Foreign Capital Flows into South Korea 1980–2008**

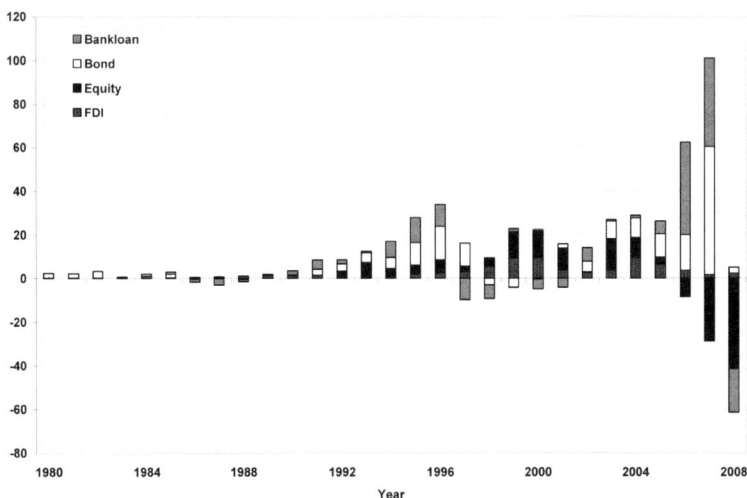

Sources: International Financial Statistics database of the International Monetary Fund; author's calculations.

Table 5-1: **Financial Liberalization in Korea after the Asian Financial Crisis, 1997–2007**

Year	Changes in regulations
1997	In December, the ceiling on foreign ownership of Korean stock was raised from 26 percent to 50 percent.[a]
1998	The first stage of restructuring aimed to restabilize the financial system and enhance the soundness and effectiveness of financial institutions; this began with large-scale restructuring shortly after the crisis in February 1998 and lasted until August 2000. Capital markets, including the short-term money and real estate markets, were completely open to foreigners.[b]
	Korean government fully removed the ceilings on shareholding by foreign investors.[c]
	Foreign investors were allowed to directly participate in Korean banks through acquisition and equity market.[d]
	Foreigners were allowed to purchase domestic collective investment securities without restrictions.[a]
	The Emergency Economic Committee agreed to allow foreigners to buy up to one-third of a company's shares without prior approval.[a]
	The deposit requirement ratio, which required that stock purchase orders be accompanied by a cash deposit, was eliminated.[a]
	Some of the foreign investment limits on Korean securities were lifted.[a]
1999	The government aggressively pursued foreign exchange liberalization in order to transform the Korean financial market into a major business hub of Northeast Asia by 2011. In the first stage of liberalization, launched in April 1999, the positive list system of the Foreign Exchange Act, governing foreign exchange transactions in Korea, was overhauled and transformed into a negative list system.[c,e]
	Investment in foreign real estate by domestic entities was permitted.[f]
	Investment in foreign financial and insurance markets by domestic entities was permitted.[f]
	Korean government allowed domestic corporations to borrow money with maturities of less than one year directly from foreign financial institution and to issue short-term foreign currency–denominated bonds.[c,f]
	Requirement that foreign-invested firms receive government approval for intrafirm transactions exceeding $1 million was abolished.[f]
	Domestic institutions were permitted to engage in derivatives transactions.[f]
	Foreigners were allowed to make deposits and open trust accounts denominated in Korean *won* with maturities of more than one year.[c]

Table 5-1: cont.

2000	Regulations on foreign direct investment were brought into compliance with Organization for Economic Cooperation and Development standards.[f]
	The financial accounting standards regarding both financial and nonfinancial firms were revised in March 2000.[g]
	Korean government began allowing financial holding companies to offer all financial services, and four companies—Woori, Shinhan, Korea Investment, and Hana—began conducting business. Other financial companies, including Kookmin Bank, Citibank Korea, and the National Agricultural Cooperative Federation, now are on the verge of conversion into financial holding companies.[h]
	The second stage of restructuring, aimed at restabilizing the financial system and increasing the soundness and effectiveness of financial institutions, was triggered by Daewoo Group's liquidity crisis in September 2000.[b]
2001	The second stage of foreign exchange liberalization followed in January 2001, accompanied by the deregulation of virtually all current account transactions.[b]
	All restrictions were lifted on foreign currency loans to residents by domestic banks.[f]
	Remaining ceilings on current account transactions by individuals eliminated.[f]
	In January 2001, over-the-counter securities transactions between residents and nonresidents were liberalized.[i]
	The ceiling on overseas payment for overseas expense for travel, education, and emigration was abolished.[d]
	Restrictions on obligatory repatriation of oversea claims were relaxed.[e]
2002	The government announced the plan for the development of a liberalized foreign exchange market. For example, the government eased procedural regulations on the foreign exchange activities of individuals and business firms.[c]
	Securities and insurance companies were allowed to participate in the interbank foreign exchange market.[c]
	The government liberalized the export of the Korean *won.*[c]
2003	Foreign investors in high-growth sectors would be exempt from corporate and income taxes for seven years.[a]
	Korean government reduced the limit on overseas direct investment in financial and insurance companies by residents.[j]
	Korean government extended the range of foreign securities eligible for investment by residents.[j]

Table 5-1: cont.

2006	Korean government announced a foreign exchange liberalization plan that advanced the schedule of completing the foreign exchange liberalization from 2011 to 2009.[c,d]
	The limit on the value of an individual's residential property overseas was removed completely.[j]
	Korean government removed the ceiling on direct investment abroad by individuals.[h]
	Korean government abolished all restriction on the types and items of overseas securities investment by residents.[d,j]
	Korean government removed licensing requirements for capital transactions; replaced by ex post reporting requirements.[c,d]
2007	Korean government exempted domestic asset management companies from capital gains taxation through overseas stock purchases in foreign investment funds.[j]
	Korean government raised ceiling on overseas properties acquired by domestic investors.[d,j]

Sources:

a. G. Bekaert and C. R. Harvey, "A Chronology of Important Financial, Economic and Political Events in Emerging Markets—Korea," 2004, http://www.duke.edu/~charvey/Country_risk/chronology/korea.htm.

b. J. Y. Lee, "Korea's Way Out of Financial Crisis," *Korea Times,* 4 April 2008, http://news.naver.com/main/read.nhn?mode=LSD&mid=sec&sid1=001&oi d=044&aid=0000072416&.

c. M. K. Kang, "Global Financial Crisis and Systemic Risks in the Korean Banking Sector," Academic Paper Series 4, no. 5 (2009).

d. K. Kim, B. K. Kim, and Y. K. Suh, "Opening to Capital Flows and Implication for Korea," Working Paper no. 363 (Seoul: Bank of Korea, Institute for Monetary and Economic Research, 2009).

e. J. E. Song, "Currency Market Needs Full-Blown Liberalization," *Korea Times,* 2 May 2008, http://news.naver.com/main/read.nhn?mode=LSD&mid=sec&sid=001&oid=044&ai d+0000073240&.

f. M. Noland, "South Korea's Experience with International Capital Flows." Working Paper no. 11381 (Cambridge: National Bureau of Economic Research, 2005).

g. J. B. Kim, "Improving Transparency in Financial Market," *Korea Times,* 9 May 2008, http://news.naver.com/main/read.nhn?mode=LSD&mid=sec&sid1=001 &oid=044&aid=0000073462&.

h. C. B. Suh and J. H. Koo, "Recipe for Success of Financial Conglomerates," *Korea Times,* 7 May 2008, http://news.naver.com/main/read.nhn?mode=LSD&mid=sec&sid1=001&oid=044& aid=0000073383&.

i. K. S. Kim, "Opening Up to Capital Flows Poses Challenges," *Korea Times,* 31 December 2008, http://news.naver.com/main/read.nhn?mode=LSD&mid=sec&sid1=001&oid=044&ai d=0000079529&.

j. Ahn B. C., "Capital Flows and Effects on Financial Markets in Korea: Developments and Policy Responses," Paper no. 44 (Basel: Bank for International Settlements, 2008).

a strong influence in changing the composition of capital flows within the short-term flows, by tilting the structure of capital flows toward portfolio investment flows. This result suggests that an increase in the degree of financial liberalization can translate into greater financial-market deepening. Korea's experience fits this general pattern.

Postcrisis Capital Flows

After the Asian financial crisis, international capital inflows to Korea reappeared, particularly in the form of equity flows and FDI flows as a result of domestic financial liberalization, capital account openness, and favorable macroeconomic conditions. Several factors contributed to large changes in the composition of capital inflows in Korea during 1999–2000, shifting Korean capital flows away from foreign loans toward FDI flows and equity flows. An increase in risk perceptions by foreign creditors as a result of the loss of confidence in Korean borrowers' ability to repay their debts was one. Another was the lessons learned by Korean borrowers from the sudden stops and the reversals of foreign loans during the crisis. After 2000, a continuing surplus in current and capital accounts, which would put upward pressure on foreign exchange rates, led Korean authorities to encourage capital outflows by relaxing restrictions on capital outflows to overseas real estate, portfolio investments, and direct investment abroad (Kim, Kim, and Suh 2009).

As we can see in *Figure 5-2,* by 1999 net capital flows had turned positive again, with especially large investments coming into the Korean stock market in 1999 and continuing on a large scale through 2004 with only the exception of 2002. Total net capital flows followed a similar pattern over these years. In 2005 total net inflows dropped, with inflows in the bond market and banking exceeding equity inflows. Bond sales and bank borrowing reached much higher levels in 2006 and 2007 while net foreign flows into the Korean stock market turned mildly negative in 2006, with net sales accelerating in 2007. At the same time, the loosening of restrictions on capital outflows led to a boom in purchases of foreign stocks and real estate by Korean residents. This led to sizable net portfolio equity outflows in 2006 and even larger ones in 2007 (*Figure 5-3*). As a result, total net capital flows turned negative in 2007 (*Figure 5-4*). Note that this shift occurred before the effects of the U.S. subprime meltdown began to be felt in emerging markets.

The other especially notable feature of Korean capital flows between the crises was the rapid buildup of short-term foreign debt by the Korean banking sector beginning in 2006. The foreign borrowing by the Korean banking sector considerably increased from $1.1 billion in 2004 to $40 billion in 2007, growing approximately 10-fold per year. In addition, during 2006–07, bank borrowing alone on average accounted for 45 percent of the capital inflows. The substantial increase in foreign borrowing was in part a consequence of the large portfolio outflows from Korean residents; Kim, Kim, and Suh (2009, 30) state that "capital outflows via overseas equity investment increased markedly, but at the same time investors (funds) sold forward exchange on a large scale to hedge against exchange rate risk, leading to a considerable increase in overseas foreign currency borrowing." The increase was also caused in part by hedging against future export proceeds, especially from shipbuilding. This buildup in short-term foreign borrowing was generated largely by the Korean branches of international banks.

This rapid buildup illustrates how quickly international financial relations can change even in noncrisis periods. This accumulation of short-term foreign debt was carefully monitored by the Korean authorities, who judged that, because of the combination of the reasons for the borrowing, its concentration with Korean branches of international banks, and Korea's ample supply of international reserves, this increase was not a major source of concern despite its large size. As will be discussed in Chapter 10, this judgment was well founded in the sense that, during the current crisis, the decline in such debt has been fairly modest in contrast with the Asian crisis, but the large headline number helped contribute to considerable investor concerns during the crisis, which helped contribute to the dramatic plunge of the *won*.

Sizable portfolio outflows continued in 2008. In contrast, short-term bank debt, which had begun to surge in 2006, has remained at high levels. This is a substantial deviation from the pattern in the 1997–98 crisis, when reversals in the banking accounts were the major factor and the falloff in stock market investment was slight. To a substantial degree we can explain these differences in the patterns of capital flows by the differences in the nature of the crises. In 1997–98, the crisis was centered in Korea and focused on problems in the financial sector. Consequently, there was considerable risk to foreign lending to Korean banks, and it is not surprising that there were considerable outflows from the banking sector. The current crisis is centered in the United States, and the Korean banking sector is much sounder, although concerns have been expressed about the recent large accumulations of short-term foreign debt and the increasing reliance on wholesale funding. The behavior of capital flows during the current crisis will be discussed in Chapter 10.

Figure 5-3: **Patterns of South Korea's Capital Outflow, 1980–2008**

In Billions of
US Dollars

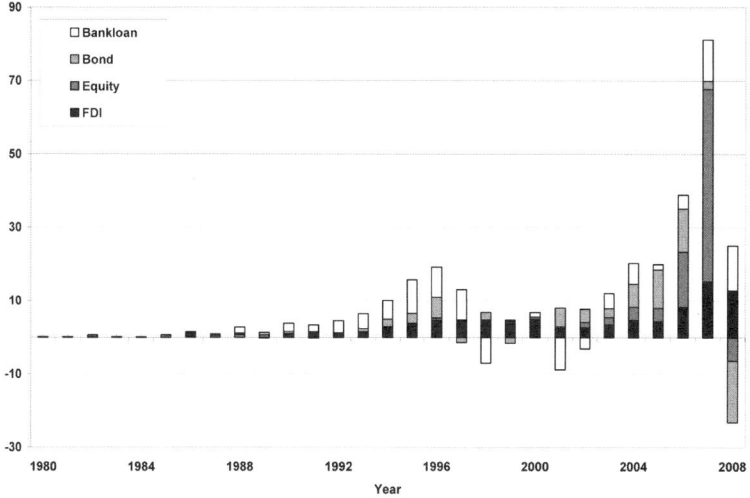

Sources: International Financial Statistics database of the International Monetary Fund; author's calculations.

Figure 5-4: **Patterns of Net Total Capital Flows for South Korea 1980–2008**

In Billions of
US Dollars

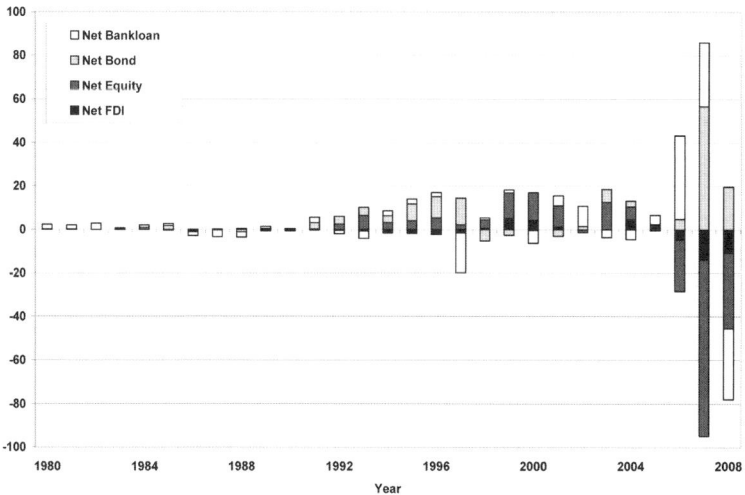

Sources: International Financial Statistics database of the International Monetary Fund; author's calculations.

6

International Aspects of
Korea's Monetary Policies

This chapter is coauthored by Alice Ouyang.

As was discussed in Chapter 5, considerable financial liberalization and capital opening was implemented by Korean authorities during the 1990s. The government conducted a series of interest rate deregulation plans beginning in 1991 and partially opened the domestic stock market to foreign investors in the following year.[30] Despite the continuation of numerous restrictions, substantial capital inflows helped keep Korea's overall balance of payments (BOP) in surplus during the early 1990s, even though the current account remained continuously in deficit because of strong domestic demand. However, the Asian currency crisis in 1997 led to huge flows of capital out of the country. The current account was improved by the substantial depreciation of the *won* in 1997 and early 1998, and it remained in surplus until into 2007 when the run-up in prices of oil and raw materials caused it to turn negative again. The capital, or financial, account turned to surplus as well. As a result of these combined current and capital account surpluses, Korea accumulated international reserves rapidly until the recent crisis.

Governments and central banks have understandable concerns that substantial international capital mobility and large swings in the BOP may harm a country's ability to follow sound domestic monetary policy. Indeed, this appears to have been a major factor underlying the slowness with which Korea liberalized its capital account before the crisis.(Noland 2005). This chapter investigates whether the substantial increase of capital account liberalization

---

30. The ceiling of overall foreign investment in any listed company was initially set at 10 percent and then gradually raised, with by far the largest increase being implemented after the outbreak of the currency crisis in November 1997 (S. Kim and W. Kim 1999).

that followed the crisis has undermined the BOK's ability to carry out domestic monetary policy.

Monetary Policy and the Balance of Payments in Korea

Korea's postcrisis policy of intervening in the foreign exchange market to strongly lean against the wind, which was documented in Chapter 2, resulted in large changes in international reserves. To keep these changes in reserves from generating corresponding changes in the money supply, it was necessary for the central bank to actively counter the automatic effects of these reserve changes on the monetary base. International reserves are an important component of the monetary base, and reserve increases expand the foreign component of the base. If reserve requirements and the money multiplier are constant, then it is necessary to take actions to reduce the domestic component of the monetary base in order to keep money growth from accelerating.

Changes in the foreign and domestic components of the base are plotted in **Figure 6-1.** This is called sterilization. Of course, changes in volatility can be quite important in today's world of liberalized financial markets; thus, changes in the money supply are not necessarily a good indicator of the stance of monetary policy. Still, few economists believe that the money supply is totally inconsequential, and prolonged substantial increases in the monetary base would be likely to lead to excessive credit growth. Thus, many central banks routinely take actions to neutralize the effects of overall payments imbalances, for example, changes in international reserves, on high-powered money.

A standard proposition in monetary analysis is that the higher the international capital mobility, the more difficult it is to carry out such sterilization effectively. Indeed, in the limit of perfect international capital mobility, effective sterilization is impossible. It is clear that there has been a substantial increase in international capital mobility facing most emerging-market countries, including Korea. Such capital mobility is still far less than perfect. Whether capital mobility is high enough to seriously undermine the ability of central banks to sterilize reserve changes and hence give them the ability to differentiate monetary from exchange rate policy in the short run is an important issue on which leading economists have offered widely differing views. It is essentially an empirical issue. Our econometric estimates find that, despite the large scale of reserve flows and payments imbalances since the 1997–98 crisis, the BOK has retained the ability to effectively sterilize these reserve flows and has actively pursued this practice.

Figure 6-1: **Monthly Annual Change in Net Foreign Assets, Net Domestic Assets, and Monetary Base in Korea, January 1985–October 2008**

Billions (won)

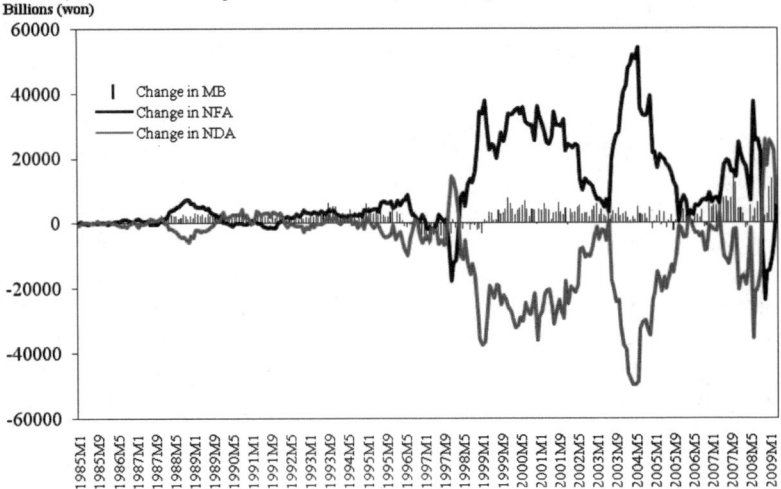

Source: CEIC data set.

Notes: MB = monetary base; NDA = net domestic assets; NFA = net foreign assets.

Monetary Sterilization Policies in Korea

Like central banks in most Asian countries, the BOK now takes price stability as the most important objective of its monetary policy, and the BOK has full discretionary power in terms of deciding the sterilization policies and choosing monetary instruments. As is shown in *Figure 6-2,* it has been rather successful in this task, although as with many other Asian countries shortly before the current crisis stronger inflationary pressures were beginning to emerge again. A variety of monetary target policies have been set since the creation the Financial Stabilization Program in 1957 (see *Table 6-1*). The earliest targets were M1, reserve money, and domestic credit. Over time the emphasis shifted toward broader monetary aggregates M2, MCT,[31] and M3, and more recently Korea joined the widespread movement to inflation targeting with increased emphasis on interest rate adjustments as an operational policy instrument.

Although the BOK has not consistently hit its inflation target of 3 percent ±0.5 percent, it has generally succeeded in keeping inflation fairly low. In 2007, however, Korea joined the trend of accelerating inflation that had developed in a number of Asian economies and that some economists have argued reflected as much excessive liquidity generated globally as it did a

---

31. MCT includes M2, certificates of deposit, and money in trust.

country's own monetary policy. The importance of this global financial ease is a topic that is unlikely to be resolved soon. Our reading of the evidence suggests to us that many countries still have sufficient monetary autonomy to counter such global trends but that the existence of global monetary ease makes it less likely that sufficiently cautious national policies will be adopted. This is our interpretation of the major way in which the global monetary and credit ease and savings glut contributed to excessive credit growth in the United States. In this chapter we investigate some of the major channels of international influence on Korea's monetary policies.

Figure 6-2: **Inflation in Korea, January 1985–March 2009**

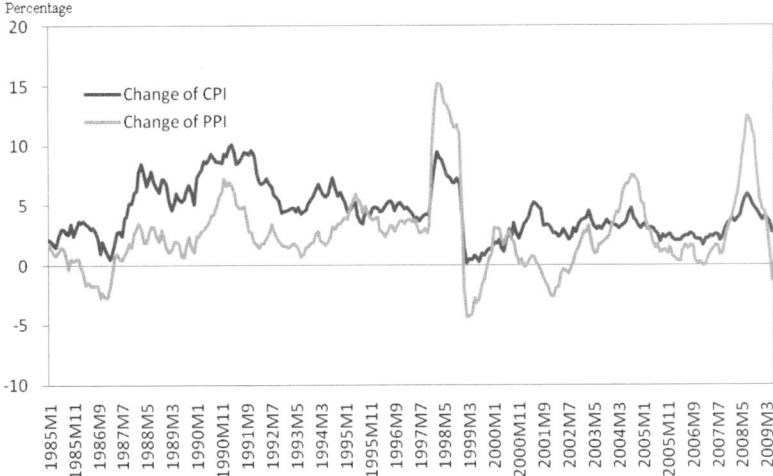

Source: CEIC data set.

Notes: CPI = consumer price index; PPI = producer price index.

To keep inflation low, reserve requirements and lending policy have been used frequently to adjust the domestic liquidity since foreign reserves began to be accumulated in the mid-1980s. But, with the development of the domestic bond market, open market operations (OMOs) have played a more important role as a monetary instrument since the early 1990s.[32] The BOK often changed reserve requirement policies during the 1970s and 1980s (***Figure 6-3***). To ease the burden on banks' earnings, the reserve requirement ratios have been lowered on several occasions since the beginning of 1980s, but they were then increased twice in November 1987 and December 1988 owing to the growing monetary expansion. Although a unified reserve requirement

---

32. However, the relationship between the BOK and commercial banks tends to be one-sided rather than coordinative because the BOK forcefully allocated the amount of bond purchases across financial institutions.

ratio was applied to all deposits in July 1981, marginal reserve requirements were again put in place in 1989 to help control the money supply.

Table 6-1: **Monetary Policy Targets in Korea, 1979–2009**

Year	Inflation target	Target figures (percent)
1979	M2 growth rate	25
1980	M2 growth rate	20 (25)
1981	M2 growth rate	25
1982	M2 growth rate	20–22 (25)
1983	M2 growth rate	18–20 (15)
1984	M2 growth rate	11–13
1985	M2 growth rate	9.5
1986	M2 growth rate	12–14 (16–18)
1987	M2 growth rate	15–18
1988	M2 growth rate	15–18
1989	M2 growth rate	15–18
1990	M2 growth rate	15–19
1991	M2 growth rate	17–19
1992	M2 growth rate	18.5
1993	M2 growth rate	13–17
1994	M2 growth rate	14–17
1995	M2 growth rate	12–16
1996	M2 growth rate	11.5–15.5
1997	Double monetary targeting system: M2 growth rate and MCT growth rate	14–19 (M2); 15–20 (MCT)
1998	Inflation rate (CPI)	9 ±1%
1999	Inflation rate (CPI); M3 growth rate	3 ±1% (inflation); 13–14 (M3 growth rate)
2000	Inflation rate (CPI); M3 growth rate	2.5 ±1% (inflation); 7–10 (M3)
2001	Inflation rate (CPI); M3 growth rate	3 ±1% (inflation); 6–10 (M3)
2002	Inflation rate (CPI); M3 growth rate	3 ±1% (inflation); 8–12 (M3)
2003	Core inflation rate	2.5 (core inflation)
2004–06	Core inflation rate	2.5–3.5 (core inflation)
2007–09	Inflation rate (CPI)	3 ±0.5% (inflation)

Source: Annual Monetary Policy Report (Seoul: Bank of Korea).

Note: Figures in parentheses are revised target figures.

In the 1990s, the implementation of interest rate deregulation gave financial institutions a much greater degree of autonomy managing their funds.[33] The reserve requirement ratios were reduced in 1996 and 1997 and have been kept at an average of 3 percent in order to increase the banks' competitiveness while open market operations have become the main instrument of monetary management. The surge in capital inflow and the high growth of money supply in 2006 caused the BOK to raise the reserve requirement, to 7 percent, for the first time since 1990.

To deal with the growing monetary expansion, the BOK in 1972 began to issue monetary stabilization bonds (MSBs) on the open market. In 1977 it allowed nonbank financial institutions to bid on the MSBs, and starting at the beginning of the 1980s it also opened MSB transactions to private investors. *Figure 6-4* shows that the BOK issued a large amount of MSBs to sterilize the domestic liquidity on account of the growing pressure for monetary expansion coming through the foreign sector in the late 1980s. But the consequence was that the government had to issue other kinds of medium- and long-term foreign exchange stabilization bonds (FSBs) to ease the burden of the redemption payments that resulted from the expansion of MSBs (see *Figure 6-5*).

Figure 6-3: **Changes in Reserve Requirement Ratios in Korea 1979–2008, percentage**

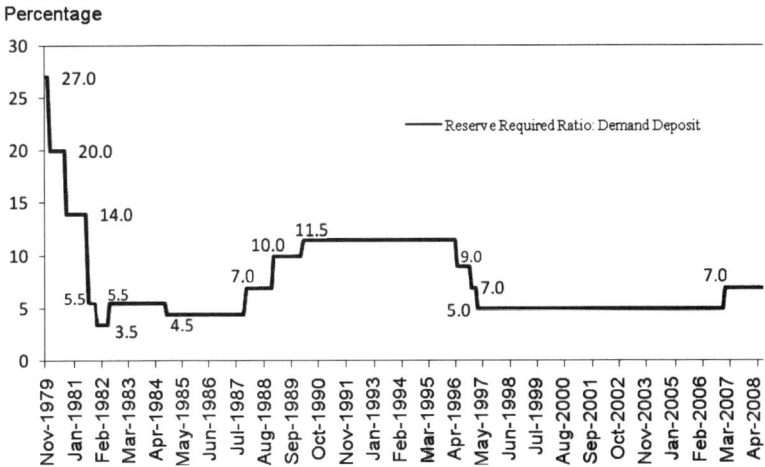

Source: CEIC data set.

The MSB issuance and outstanding levels had a significant fall during 2007 and 2008 because of the depreciation during this period. But, around the time

33. For more detailed discussion of the development of Korea's money market, see Dwor-Frécaut (2008).

when the exchange rate began to appreciate again in 2009, the BOK started to increase the issuance of the MSBs as well. The level of outstanding MSBs built up quickly, and reached 156.8 trillion *won* by May 2009.

The BOK also used OMOs to provide funds to the institutions that were short of liquidity. The BOK, for example, provided a total of 1.5 trillion *won* of liquidity to the banks during the period from June to September in 2000, enabling them to provide financial support to the Korea Deposit Insurance Corporation. In the same year, the BOK also provided the same amount through repurchase agreements to the Kookmin Bank and the Housing and Commercial Bank of Korea, which faced a temporary outflow of deposits caused by strikes at the end of the previous year. In 2004, when a strike broke out at KorAm Bank, the BOK immediately formed a special task force to monitor the impact on the financial markets and conducted its daily OMOs to facilitate the stricken bank's trouble-free borrowing of call funds so as to guard against possible liquidity problems owing to large-scale withdrawals of deposits.

By the late 1980s, OMOs had become the most important instrument that the BOK used to manage the money supply. With the development of domestic bond markets, MSBs of different maturities (28, 91, 371, 392, and 546 days) were introduced. In addition to government bonds and government-guaranteed bonds, the BOK in 1998 added repurchased MSBs and land development bonds, issued in connection with the redemption of corporate debt to financial companies, to the list of eligible OMO securities. The level of outstanding MSBs built up quickly and reached 127.8 trillion *won* as of the end of October 2008. The accumulating issuance of MSBs brought upward pressure on market interest rates. To reduce the issuance of MSBs, the BOK introduced currency swap transactions with the National Pension Fund, absorbing Korean *won* in exchange for foreign reserves to be repurchased at maturity in May 2005.

In addition to reserve requirements and OMOs, lending policy has been used often by the BOK as a monetary instrument since the 1950s. It has been used more as a means of policy financing than as a tool for liquidity adjustment during the period of rapid economic growth. During the 1980s, lending policies mainly focused on financial support for export industries and small- and medium-size enterprises (SMEs). When the second oil shock occurred in the mid-1980s, the BOK created industrial restructuring funds to a total amount of 1,722.1 billion *won* to support the institutions that suffered from the shock.

In the 1990s, a total of 2.9 trillion *won*, in the form of funds for the managerial stabilization of investment trust companies, was injected into three in-

Figure 6-4: **Issuance of Monetary Stabilization Bonds and Total Outstanding Monetry Stabilization Bonds in Korea January 1985–January 2009**

Billions (won)

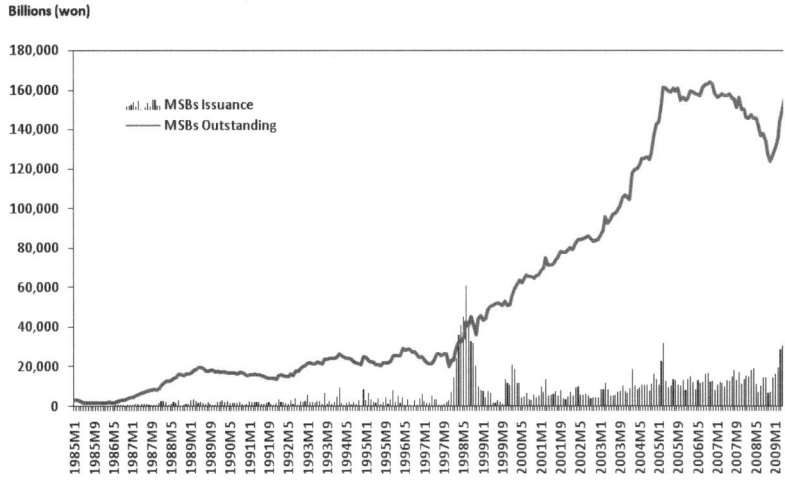

Source: CEIC data set.

Note: MSB = monetary stabilization bond.

Figure 6-5: **Issuance of Foreign Exchange Stabilization Bonds and Total Outstanding in Korea, January 1985–December 2008**

Billions (won)

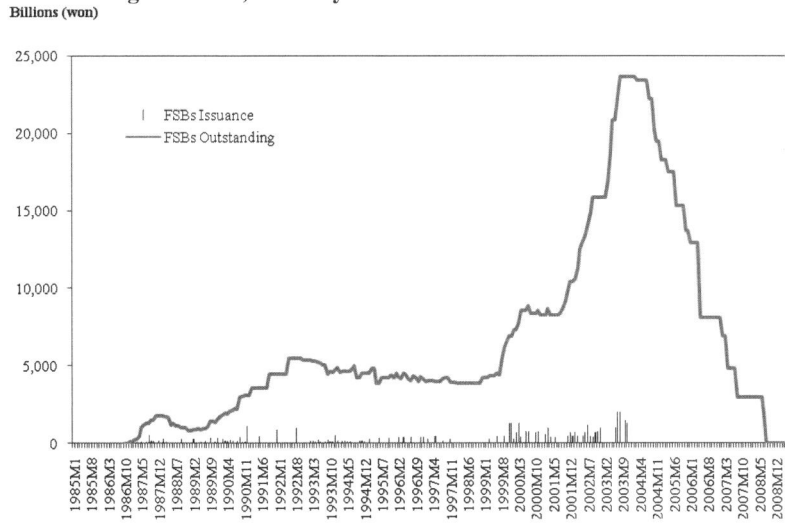

Source: CEIC data set.

Note: FSB = foreign exchange stabilization bond.

vestment trust companies, Hanguk, Daehan, and Kookmin, which were experiencing difficulties because of increased beneficiary certificate redemptions and weakening earnings. The BOK even issued a large amount of MSBs and FSBs to sterilize the increasing monetary expansion that resulted from these loans. Because of growing criticism of the BOK for placing too much emphasis on policy financing, an aggregate credit ceiling system was introduced in March of 1994 to strengthen its function of management of the money supply. Since then, this system has been used to provide financial support for SMEs or some specified industries. Finally, several special loans were also introduced and extended by the BOK during the Asian currency crisis as part of the BOK's role as lender of last resort.

In addition to the aggregate credit ceiling system, a liquidity adjustment loan system and an intraday overdraft system were introduced in 2000 to finance applicant banks that faced temporary shortages of liquidity. To strengthen the financial support for regionally based SMEs in the last two years, the quota under the aggregate credit ceiling system allocated to the Bank's regional branches for the support of local SMEs was increased by 400 billion *won*. In addition, another 400 billion *won* was raised on the ceiling for trade finance to counter the SMEs' weakening profitability owing to the increasing international raw materials prices. Furthermore, a system of currency swaps linked to foreign currency loans was launched in July 2005 to make use of part of the foreign reserve as a resource for banks' facilities investment lending.

As the effectiveness of monetary aggregates as an intermediate target continued to weaken, the operating target for monetary policy was switched from reserves to the overnight call rate target after the 1997 currency crisis. The BOK used interest rates as its official operating target for the first time in September 1998 after the foreign exchange market recovered from the currency crisis: it reduced the interest rate for OMOs from 8.1 percent to 7 percent in order to initiate a more expansionary monetary policy. Because the overnight call rate moves closely with the rate applied in OMOs, this policy change consolidated the overnight call rate as the operating target of monetary policy. Subsequent changes in target interest rates are reported in *Table 6-2.* Because of considerable slippage in the effects of changes in the call rate on longer-term interest rates, the BOK grew concerned about the limited effectiveness of the overnight call rate on credit growth and hence has been reluctant to give up entirely the use of changes in reserve requirements. In 2008 the Bank shifted its target interest rate to the seven-day repurchase rate in part to help stimulate further development of the money market.

As we see in Table 6-2, these interest rate changes were generally reductions from 2000 until 2005. Then, as inflationary concerns began to mount, all of the interest rate adjustments were upward until October 2008 when Korea began to be hit hard by the global economic slowdown. Since then, and unlike in the 1997–98 crisis, the BOK has moved aggressively to lower interest rates and stimulate the economy.

Empirics

In Appendix A, we estimate the extent of sterilization and the de facto extent of capital mobility in Korea. We estimate what the literature refers to as the "sterilization coefficient," that is, how much domestic credit changes in response to a change in international reserves. Theoretically, higher financial integration makes sterilization more difficult. The sale of government securities tends to raise interest rates, attracting further capital inflows. If capital mobility is very high, the central bank may not be able to neutralize such capital flows. To reduce the possibility of serious statistical bias, we follow modern practice and make use of an equation system that simultaneously estimates the sterilization coefficient and a measure of international capital mobility that the literature refers to as the "offset coefficient," that is, how much BOP changes in response to a change in domestic monetary policy. Because the foreign exchange market and the domestic monetary market are tightly interrelated, ignoring such interrelationships can lead to highly biased results. The theoretical absolute values of both the sterilization and offset coefficients run from zero to one. For the sterilization coefficient, zero implies no sterilization, and one implies full sterilization. Similarly, an offset coefficient of zero implies no international capital mobility, while a value of one implies perfect capital mobility.

It is important to emphasize that looking directly at the amount of sterilization notes issued by the central bank does not give us direct information on the question we are investigating: To what extent do international capital flows undermine the ability of the central bank to conduct domestic monetary policy? Where the issuance of sterilization notes is the only method of sterilization used, what their volume can tell us is how much international flows contributed to the growth of the money supply. But the relevant policy issue is to what extent international flows caused the money supply to grow more or less rapidly than was deserved by the central bank. To answer this question requires estimates of appropriate domestic money growth, which is what is in effect done by the simultaneous equations estimation presented in Appendix A.

We estimate separate regressions for before and after the 1997–98 crisis. Starting in 1985 we find a precrisis offset coefficient of approximately 0.5, indicating considerable but far from complete capital mobility and substantial but less than complete sterilization on the order of 0.65. These are substantially higher than the estimates of Fry (1996) for the earlier period of 1960 to 1991 of about 0.25 for each, suggesting a substantial increase in both capital mobility and sterilization in the latter part of the precrisis period.

Table 6-2: **Changes in the Bank of Korea Standard Target Interest Rate May 1999–February 2009**

Target change date	Target rate (percent)
Thursday, 6 May 1999	4.75
Thursday, 10 February 2000	5.00
Thursday, 5 October 2000	5.25
Thursday, 8 February 2001	5.00
Thursday, 5 July 2001	4.75
Thursday, 9 August 2001	4.50
Wednesday, 19 September 2001	4.00
Tuesday, 7 May 2002	4.25
Tuesday, 13 May 2003	4.00
Thursday, 10 July 2003	3.75
Thursday, 12 August 2004	3.50
Thursday, 11 November 2004	3.25
Tuesday, 11 October 2005	3.50
Thursday, 8 December 2005	3.75
Thursday, 9 February 2006	4.00
Thursday, 8 June 2006	4.25
Thursday, 10 August 2006	4.50
Thursday, 12 July 2007	4.75
Thursday, 9 August 2007	5.00
Friday, 7 March 2008	5.00
Thursday, 7 August 2008	5.25
Thursday, 9 October 2008	5.00
Monday, 27 October 2008	4.25
Friday, 7 November 2008	4.00
Thursday, 11 December 2008	3.00
Friday, 9 January 2009	2.50
Thursday, 12 February 2009	2.00

Source: Bank of Korea; table modified by the author.

Note: Until February 2008 table shows overnight call rate target; beginning in March 2008 table shows Bank of Korea base rate target.

Using a slightly earlier period than ours, 1980–1994, G. Kim (1995) finds a little lower offset coefficient and a modestly higher sterilization coefficient. Several other studies discussed in the appendix find broadly similar results for the precrisis period. For the postcrisis period we find a fairly substantial increase in the offset coefficients to almost 0.7, suggesting that further capital account liberalization has more than offset the effects of increased exchange rate uncertainty.[34] Our estimates of the sterilization coefficient rose even more, implying full sterilization in the postcrisis period.

Note that, although these estimates imply that international flows in the liberalized postcrisis period have not undercut the BOK's ability to conduct monetary policy, the estimates do not imply that the Bank pays no attention to international developments in setting monetary policy.

In a 2004 study, Barry Eichengreen (2004) estimates a policy reaction function for Korea's overnight call rate from 1998 (when inflation targeting was initiated) through mid-2003 and finds that the call rate has responded to movements in the dollar-*won* exchange rate as well as to expected inflation and the output gap. He also finds a strong tendency to smooth interest rate variability. His statistical results suggest that in practice the BOK has paid more attention to the dollar-*won* exchange rate than would be suggested by its written reports and more than would be implied by the exchange rate effects on expected inflation alone. In a more recent study covering the period beginning in January 1999, Parsley and Popper (2009) use more advanced statistical techniques and also find that the exchange rate plays an important role in the setting of Korean monetary policy, but that it does not appear to have an independent influence over and above its effects on inflation; that is, they find no evidence that concerns with the behavior of the exchange rate have interfered with the BOK's pursuit of inflation targeting.[35]

This result, combined with our findings of substantial official intervention in the foreign exchange market and heavy sterilization of this intervention, suggests that the BOK has had independent concerns about the behavior of the exchange rate over and above its effect on inflation but that its strategy has

---

34. Further evidence of the less-than-complete capital mobility facing Korea are continuing deviations from covered interest rate parity that have been instrumental in stimulating the yen carry trade and estimates of the intermediate degree of interest rate interdependence between Korean interest rates and those in the United States and in other Asian countries (Keil, Rajan, and Willett 2009).

35. With simple estimation techniques, Parsley and Popper (2009) find substantially the same result as Eichengreen. Using a broader range of data than Eichengreen (2004), they are able to better specify the relevant relationships and offer convincing evidence that in setting interest rates little if any weight has been given to the won-dollar exchange rate by the BOK beyond its expected effect on inflation.

been to deal with those concerns through sterilized intervention rather than adjustments in domestic monetary policy.

As we argued in Chapter 2, given the substantial degree of openness of the Korean economy, it is quite appropriate that the BOK pay attention to exchange rate and other international developments in setting monetary policy. We concur, however, with the recommendation in Eichengreen (2004) that the BOK offer more clarity about the role the exchange rate plays in the formulation of monetary policy.

7

Creating a Common Asian Currency Is the Wrong Approach to Asian Monetary and Exchange Rate Cooperation

This chapter is coauthored by Orawan Permpoon.

Since the Asian currency and financial crises of 1997–98, Asian countries have begun to pay much greater attention to issues of regional monetary and financial cooperation. While earlier progress toward greater economic integration is usually described as having been primarily market led, the high costs of the crises and perceived failures of the help from the IMF and major industrial countries have led to a major increase in government-led cooperation in the monetary and financial areas. Regional initiatives such as the Asian bond funds and the Chiang Mai agreements on crisis financing have been accompanied by a substantial increase in the frequency and scope of regional meetings of central bankers and finance ministry officials.

Such progress is extremely encouraging. Less promising is the amount of attention being paid by a number of academics and some officials to calls for a common Asian currency as a solution to regional monetary, financial, and exchange rate issues. There would be many advantages to such a common Asian currency, and support for this approach can appear to put one on the side of the angels as a supporter of the strongest form of regional monetary cooperation. While calls for Asian monetary union can seem quite farsighted and statesmanlike, the true statesman seeks to lead toward the best feasible outcomes and does not forget to look at the costs as well as the benefits of alternative strategies. This is where proposals for creation of a common Asian currency meet their doom; although the economic benefits could be substantial, the costs would be likely to be greater still because such a venture would involve giving up a country's ability to use national monetary policies to offset major shocks to the economy. A common currency would imply a single monetary policy for all members. This would be little sacrifice if all the economies were similar and faced the same shocks, but this is far from being the case. It is essential not to confuse increases in economic integration and a high degree of similarity of shocks (which have been occurring) with the conclusion that a single monetary policy would be efficient for all of Asia.

Even if this were desirable on economic grounds, there are strong political obstacles to reaching agreement on a common currency in the medium-term future. Nothing is wrong with planning now for the longer-run future, but only if this does not deflect attention excessively from shorter-run opportunities to make real progress. If history is any guide, improving Asian monetary, financial, and exchange rate cooperation will be quite a long-term project that must overcome many obstacles. Thus, one can understand the attractions of theories that argue that this long, difficult path can be avoided by jumping immediately to monetary union. As we shall discuss, however, there is little empirical evidence to support such theories and a good deal that calls them into question.

It is now generally recognized by economists and most knowledgeable monetary officials that there is no one ideal exchange rate regime for all countries at all times. Most early debates about fixed versus flexible exchange rates took place in the abstract. Today most analysis is more nuanced. There are both costs and benefits to all exchange rate regimes. The ratio of the costs to benefits may vary systematically across countries on the basis of their characteristics. The major factors influencing these costs and benefits are delineated in the literature on the theory of optimum currency areas.

Although this may sound like just esoteric academic theorizing, it is in fact of quite practical importance. Just as with monetary policy and macroeconomics more generally, not all economists agree on particular policy prescriptions or even on the relative importance of different factors, but this approach gives us a valuable framework within which issues can be investigated. It illustrates, for example, that it can make perfect sense for a huge economy like that of the United States to adopt a flexible rate while a small, open economy like Estonia's or Hong Kong's may be much better off adopting a fixed exchange rate. As will be discussed later in the chapter, it is not always understood that monetary integration in the form of a common currency is fundamentally different from trade and financial integration. For the latter, while some individuals and groups may lose, there is a strong presumption that all countries that reduce artificial barriers to trade and financial flows will gain in aggregate.[36] Monetary integration, in contrast, is not about removing restrictions on trade but about determining the rules for monetary policy, and here there is no presumption from economic theory or empirical evidence that all countries will gain in aggregate.

Most research studies on issues of establishing fixed exchange rates and common currencies now draw on the optimum currency area (OCA) approach. Unfortunately, however, a number of these studies have placed questionable interpretations on their results, and, as a result, there has been a tendency for many of these studies to give overly optimistic pictures of how well various groupings of Asian countries meet the OCA criteria for making a common currency economically desirable.

This chapter begins with a brief exposition of the basic ideas of the OCA approach and then discusses problems with the technical studies that have purported to find evidence supporting the formation of a common currency in Asia. Although some of these studies are technically quite sophisticated, the basic problems with their interpretations can be explained in simple ways. Probably the most important of these is that most of the studies have focused on a quite limited range of criteria selected primarily for the ease of getting data and applying popular econometric techniques rather than their economic importance. In some cases there are serious questions about the stability of the resulting estimates. This problem is illustrated with respect to a new set of calculations on several of these criteria. It is argued that a broader overview of relevant criteria suggests that in general the economic case for a broad-based common currency area in Asia is quite weak and that this is particularly true for Korea. Some Asian economies would likely gain from a common Asian currency, but Korea is not one of them.

Chapter 8 turns to analysis of the political conditions necessary for a successful monetary union. Particular emphasis is placed on the European experience. Some have looked at the historical time line of regional economic integration in Europe and concluded that high levels of economic integration will also almost inevitably lead to monetary integration. The fact that economic integration in Asia has been growing rapidly has led some to believe that monetary integration should soon follow. It will be argued that such views are based on a serious misunderstanding of the history of European integration. The process was driven not primarily by economic objectives but by the use of economic means to promote geopolitical objectives. The geopolitical situation is quite different and at least for the near future is more likely to

---

36. As was discussed in Chapter 5, this presumption in favor of removal of restrictions on international capital flows is based on the assumption of adequate micro and macro prudential supervision. Where this is absent, there can be a strong second-best argument for some restrictions on capital flows.

hinder than to promote monetary integration even if it were economically desirable.

The negative conclusions drawn on both the economic desirability and political feasibility of an Asian monetary union in the mid-term future do not imply, however, that there may not be substantial gains from other types of efforts to promote greater Asian monetary and financial cooperation. Chapter 5 reviewed a number of aspects of such cooperation and recommended a positive program for increased short- and medium-term cooperation, including the development of a stronger institutional framework. It is argued that it is in this area rather than in the more headline-catching proposals for a common Asian currency that the strongest prospect for mutual gain lies. And in this area the experience of European integration offers a number of important lessons, some positive and some negative.

OCA Approach

Some of the literature on OCA theory has become quite technical, and the number of criteria that can be relevant is now well into double figures. Some of the most important ideas can be explained quite simply, however.[37] When economic or financial developments generate a conflict between internal and external balance, the basic issue becomes how to adjust with the lowest costs.[38] With exchange rate adjustments, the major part of the adjustment falls on the external sector. With a fixed exchange rate, domestic macroeconomic policy adjustments are required, and these usually fall most heavily on the domestic sectors. Which approach to adjustment is better will then depend on the comparative effectiveness and costs of exchange rate versus domestic policy adjustments and the relative importance of the domestic and international sectors.

All of these considerations suggest that the case for a fixed exchange rate or common currency is greater if the international sector is relatively more important than the domestic sector of a country's economy. The importance of the external sector is greater depending on how much larger it is than the domestic sector. Thus, if adjustment costs in both sectors are equal, more of the adjustment should be done by the smaller sector to minimize the total costs of adjustment.

Furthermore, the relative sizes of the external and domestic sectors influence the relative effectiveness of exchange rate and macro policy adjustments in a manner that further increases the case for small, open economies to have

---

37. For overviews of the OCA literature see De Grauwe (2003) and Willett (2003b).
38. In standard economics jargon, external balance refers to balance of payments equilibrium and internal balance refers to macroeconomic stability.

fixed rates and large, relatively closed economies to have flexible rates. Where wages and prices are sufficiently sticky so that there are important Keynesian aspects to the macro economy in the short run, then large economies would have to generate bigger recessions for a given amount of trade balance correction than would small economies. This is because the smaller economies would have higher marginal propensities to import. A reduction in the rate of growth of real income for smaller economies would generate larger reductions in imports. For a large economy, however, the marginal propensity to import would be low, so greater lost income would be required to reduce imports by a given amount than would be necessary for a small, open economy. Thus, domestic income adjustments are a less costly mechanism for small economies.

For small economies, however, exchange rate adjustments are likely to be less effective. The more important that international trade is for the economy, the greater the feedback effect that a depreciation will have on domestic prices. And the greater this feedback effect, the larger the change in the nominal exchange rate that would be required to bring about a given change in the real exchange rate; that is, the more the effects of a given depreciation would be offset by an increase in domestic prices. In the extreme of a tiny, highly open economy, exchange rate adjustments should almost completely lose their ability to affect the relative prices of traded versus nontraded goods and hence to promote adjustment through expenditure switching rather than expenditure reductions. And the recessions caused by large expenditure reductions are far more costly than the adjustments needed for switching consumption and production patterns to stimulate more exports and fewer imports.

Another key factor is the flexibility of the domestic economy. If adjustments were costless, there would be a strong presumption in favor of a common currency because this would be more conducive to international trade and investment and the efficient allocation of resources. Thus, in the 19th century when wages and prices were much more flexible, the widespread system of fixed exchange rates based on the gold standard worked rather well during the periods in which that system was in use. The monetary contractions required of countries in BOP deficit would result primarily in falling nominal wages and prices rather than rising unemployment. Substantial labor mobility similarly lowers the cost of the domestic adjustments that may be required to maintain fixed exchange rates. Thus, wage and price flexibility and factor mobility are also important OCA criteria.

A third important type of criteria concerns the nature of shocks to the economy. Recall that this discussion began with analysis of a case whether the internal and external balance requirements in the economy conflicted with each other. This need not always be the case, however. Depending on the nature of the shocks hitting an economy, the conditions for internal and external balance may coincide or conflict. In general, fixed exchange rates are more desirable when these requirements coincide, and exchange rate adjustments are more desirable when they conflict. The time dimension of shocks can also be relevant. As was discussed in Chapter 6, if a disturbance is temporary, a conflict between internal and external balance can be financed rather than requiring adjustment. In general fixed exchange rates will work better if shocks are temporary instead of permanent. This is not always the case, however: depending on the degree of capital mobility and the nature of the shock, flexible rates will sometimes be superior to fixed rates as an automatic stabilizer in the face of domestic shocks and as a mechanism of insulation against foreign shocks. The analysis of the various possibilities has been the subject of countless research papers.

When the formation of a common currency area is being considered, it is important to recognize that this type of analysis is of secondary importance. Such considerations are primarily relevant for the conduct of discretionary policy, where a government may decide to intervene to limit exchange rate fluctuations in the face of particular types of shocks. With a managed float, officials have the discretion to let some types of shocks affect mainly the exchange rate while another type might be largely buffered by the purchase or sale of international reserves. With a common currency, individual members lose their ability to conduct discretionary monetary and exchange rate policy. Indeed, this is the major cost of adopting genuinely fixed exchange rates.

OCA analysis has traditionally been framed in terms of fixed versus flexible exchange rates, but this can be misleading. The key issue to which most of the OCA literature is actually relevant is whether or not to allow exchange rate adjustments, that is, whether or not to adopt a genuinely fixed rate regime. There is a wide range of options for how exchange rate adjustments might be made if a hard fix is not adopted. Thus, fear of floating need not imply a preference for fixed exchange rates (Willett 2003a). There may be many good reasons why a country does not want to adopt a freely floating exchange rate that do not present a case for adopting a hard fix.

Some of the key considerations for the choice among regimes that allow for exchange rate adjustment were discussed in Chapters 2 and 3. The key point here is that the adoption of a common currency or other forms of a hard fix implies that discretionary monetary and exchange rate policy can be undertaken only collectively. In this context an important consideration is the extent to which optimal discretionary policy for a country considering joining a common currency area is likely to differ from that of the other members; or, phrased in more practical policy terms: How great are the likely costs of giving up the independence of individual discretionary policy to follow the common policies of the group?

Clearly such a commitment is worth contemplating only if the group policies are expected to be sensible. A point that has been insufficiently emphasized in the OCA literature is that the standard OCA criteria assume that a country has the option of fixing to a stable country with which it has a high proportion of its international trade. A country may meet the small, open economy criteria but still have much of its trade with an unstable partner. This situation faced the Baltic states right after the breakup of the Soviet Union. There was initially talk of forming a Baltic currency union because Estonia, Latvia, and Lithuania were all small, open economies. They had relatively little trade with one another, however. Under the Soviet Union's hub-and-spoke regime, most of the trade of each one had been with Russia, but, besides the political objections to fixing to the ruble, Russia after the breakup of the Soviet Union was undergoing hyperinflation. Thus, there were initially no ideal candidates for the Baltic states to fix their currencies to. Over time this problem has been resolved with changing trade patterns and the creation of the euro. This example vividly illustrates the need to undertake OCA analysis in a multi-country context.

European monetary integration after 1973 evolved with the large size and stability of the German economy providing a centerpiece. Initially several smaller countries began to fix their exchange rates to the deutsche mark. Although these were technically adjustable pegs, they soon evolved into hard fixes. Asia does not have an equally strong candidate to play a similar role. Japan has come the closest, and numerous proposals have been put forward for a *yen* zone in Asia, but the geopolitical resentments in Asia toward Japan stemming from World War II (and before) have lingered much more strongly than did those in Europe toward Germany. The rapid rise of China further complicates the situation from this standpoint.

China has been rapidly overtaking Japan as the most important trading partner for many Asian economies. The underdevelopment of China's financial sector and its continued use of an array of capital controls make it unattractive as a monetary center for the region. Thus, it appears unlikely that there would be a natural path toward a dominant national currency in Asia to which a common Asian currency would be a successor as the euro was viewed as the successor to the deutsche mark.

Because one of the greatest costs of joining a currency area is giving up independent monetary policy, a major focus of the empirical OCA literature has been on different desirable discretionary monetary policies for different countries. If countries face fairly similar shocks, then there should be fairly similar desired responses of monetary policy, making the cost of giving up independent policy lower.[39] But, where economies face quite different shocks, they would typically want to follow different monetary policies, and hence the costs of being in a monetary union would rise.

Similar considerations apply to exchange rate policy with respect to shocks to the equilibrium real exchange rate. For example, if the exports of most of the members of a currency union are booming while those of a particular country are slumping, the appreciation of the common currency would worsen that individual country's export slump. With its own currency, however, depreciation would likely take place, which would help to dampen the slump. While Korea's initial depreciation during the current crisis went further then was desirable, this did help protect the real economy.

Recent Empirical Studies

Because of such considerations, a number of empirical studies have investigated the behavior of countries' real exchange rates, estimated patterns of demand and supply shocks, and looked at the degree of synchronization of countries' business cycles to see whether they would be good partners for a currency union. Indeed, this type of analysis has become the most common form of recent empirical analyses of OCA issues.

To illustrate this approach and some of the difficulties in its application, we will focus in this section on measures of business cycle synchronization. The less divergent the business cycle conditions among a set of countries, the fewer the expected conflicts about the course of joint monetary policy.

Based on this type of analysis, a number of studies have reached optimistic conclusions about the feasibility of a common Asian currency. Studies have suggested that the degree of synchronization of business cycles in Asia has increased substantially in recent years and that, as a survey paper (Watanabe and Ogura 2006) puts it, "subsets of Asian currencies meet the optimal currency area criteria to the same degree as European countries did in their pre-euro phase."

This is a fair summary of the conclusions drawn by the authors of a number of studies, but these conclusions are themselves open to considerable question. In the first place, it should be emphasized that these findings apply only to a small set of the OCA criteria, typically patterns of shocks or degree of business cycle synchronization. Although no general consensus exists about

---

39. Even with the same shock, differences in economic and institutional structures could generate some differences in optimal policy responses, as could different preferences.

the exact relative importance of the various OCA criteria, it should be clear that, for a fixed exchange rate regime to work well, the member countries need to meet more than just one or two of the criteria. This point was vividly albeit tragically illustrated by the experience of Argentina with its fixed exchange rate currency board. Argentina did meet some of the criteria of the OCA theory, such as having a high degree of currency substitution, but it was a rather closed and rigid economy, and trade with the United States, to which Argentina had fixed its exchange rate, represented only about 1 percent of Argentina's economy. Thus, it is not surprising that various shocks led to a severe recession in Argentina and the ultimate abandonment of its fixed exchange rate regime.[40]

Not all experiences with fixed exchange rates are so devastating, and, as the European experience with the euro shows, a country need not meet completely all of the OCA criteria to have a reasonably satisfactory experience. As we will discuss below, joining a fixed rate regime may set in motion developments that make economies closer to being OCAs. Thus, recent developments in what is called endogenous OCA theory suggest that the ex ante requirements for successful currency areas are less stringent than had been previously thought. Argentina presents a strong counter example, however, to the exaggerated claims sometimes made that endogenous OCA theory shows that any group of countries can become an OCA ex post.

In evaluating the conclusion that most studies find that a subset of Asian countries meet the OCA criteria (as judged by the degree of business cycle synchronization compared with pre-euro Europe), it is crucial to recognize that different studies find different subgroups meeting the criteria. In part this reflects different methodologies and time periods used, but also quite important is that we have no good reason to expect that the patterns of synchronization will remain constant over time, so the use of different time periods can sometimes yield quite different results. It is clear that economies that are more highly integrated with each other will generally tend to move more closely together,[41] but the degree of business cycle synchronization is also heavily influenced by the patterns of shocks, and these may show considerable variability over time. For example, discussing the different groupings found by different studies on OCA analysis for Asia, Wyplosz (2001) argues "this difference reveals the limited reliance that one can put on historical shocks as a guide to the choice of an exchange rate regime."

---

40. On the Argentine case, see the analysis and references in Willett (2002).
41. The exception is where greater integration generates more specialization. Thus, increases in intraindustry trade would cause economies to move more closely together at the macro level than would increases in interindustry trade.

This critique also applies to the conclusion that increasing regional trade integration in Asia has led to a substantial increase in the degree of macroeconomic synchronization. As *Table 7-1* shows, this conclusion certainly applies to Korea's degree of growth rate synchronization when the 1968–91 period is compared with the 1992–2005 period. The average one-year correlations of Korea with East Asia (China, Hong Kong, and Japan) increase from 0.228 to 0.488 while the correlations with Southeast Asia (Indonesia, Malaysia, Philippines, Singapore, and Thailand) increase from –0.062 to 0.652.

Table 7-2 shows the increase in Korea's trade with a number of its Asian partners. Some increase in business cycle synchronization was to be expected, but not by as much as these numbers suggest. Also interesting to note is that in the most recent period the correlations are lower with East Asia, with which Korea trades the most, than with the Southeast Asian countries, with which Korea's trade is less.

Table 7-1: **Unweighted Average Correlations of Real Output Growth Rates for Korea, Southeast Asian Countries, and East Asian Countries over Different Time Horizons and Different Periods**

Correlation coefficients of real output growth rates	Average correlation of Korea and Southeast Asian countries	Average correlation of Korea and East Asian countries
A. 1968–91		
Annual growth	−0.0623	0.2279
Two-year growth	−0.1479	0.2011
Three-year growth	−0.0065	0.0231
B. 1992–2005 (including 1997 and 1998)		
Annual growth	0.6517	0.4882
Two-year growth	0.6425	0.5195
Three-year growth	0.6161	0.6131
C. 1992–2005 (excluding 1997 and 1998)		
Annual growth	0.3697	0.1740
Two-year growth	0.4046	0.1894
Three-year growth	0.2875	0.0929

Source: World Bank, World Development Indicators; author's calculations.

An alternative hypothesis is that much of the recent increase in correlations was due to the common shock of the Asian crisis. To the extent that this was the cause, the increased correlations would not be evidence of increased suitability for a common currency. This is easily checked by excluding the crisis years of 1997 and 1998 from the calculations. This is done in Part C of Table 7-1. Now we still find increased correlations, from -0.062 to 0.370

with Southeast Asia, and an actual decline in the correlations with East Asia from 0.228 to 0.17.

Table 7-2: **Comparison of Trade Statistics of Korea with Selected Trading Partners, 1991 and 2005, percentage**

Korea's trade with partners	1991	2005
Exports/GDP		
China	0.33	7.86
Indonesia	0.44	0.64
Japan	4.01	3.05
Thailand	0.43	0.43
Hong Kong	1.55	1.97
Singapore	0.88	0.94
Exports to Asia/GDP	8.25	16.34
Total exports/GDP	23.49	36.10
Imports/GDP		
China	1.12	4.91
Indonesia	0.67	1.04
Japan	6.85	6.15
Thailand	0.18	0.34
Hong Kong	0.25	0.26
Singapore	0.33	0.68
Imports from Asia/GDP	10.13	14.51
Total imports/GDP	26.55	33.16

Source: World Bank, World Development Indicators; International Monetary Fund, Direction of Trade Statistics; author's calculations.

Notes: Asia = members of the Association of Southeast Asian Nations (ASEAN), China, Japan, Hong Kong, and Singapore; GDP = gross domestic product.

Similar patterns are found using two- and three-year correlations. While most studies have focused on annual growth correlations, for the purpose of comparing the need for different monetary policies across countries, these two- or three-year growth correlations are likely more relevant. Given the imperfections of forecasting and the lags with which changes in monetary policy affect the economy, it is likely beyond the technical power of discretionary monetary policy to do a great deal to smooth out very short-run fluctuations in the macro economy. For evaluating countercyclical policies, a longer time horizon than just one year seems more relevant. In Table 7-1, however, we find that the differences between one-, two-, and three-year correlations are often small, especially with Southeast Asia. With East Asia, however, there is a sharp decline between the two- and three-year correlations that exclude the crisis years.

This conclusion of little difference across time horizons does not hold up across all time periods. Table 7-1 shows a decline rather than increase in the correlations with East Asia and larger differences between the one- and three-year correlations. For three of the cases, the longer-term correlations are lower, but in the later period the three-year correlations of Korea with the Southeast Asian countries are much higher.

This lack of stable results holds up when we look at Korea's correlations with individual countries. Here we will just offer a few illustrations. For annual correlations with China, extending the 1968–91 period to 1996 leads to a modest increase in correlations from 0.10 to 0.17, consistent with the increasing-integration thesis (Permpoon 2008). We get a roughly similar result of 0.24 when we use the 1992–2005 period excluding the crisis years, but if we take the shorter 1999–2005 period excluding the crisis years we find a high 0.51 correlation. For 1999–2005, however, the correlation turns negative. Correlations with Japan are low for both periods but also change sign. We could go on, but we believe these examples should be sufficient to establish that such correlations need to carry a warning sign: Danger—Highly Unstable—Handle with Care.

Broader Perspective

Such synchronization estimates sometimes place Korea in a grouping with Southeast Asia as the basis for a sub-Asia currency area (Bayoumi and Eichengreen 1994; Loayza, Lopez, and Ubide 2001). Even if we believed that such correlations were stable, this conclusion should almost certainly be overridden by other criteria. As shown in Table 7-2, Korea's trade with both Asia and the world has grown substantially, and it has become a large proportion of Korea's GDP. Between 1991 and 2005 Korea's exports as a proportion of its GDP grew by more than 50 percent. Within Asia the rankings of Korea's trade with other countries have remained fairly stable, with the exception of China, which has taken on a greatly increased importance. Korea's trade with the economic giants of Northeast Asia—China and Japan—is much stronger than with the Southeast Asian countries. China and Japan are also of much greater geopolitical importance to Korea.

Some economists have suggested that Asia begin with one or two subregional currency areas that might then combine over time. Apart from the economic merits and limitations of such an approach, this proposal would face huge hurdles from a political standpoint. The formation of several small currency areas might make sense with tiny open economies like Hong Kong and Singapore joining a currency area with a larger neighbor in the historical tradition of such countries adopting currency boards. This could likely be done without invoking seriously disruptive geopolitical pressures.

Singapore, however, has prospered with its managed float; Singapore's experience as well as the experiences of New Zealand, Switzerland, and Sweden suggest that fairly small economic units can have viable national currencies if they are managed well. Hong Kong has likewise done rather well with its currency board based on the dollar. It has not been free of crises, but on the whole it has produced reasonably good economic results. Both Singapore and Hong Kong nicely illustrate the dilemmas that can face a small, open economy concerning which currency to fix to. With its diversified trade and financial activities, Singapore had good reasons not to fix to its closest neighbor, Malaysia. Fortunately, despite its high level of openness, Singapore has been able to manage a flexible regime quite successfully.

With its strong role as a regional financial center, Hong Kong has found it makes considerable sense to base its choice of the currency on which to fix on financial flows, not trade flows. Thus, Hong Kong's fix to the dollar was the obvious choice in the 1980s. Early in the past century the choice of the British pound would have been obvious. Today the situation is much more complicated. The declining (albeit still strong) international role of the dollar combined with the rapid economic rise of China have led to proposals that Hong Kong should adopt China's renminbi. The underdevelopment of China's financial system creates strong arguments against such a switch. Thus, it seems unlikely that in the near future the small economies in Asia will start a move toward currency consolidation. Nor, even if this would occur, would it be likely to start a process of further consolidation, any more than Ecuador's adoption a few years ago of a currency board based on the dollar or any more than Argentina's earlier currency board started a movement for currency consolidation in Latin America.

Such a consolidation dynamic has clearly been at work in Europe, but this is because there is already a large euro bloc with which to fix. Despite the high level of openness of many Asian economies, the considerable diversification of trade and financial relationships makes it extremely unlikely that such a dynamic would result from a process of independent national decision making. Such a dynamic did play a role in Europe in creating stronger pressures for the euro as the increasing number of small countries that adopted hard fixes with the deutsche mark created a growing currency area that in turn increased the attractiveness for others to join (Andrews 2008). Germany has no equivalent in Asia. Although at one time it looked like Japan might possibly take on that role, the combination of its economic stagnation in the 1990s and the rise of China has effectively destroyed any chance of Japan playing that role. Even apart from political considerations, the underdevelopment of China's financial system would keep it from being able to play such a role for decades at least.

Some have recommended the formation of a Southeast Asian currency area, but this would have severe disadvantages from a geopolitical standpoint. ASEAN Plus Three (the ASEAN countries augmented with China, Japan, and Korea) has become by far the most effective regional grouping in Asia, and many of the Northeast Asian countries are becoming increasingly economically and financially important for ASEAN. In geopolitical terms, only a large currency area including the East Asian countries would make sense.

ASEAN Plus Three is clearly a natural unit to form stronger economic and financial ties, and efforts to promote greater regional trade and investment integration make great sense as long as they do not come at the expense of creating barriers to trade with broader Asia and the rest of the world. In popular discussions of regional integration, it is often not recognized that the case for trade and investment integration is fundamentally different from monetary integration.

Economic analysis convincingly shows that with rare exceptions the reduction of barriers to trade and direct investment increases the aggregate economic productivity of all the countries participating. This, of course, does not mean that all parties in every country gain. Some domestic firms and workers will lose from the increased competition, but in aggregate greater gains than losses will be generated. The fact that there may be a substantial number of losers in the short run and some even in the long run helps explain the political opposition to trade liberalization and suggests the need for such liberalization be combined with other policies such as adjustment assistance to reduce the unevenness of the distributional effects. But this does not undercut the presumption that aggregate gains are generated for all participating countries.

Monetary integration, that is, monetary union or any other form of a genuinely fixed exchange rate, is fundamentally different. Although the effects of a common currency in stimulating trade and investment are similar to trade liberalization, this is as far as the similarity goes. Unlike trade integration, monetary integration also sets the course for national monetary policy, and here there is no presumption that there will be aggregate gains. With mon-

Table 7-3: **Historical Growth Rates of Selected Asian Countries, 1990–2005**

Country	1990	1991	1992	1993	1994	1995	1996	1997	1998	1999	2000	2001	2002	2003	2004	2005
Cambodia	n.a.	n.a.	n.a.	n.a.	9.2	6.5	5.3	5.7	5.0	12.6	8.4	7.7	6.2	8.6	10.0	13.4
China	3.8	9.2	14.2	14.0	13.1	10.9	10.0	9.3	7.8	7.6	8.4	8.3	9.1	10.0	10.1	10.2
Hong Kong, China	1.9	5.6	6.6	6.3	5.5	3.9	4.3	5.1	-5.0	3.4	10.2	0.6	1.8	3.2	8.6	7.3
Indonesia	9.0	8.9	7.2	7.3	7.5	8.4	7.6	4.7	-13.1	0.8	4.9	3.8	4.4	4.7	5.1	5.6
Japan	5.2	3.4	1.0	0.2	1.1	1.9	2.6	1.4	-1.8	-0.2	2.9	0.4	0.1	1.8	2.3	2.6
Korea, Rep.	9.2	9.4	5.9	6.1	8.5	9.2	7.0	4.7	-6.9	9.5	8.5	3.8	7.0	3.1	4.7	4.0
Lao PDR	6.7	4.1	6.9	5.9	8.2	7.0	6.9	6.9	4.0	7.3	5.8	5.8	5.9	6.1	6.4	7.0
Malaysia	9.0	9.5	8.9	9.9	9.2	9.8	10.0	7.3	-7.4	6.1	8.9	0.3	4.1	5.7	7.2	5.2
Philippines	3.0	-0.6	0.3	2.1	4.4	4.7	5.8	5.2	-0.6	3.4	6.0	1.8	4.4	4.9	6.2	5.0
Singapore	9.2	6.6	6.3	11.7	11.6	8.1	7.8	8.3	-1.4	7.2	10.0	-2.3	4.0	2.9	8.7	6.4
Thailand	11.2	8.6	8.1	8.3	9.0	9.2	5.9	-1.4	-10.5	4.4	4.8	2.2	5.3	7.0	6.2	4.5
Vietnam	5.1	6.0	8.6	8.1	8.8	9.5	9.3	8.2	5.8	4.8	6.8	6.9	7.1	7.3	7.7	8.4
Average	5.42	4.45	2.90	2.62	3.47	3.96	4.23	2.99	-1.3	2.02	4.67	2.10	2.65	3.77	4.56	4.68

Sources: World Bank, World Development Indicators; author's calculations.

etary union, a country loses control of its national monetary policy. It operates like the gold standard. If a country runs a payment deficit with the other members of the union, then its money supply will automatically contract. That will be fine if the domestic economy is overheated but not if it is already in recession. In this case the gains from increased trade with the currency area members may be swamped by the losses from the increased severity of the recession. If Korea had been in an Asian currency area when the current crisis hit, then, instead of its currency depreciating, it likely would be running a payments deficit with the currency union, its money supply would be forced to contract, and recessionary pressures could be much worse. This example is given in terms of the standard textbook exposition of the operation of the gold standard. Today monetary policies generally focus much more on interest rates than money supplies, but the major conclusion of loss of control over national monetary policy still holds.

The balance of gains and losses is determined by the combination of considerations delineated in OCA theory. As noted above, where the domestic economy is highly flexible, a payments deficit would result primarily in falling wages and prices, and the aggregate costs might be slight. To a considerable extent, this was true for the countries on the gold standard in the 1800s. Modern economics tends to be much less flexible, however, so the costs can be considerable. One clear example is the long, painful decade of stagnation in Japan after its financial bubble burst.

In new classical macro models, economies are assumed to be quite flexible, so the costs of giving up independent monetary policy are low. Indeed, it may even be positive if this allows a country to overcome the inflationary biases generated by short-run political pressures. This combination of discipline and low cost of deflation helps explain why many new classical and global monetarist-oriented economists such as Ron McKinnon (2005) and Robert Mundell (2003) are strong advocates of broad monetary unions. Their logic is impeccable, but their empirical assumptions are highly questionable. One of the most crucial questions for Koreans in evaluating whether an Asian currency union would be in Korea's interest is whether the flexibility of Korea's economy is closer to that of most advanced industrial nations that display considerable wage and price stickiness and limited labor mobility or closer to the highly flexible economies of the new classical and global monetarists' macroeconomic models.

Some indirect evidence on the issue is found in the econometric studies that estimate speeds of adjustment to economic shocks. Such studies generally find the speeds of adjustment for Japan and Korea to be quite low. In a recent Claremont dissertation, Peter Han (2009) finds that for Korea only about 25 percent of the adjustment to a demand shock takes place during the first two years. This is similar to Han's findings for Japan, but the adjustment is much slower than the averages for the rest of Asia and also less than for the average of the euro countries. Roughly similar results have been found in studies by Baek and Song (2001) and Ahn, Kim, and Chang (2006).

Such stickiness highlights an OCA criterion—differences in economic growth rates—for which data are easily available (see *Table 7-3*) but are not usually used in empirical OCA analysis; De Grauwe (2003) is an important exception. Synchronization studies focus on fluctuations around trend rates of growth, which is appropriate for considering countercyclical monetary policy. Substantial differences in trend rates of growth among participants can also generate considerable problems for the operation of a currency area, however. As is well known from the Balassa-Samuelson analysis of the effects on differential productivity growth on purchasing power parity, in an integrated area with constant prices of internationally traded goods, the higher the rate of productivity growth in a country, the greater the increases in the prices of the country's domestic goods and services and hence the country's overall rate of inflation. Thus, the greater the divergence in growth rates among countries in a currency area, the greater will be the divergence in national inflation rates. With highly flexible wages and prices such as are assumed in the strong form of the new classical macro models, this is not a problem because the monetary authority can pursue an appropriate inflation target for the group as a whole, with the result that some countries will have higher inflation and others may have declining prices.

There is considerable evidence, however, that, contrary to the new classical assumptions, deflation tends to reduce growth in many real economies (Burdekin et al. 2004; Burdekin and Siklos 2004). If costly deflation is to be avoided, then greater disparities in growth rates will force higher monetary expansion and inflation for the group. Just as with growth correlations, growth trends can change over time, so historical statistics are no sure guide to what will happen in the future. Variations in trend rates of growth tend to be much less variable than synchronization correlations, however; and it seems pretty certain that for the coming decade China will have a much higher trend growth rate than Japan, with Korea likely being in between. Thus, it seems likely that a currency combining these key countries would face enormous pressures coming from differences in growth potential.

From the perspective just presented, the patterns of short-run shocks and degree of business cycle synchronization emphasized in many empirical OCA studies are of secondary importance. Considerations of other important criteria paint a much less positive picture for the desirability of adopting a common Asian currency in the medium-term future. Furthermore, Korea would likely be one of the countries for which a common Asian currency would be most costly. There is, however, one powerful type of argument that could reverse this conclusion: the possibility of the changes that would be generated by joining a currency area to convert members' economies to close approximations of OCA conditions.

Endogenous OCA Analysis

The endogenous OCA approach is unquestionably the correct theoretical perspective. What is relevant for the successful functioning of a currency area is the behavior of economies after they join, not what they were before. So the key question becomes how joining a currency area will change the behavior of economies. Although there are some conflicting theoretical considerations, there is a strong presumption that joining a currency area would induce endogenous responses that would make the member economies more closely approximate OCA criteria (De Grauwe and Mongelli 2005; Willett, Permpoon, and Wihlborg 2008).

The case is strongest and most straightforward with respect to trade. Joining a currency area should expand trade among the members; and because trade openness with respect to other members of the group is an important OCA criterion this would make the case for a currency union stronger ex post than ex ante. Similarly many economists have argued that, because fixed rates would increase the cost of domestic rigidities, joining a currency area would induce structural reforms that would increase the flexibility of economies.

Such possibilities have led some economists to go so far as to suggest that the traditional OCA criteria are irrelevant and that any group of countries can become an OCA ex post.[42] Such views are also used to propose a reversal of the traditional sequencing of regional integration such as was followed in Europe when increased trade integration led to monetary integration. In this view, the long, slow journey through increasing trade integration can be skipped. A more efficient path, this view argues, is to go directly to monetary integration, and this will in turn generate trade integration, increased economic flexibility, and closer synchronization of business cycles.

This is certainly an attractive vision. But, for it to be relevant, it is necessary not just that developments move in the right direction; they must move sufficiently to approximate the OCA conditions. Unless countries are already quite

---

42. As Watanabe and Ogura (2006, 16) write, "therefore, as this argument goes, there is little point in debating whether or not the optimal currency area conditions are satisfied ex ante." Another example is the statement by Masahiro Kawai (2007, 111) that "once a group of countries permanently fixes its exchange rate, the degree of intra-area economic integration will rise and shocks will become more symmetric. One need not worry too much, then, about the OCA criteria since these will obtain endogenously.... Only political commitment is required." This is much too strong. For a detailed critique, see Willett, Permpoon, and Srisorn (forthcoming).

close to meeting these conditions, the endogenous responses, while likely to be in the right directions, are unlikely to be of sufficient magnitude to make a huge difference. It appears, for example, that the adoption of the currency board by Argentina did lead to some increase in labor market flexibility, but that the changes were clearly not sufficient to avoid a horrible recession.

In the euro area, there has been much talk of the need for structural reform to increase the flexibility of economies, and some actions toward this goal have taken place, but overall the degree of progress has been quite disappointing to most supporters of the euro.[43] What was overlooked in the economic efficiency models that predicted large increases in flexibility were the political economy obstacles to change. Many if not most rigidities in economies are there because some group is gaining from them. Concern about aggregate efficiency may carry little sway with such interests. Of course, we would expect joining a currency area to tilt the balance of political pressures in the direction of more flexibility, but the strength of this movement will often be sharply damped by political economy considerations, including reform fatigue. Indeed, it appears from the euro experience that considerably more reform was generated during the process of meeting the conditions set for entry than have been stimulated endogenously after joining.

The effects of a common currency in stimulating trade should not face as strong a political economy damper, but the size of the effects to expect is open to considerable uncertainty. Some estimates have projected gains in trade volume of 100 to 200 percent, but it turns out that these were based on the experiences with very small economies, and we would expect that the smaller the economies involved, the greater the proportional effects. Thus, for good-sized economies like Korea's we would expect considerably smaller effects. Many estimates of the expected effects of the euro on trade have run up to a 50 percent increase over perhaps 20 years. Based on the early evidence, this appears overly optimistic. The creation of the euro was associated with a jump in trade, but trade also grew with non-euro Western European countries. Some put a positive spin on this development that the euro had generated trade creation without trade diversion. A more plausible interpretation is that something else besides the euro creation was increasing trade.[44]

This interpretation is reinforced by business cycle correlations. These also rose substantially for the euro countries, consistent with a strong endogenous OCA effect. However, the correlations among non-euro western European countries and among the euro and non-euro countries rose as much or more. Thus, it is not easy to interpret this early euro experience. Perhaps the best judgment that we can render on the euro experience to date is that it has been

---

43. See the references in Willett, Permpoon, and Wihlborg (2008).
44. On the issues, see the analysis and references in Willett, Permpoon, and Wihlborg (2008).

neither as successful as expected by its strongest supporters nor as disastrous as predicted by its strongest critics. Although it has not provided the substantial boost to growth predicted by supporters, neither has it generated the high unemployment in out-of-sync countries that was feared by opponents. Until the current financial crisis, the economic environment had been unusually benign so the euro area had not had a severe test. Perhaps the major danger sign has been the growing real exchange rate appreciation of several of the southern European members.[45] These may generate serious deflationary pressures on these countries during the next few years on top of the general recessionary pressures that have been generated by the financial crisis. The euro's second decade may give us clearer evidence on the strength of various endogeneities than did its first decade. In the meanwhile, risk-averse policymakers would be wise to not put their faith in expectations of enormous endogenous OCA effects. Given the evidence of reform fatigue in the eurozone, most needed policy harmonization and structural reforms should be undertaken before a common currency is adopted.

---

45. See the analysis and references in Wihlborg, Willett, and Zhang (2009).

8

Geopolitical Considerations and Lessons from Europe for Monetary and Financial Cooperation in Asia

This chapter is coauthored by Lalana Srisorn.

The previous section concluded that it was quite unlikely for it to be in Korea's economic interest to support the creation of a common Asian currency, at least not in the near- or medium-term future. There is unlikely to be political support for such a move in any event. The dynamic that led to monetary union in Europe was extremely unusual and stemmed largely from geopolitical considerations. Europe responded quite differently from Asia in the early postwar period. A number of European leaders came to adopt a common view that to avoid future devastating wars in Europe it was essential to bind Germany more closely to the rest of Europe through strong economic ties. This view was accepted as strongly in Germany as in the rest of western Europe. This approach was also strongly supported by the United States, both to reduce the probability of another war among European nations and also to counter the danger that one or more western European countries would embrace communism. The result of this strategy has been wildly successful. While the process of European economic integration moved forward in fits and starts, it generated substantial economic prosperity; just as important, or possibly more important, European economic integration cemented West Germany so strongly to the rest of western Europe that the prospect of a new round of warfare among these nations is widely viewed as an impossibility.[46]

This did not mean that other European countries, especially France, were unconcerned with Germany's growing economic power. The prospect of the reunification of East and West Germany after the fall of the Berlin Wall

---

46. For histories of European integration, see Ungerer (1997) and Gros and Thygesen (1998).

greatly increased such concerns in some quarters in Europe. While a strong case could be made that reunification would reduce West Germany's effective external power because of the huge allocation of resources required to help integrate East Germany into West Germany's economy, many European leaders reacted with fear at the prospect of a united Germany. This combined with beliefs that it was important to keep moving forward on European integration to generate greatly increased political interest in European monetary union. This also coincided with the last generation of German political leaders who felt a strong need to bind Germany more strongly to Europe and who were willing to make major concessions to do so. The result was a German agreement to give up the deutsche mark and join a common European currency.[47] Germany retained the power to heavily influence the terms on which the euro was created, including the strong independence of the European Central Bank, but it gave up the right to maintain its national currency, a move that was deeply unpopular with a large majority of the German people. France pushed hard for this agreement because it had already adopted a fairly hard peg to the deutsche mark and hence had already largely given up its effective monetary independence. From the French perspective, giving up monetary sovereignty to a European Central Bank was far preferable in geopolitical terms than giving up sovereignty to Germany.

The puzzle here was why France had been willing to give up its monetary sovereignty in the first place. The answer comes from the macroeconomic excesses of the early years of the government of François Mitterrand. Following its socialist agenda as it came into power in 1981, the Mitterrand government began a series of overly expansionary crises that resulted in a series of currency crises. A combination of misinterpreting the results of these crises as showing that flexible exchange rates were not workable for France and a belief that linking a fixed exchange rate for the franc to the European project could induce French voters to accept more austere macroeconomic policies were the key pieces that generated a complete turnaround in the Mitterrand government's economic policies and the resulting surrender of monetary sovereignty (Andrews and Willett 1997). Had this shift in French policy occurred a decade later, it is extremely unlikely that the new generation of German leaders, born after the end of World War II, would have been willing to give up the deutsche mark.

Drawing Lessons from Europe

This analysis suggests that, rather than being a historical inevitability, the creation of the euro was in fact a low-probability event that relied on a highly

---

47. Also important in securing agreement were changing beliefs about inflation-unemployment trade-offs; for more detailed discussions of the creation of the euro, see Marsh (2009) and McNamara (1998).

unusual combination of circumstances and interpretations. From this perspective, if the euro had not already been created it is unlikely that under current circumstances it would be recreated.[48]

The geopolitical configuration makes the prospects for political agreement to give up national monetary sovereignty and create a common currency in Asia even more remote than for Europe if it did not already have the euro. The United States adopted a very different postwar strategy toward Asia than it did toward Europe. In contrast with its support for a more integrated Europe, in Asia the United States followed a hub-and-spoke strategy based on emphasizing bilateral relations with the United States rather than a more group-based approach. This was likely a sensible strategy for enhancing U.S. power and influence in Asia in the short run, but the result has been that geopolitical grievances among a number of Asian countries have remained much stronger than in Europe. This legacy makes the development of substantive economic cooperation in Asia considerably more difficult than in Europe.

It may not be too late, however, for Asia to adopt aspects of the European strategy of using economic integration to promote more harmonious political relations. Certainly one of the prime objectives of most countries should be to encourage the peaceful integration of China into the world economy.

We interpret the European experience as showing the wisdom of a gradualist approach based on taking a number of steps over time. Efforts to move too quickly run the serious risk of promoting more political conflict than cooperation. It is sensible to begin, as Asia has, with gathering the low-hanging fruit, concentrating on areas where the ratio of benefits to lost sovereignty is high. Such efforts may draw disdain from visionaries who favor a big-bang approach, but the prospects for both economic and political gains are much higher.

The judgment that the economic gains from creating a common Asian currency any time in the near future would be negative does not imply that there is not considerable prospect for gains from monetary and financial cooperation as well as trade integration. Out of such cooperation the conditions for a common currency to be desirable might finally emerge, but making this an explicit objective would be a mistake. It would implicitly downgrade perceptions of the benefits of more modest (and feasible) advances.

---

48. Note that this analysis does not imply a prediction that the euro area will break up. There is strong path dependence in such institutional arrangements, and the political and economic costs to a country that exited from the eurozone would be enormous. Although there has been anti-euro talk by some European political leaders from time to time, this is largely just talk. It would take a huge recession to make an exit from the euro worth contemplating seriously (Eichengreen 2007b).

From both the European experience and that of monetary and financial cooperation among the United States, Japan, and the major European countries, it is clear that it is much easier to get cooperation on provisions for short-term financial help to one another than on coordination of monetary and fiscal policies. Considerable progress has been made since the Great Depression of the 1930s in averting the types of blatant beggar-thy-neighbor devaluations and increases in trade barriers that made the worldwide depression so much worse. As a result, the huge oil shocks of the 1970s and 1980s were handled without a repeat of such behavior, and it is encouraging that, although the November 2008 meeting of the Group of 20 heads of state to deal with the current global financial crisis did not agree on the coordinated expansion measures that some had urged, the leaders showed acute awareness of the danger of beggar-thy-neighbor policies and made a strong pledge to avoid them. While not the stuff of headlines, such negative cooperation is of great importance, likely even greater than the potential gains from more actively coordinated policies. The central banks of a number of major countries did undertake coordinated interest rate cuts in November 2008, but such actions are quite unusual.

A large literature has developed, primarily by political scientists (Haas 1958; Schmitter 2004; Sandholtz and Sweet 1998), discussing the process of European integration. Clearly those in favor of European integration believed in the power of spillovers from one area of cooperation to another. This neofunctionalist view has gone in and out of favor and back in again as the process of integration sped up, slowed down, and sped up again.

Spillovers can operate through several different mechanisms (Schmitter 2004).[49] One is technical. Agreements in one area may create a need to cooperate in another area. For example, allowing greater movement of individuals and firms across national borders can greatly increase the need for harmonization of regulations and standards in a broad range of areas.

Likewise, limiting the variability of exchange rates increases the need for coordination of monetary policies. Such technical spillovers are a double-edged sword. They increase the pressure for coordination, but this can result in either greater cooperation or greater conflict. The European experience gives many examples of both, and interpretations about the mix often disagree. For example, the ERM of the EMS that provided substantial limits on exchange rate fluctuations has been hailed by some as an important contributor to monetary policy coordination and is advocated as a model for Asian monetary cooperation. Others, however, view it as a major cause of the European currency crisis of 1992 and 1993, which was characterized by major policy con-

---

49. On the similarities between spillovers and endogenous OCA analysis, see Srisorn and Willett (2009).

flicts rather than cooperation. Perhaps the best way to think of such technical spillover is that, where the costs to national sovereignty are not viewed as great, then they are likely to promote increasing cooperation over time; that is, they can provide useful nudges. It is unwise, however, to adopt strategies that will require subsequent large increases in coordination for them to work. This runs the danger of leading to more conflict than cooperation and can set back the integration process.

There is considerable disagreement about how well such linkage strategies can be planned. It is clear, however, that unintended consequences abound, so that detailed blueprints for a long process of integration are of quite limited value. Path dependence plays a strong role, and various windows of opportunity for cooperation open and close. Thus, for supporters of increased cooperation, perhaps the best strategy is to develop a sizable set of contingency plans that can be brought out quickly as opportunities present themselves.

Asia and Europe show substantial differences in legal and cultural traditions, so one should be careful in attempting to draw lessons for Asia from many of the specifics of the European integration process, but some insights are transferable.[50] One is that the process will inevitably proceed in fits and starts, and one should become neither too ecstatic during periods of rapid progress nor too depressed during lulls.

Another key lesson is that we should not underrate the longer-run importance of developing forums for more frequent contact among officials. This can bring important benefits in developing shared perspectives and the buildup of trust. We should not expect to see huge results overnight. But recent efforts have resulted in substantial increase in contact and discussion among central bank and government officials. Over time the value of such increased discussion can be immense, even when few dramatic actions result as demonstrations of success. Experiences with the evolution of cooperation through the Bank for International Settlements, the OECD, and the EMS all suggest the importance of building up institutional structures to support such dialogue. International contacts should not be limited to the most senior officials. Forums for more technical-level analysts to get together are also quite important as is the development of a high-quality staff that can serve as a trusted secretariat for a regional monetary and financial institution. It is easy to deride such institutions as bureaucratic boondoggles that waste scarce resources, but in fact the costs of fairly frequent meetings among senior officials and a moderate-sized secretariat are quite low compared with the prospective benefits that can be generated. Many of these benefits will take time to be felt, so dramatic early relations should not be expected. Building respect, trust, and

---

50. Several recent papers have dealt with lessons for Asia from the European experience; see, for example, Wyplosz (2001) and Eichengreen (2007a).

cooperation is usually a slow process. More important than speed is attention to quality. It is better to have no secretariat at all than one that turns out defective work.

It is also important that efforts at greater regional cooperation do not cause the rest of the world to be neglected. Some believe that this was the case with Europe and the creation of the euro. Asia should be on guard against such development.

Strategies and Proposals for Monetary Cooperation in Asia

In general Asian officials have been quite wise in their choice of monetary and financial topics on which to work initially. The Chiang Mai Initiative (CMI) for short-term financing, the Asian Bond Fund, and market development initiatives have created an important perception of progress. Generally it is easier to get an international agreement on financing than on adjustment issues because financing tends to carry lower political costs. Although the initial Chiang Mai arrangements have been followed by further agreement to expand and improve them, they still have never been used. This naturally raises the issue of whether more effort should be put into making them user friendly or whether, like the IMF's never-used Contingent Credit Lines that was created after the Asian crisis, it will be more productive to put efforts elsewhere.

Likewise, one can question whether it is worth increasing efforts to get agreement on the establishment of an official Asian currency unit (ACU) since this approach was not very successful in Europe. A key problem is political. Which currencies should be included in the basket that makes up the ACU, and what weights should they be given (Pontines and Rajan 2008)? As with the relative size of IMF quotas, various technical formulas can be used to give the weights. But that is just the problem. Many different formulas can be used, and one is not clearly superior to the others. As a result there is no reasonable hope of depoliticizing the debate over weights. Many countries see their influence at stake, so, unless there is a clear agreement on the pecking order of countries' influence, this type of topic is likely to be highly contentious.

As the political science literature indicates, such problems are especially severe when major transitions in power are under way (Grieco 1997; Mansfield and Milner 1997). Because this is clearly the case in Asia today with the economic rise of China, reform efforts should attempt to minimize the need for agreements that highlight issues where relative weighting is required. On this score bilateral swap lines score better than shares in a regional financing mechanism. Of course, such a multilateral regional facility would also have advantages over networks of bilateral swaps. The two approaches might even be developed in parallel.

Korea's recent swap agreements with China, Japan, and the United States need not undermine the usefulness of the recent agreement to multilateralize the CMI for short-term financing. If the Chiang Mai agreements are not used in the near future, however, they will run a serious danger of fossilizing. Such issues cannot always be avoided, but, given the likely strong limits to the short-run benefits from establishing an official ACU, it would have been wiser to push for it early in the process of developing stronger international financial cooperation in Asia. Advocates also failed to do sufficient preparation to build up support before officially proposing the ACU. The result was that the ASEAN Plus Three ministers showed considerable lack of collective enthusiasm. Officially it was referred to a study group, but unofficially it was widely considered that the proposal was being effectively shelved for the present.

Another of the problems with the ACU proposals is that they vary a great deal in how the ACU is expected to be used. The major danger lies in using it as the basis for a system of collective exchange rate bands that more or less approximate the arrangements in the EMS. As was argued above, if such a regime is not backed by effective monetary coordination, then it is likely to be highly crisis prone. When confronted with such arguments, advocates often back off to a position that what they want is a much more flexible system that would avoid the rigidities of past pegged-rate regimes.

Such more flexible arrangements should not be rejected out of hand. There is, however, a real question of whether a mix can be found that promotes a substantial reduction in exchange rate volatility without leading to the excessive rigidities that induce crises. The typical strategy has been to get agreements on exchange rate commitments and hope that sufficient monetary policy coordination will follow. As will be discussed in the following chapter, this approach has all the hallmarks of the time-inconsistent strategies that front-load the political benefits and then generate greater longer-run costs in the form of higher inflation, crises, or both. And it is likely to be especially difficult for a group of countries at quite different stages of development.

Prompting greater monetary and financial cooperation in Asia is clearly going to be a long-term process. The process has generally gotten off to a good start with substantially increased communication and agreements such as the Asian Bond Fund initiative. These have not yet brought great benefits, but neither have they imposed substantial costs; and they have clearly helped provide focal points to keep up momentum.

In such circumstances, it would be ill advised to attempt to negotiate agreement on exchange rate regimes before considerable progress is made on coordinating monetary policies. In light of the historical evidence, it seems clear that, from a longer-term perspective, the coordination of exchange rate regimes should follow rather than lead a substantial increase in coordination of monetary policies.

This is not to argue against immediate efforts for short-run coordination of intervention and exchange rate policies in the face of particular shocks such as local currency and financial crises and the projected global recession. It is against proposals to create group regimes limiting exchange rate flexibility before substantial progress in monetary coordination is made.

Another lesson from recent theoretical analysis and experience is that, if, down the road, such regimes are being seriously contemplated, they are much more likely to work in a crisis-free manner if the conduct of both monetary and exchange rate policy is given to independent central banks that are sufficiently insulated from short-run political pressures that they can take a longer-run perspective. Indeed, the case for such arrangements need not rest on the contribution to the stability of regional exchange rate regimes. Such arrangements should also speed progress in increasing international cooperation on monetary and exchange rate policy responses to major shocks. Note that what is required is effective, not just formal, independence. Just how independent the BOK is in practice is not completely clear. This is also true for a number of other formally independent central banks in Asia.

A final comment on regional monetary and financial cooperation is that considerable priority should be given to putting the CMI into use. The recent agreements to enlarge and multilateralize the agreements are useful, but lack of use of these financial arrangements over a prolonged period could send negative signals about their value. Some type of policy agreements can be useful even if they are never used. This was the case with the scarce-currency clause that Keynes and White negotiated at Bretton Woods. Although never used, its shadow likely prompted at least somewhat more cooperative behavior on exchange rates.

With financing facilities, if there are no serious shocks, then their lack of use does not undermine their credibility. But it would be hard to argue that this is currently the case. In large part because it was ill designed, the IMF's Contingent Credit Line set up after the Asian crisis was never used, and it died an inglorious death. The CMI does not suffer from the same design flaws, and it would be a shame to see it follow the same course. Making the CMI operational should be high on the list of short-run priorities for Asian monetary and financial cooperation. And the current global crisis provides a perfect opportunity to make use of it in a way that does not impose a stigma on the borrowers. Korea is well placed to get the ball moving.

9

Similarities and Differences between the 1997–98 Crisis and the Current One

The year 2007 marked the 10th anniversary of the beginning of the Asian currency and financial crisis. International conferences were held with this theme, reexamining the causes of the crisis, the crisis policy responses, and steps taken to establish a safer financial environment. Few of us participating in such conferences realized that we were already in the beginning of what in 2008 would become a full-fledged global financial crisis.

The origins of the current crisis in many ways look quite different from the Asian crisis. The epicenter of today's crisis is the United States, not Thailand, and the problems were generated in what had generally been considered to be the most sophisticated centers of finance, not in less-developed ones going through the process of learning to cope with a newly deregulated environment. And certainly Korea is much better positioned to deal with the current crisis than it was in 1997.

1997–98 Korean Crisis Primarily Caused by Financial Problems, Not Exchange Rate Problems

Although many of the particulars are quite different, the root causes of the 1997–98 Asian crisis and today's crisis are amazingly similar. In each case the fundamental problem was one of perverse incentives and tendencies toward herding by financial-market participants that resulted in excessive risk taking and overinvestment in particular areas. The widespread nature of these problems also explains why in both cases there was so much contagion from the epicenter to other markets and countries.

At first look it seemed scarcely possible that problems in the subprime mortgage market in the United States could have such serious worldwide ramifications. The first explanation that comes to mind is that the resulting widespread contagion reflected serious psychological failures of market participants, who were irrationally panicking in the face of a market downturn. In the Asian crisis such a negative judgment on market behavior was widespread, especially while the crisis was in full force. Perhaps the most common initial interpretation of the spread of the crisis that originated in Thailand was that this was caused by irrational contagion. According to this view, Korea was an innocent victim, a proposition that was put forward by many outside Korea as well as within (Radelet and Sachs 1998).

Undoubtedly there was some truth to the stories of irrational panic, but the slowness with which the Asian crisis hit Korea and the even slower unfolding of the current crisis suggest that much more than irrational panic was at work. Subsequent detailed analysis of the Asian crisis suggests that most of the flight from the *won*, the Indonesian rupiah, and several other Asian currencies was quite justified (Willett et al. 2005). Korea was following sound macroeconomic policies, and, although some economists argued that Korea's de facto crawling peg exchange rate regime had led to overvaluation of the *won*, others argued that it might even have been slightly undervalued. In any event, it had not become clearly overvalued before the crisis as had the Thai baht. Inflation was low, and government finances looked solid. Thus, the condition of these traditional fundamentals makes it is easy to see why so many initially argued that the flight from the *won* was unjustified.

Closer investigation, however, revealed serious problems in Korea's financial sector. As was discussed in Chapter 3, regulation had not been carried out with sufficient focus on the risks involved, and prudential regulation had not been strengthened sufficiently. Connected banks felt that they had little incentive to monitor carefully the quality of their loans, and the increased competition resulting from deregulation had greatly reduced the market value of some financial institutions, generating incentives for them to undertake risky loans to gamble for redemption (Dooley and Shin 2000). The use of high levels of debt was pervasive among Korean corporations, and debt-equity ratios reached extraordinary levels.

On top of this, international liberalization had not followed the standard sequencing of decontrolling long-term capital flows before short-term ones. Consequently short-term foreign borrowing increased enormously. As in Thailand, Indonesia, and several other Asian countries, many Korean banks and businesses believed that they had an implicit government guarantee against a large depreciation of the currency; thus, foreign currency borrowing was for the most part unhedged. And various deficiencies in financial reporting led to the government's and the central bank's serious underestimation of the level of the nation's short-term foreign debt relative to its level of usable international reserves.

Deficiencies in Risk Analysis

On the supply side, international investors had become understandably enamored of the Asian miracle. This, combined with managerial incentives to follow the herd, led international investors to focus on the bright spots in the Asian economies and worry insufficiently about the weak spots. Adding to this tendency was that the strengths of the Asian economies tended to lie largely in the macro areas where reasonably good statistics were readily available, while the weak spots were in the financial sectors where good data are hard to find and one needs on-the-ground observation not available on the computer screens in New York, London, and Frankfurt. Data on nonperforming loans are available but are often unreliable and are much more helpful for ex post explanation than for giving ex ante warnings.

Risk management systems also failed. The first Basel agreement on international standards on bank capital had some serious deficiencies (as will be discussed below, so does the revised Basel II). When Korea became a member of the OECD, this automatically put it in a much lower risk category for banks in countries following the Basel rules and contributed to the excessive inflow of capital into Korea. At the same time, the large international banks were placing increased reliance on quantitative models to manage their risk positions. While quite mathematically sophisticated in some respects, these value-at-risk models were surprisingly naive in others. They relied on relatively short-run historical data to be manipulated by the sophisticated models. The old adage "garbage in, garbage out" applied with a vengeance.

In fact, these models do tend to be highly useful for managing risk during normal periods. But, as has been demonstrated again during the current global crisis, they are poor at giving early warning signals of the danger of crisis; neither do they do well for managing during a crisis. The reason for both types of poor performance is the same: historical correlations break down during crisis. A position that is well diversified with respect to the smaller fluctuations during good periods will often find that in a crisis a wide range of investments are behaving in a similar manner, hence the adage that during a crisis the only thing that goes up is the correlation among different investments.

With their backward-looking approach, such models are particularly inappropriate for judging risk under regimes of pegged exchange rates. An exchange rate that has varied little over several years also gives zero information about the probability that there will be a change in the peg in the future. For this question, much more detailed analysis of BOP trends and other factors is needed. Thus, the standard risk management models continued to signal safety while fundamental analysis saw increasing probabilities of devaluation of the Thai baht as 1997 progressed. The IMF as well as my students from Thailand had been warning for well over a year that the baht was in trouble, and an increasing number of international investors began pulling their money out, but large segments of the market both in Thailand and abroad were caught by surprise in July 1997 when Thailand essentially ran out of reserves and the baht was floated.

Contagion Owing to Similar Problems in a Number of Countries and Markets

The reason that the Thai crisis spread so wildly throughout Asia was that the financial-sector problems and excessive unhedged foreign borrowing and other capital inflows that helped bring down the baht existed in a number of other Asian economies, including Korea. The Thai crisis served as a wake-up call to market participants to reevaluate their positions.[51] Many foreign investors realized that they did not really know as much about the economies in which they were invested as they thought. The assumptions of many Asian businesses and financial institutions that there would be no major currency depreciation were called into doubt. The rational response to the realization that the world is really quite different from what had been thought—what I have called broken mental models (Willett 2000)—is to turn quite conservative until a better understanding of the new situation can be obtained. In Asia in 1997–98, the situation was not so much like an especially bad draw from a known probability distribution but rather a recognition that perceptions of the probability distribution had been seriously flawed. What had been seen as a situation of risk turned into one of uncertainty. Similarly in today's crisis, much of the flight to safety is due to recognition that lenders and investors had fundamentally misjudged their situation.

There was panic, but most of it was quite rational. Certainly for institutions with large unhedged foreign debts, seeking to hedge these open positions was only prudent. Even where exchange rates were at roughly equilibrium levels before the crisis, the growing recognition of serious financial-sector problems generated by the wake-up call from Thailand would substantially reduce the levels of expected capital inflows. For countries with sizable current account deficits, this would change an equilibrium exchange rate into a seriously overvalued one.

---

51. The Mexican crises in 1994–95 also generated a wake-up call, but most large international investors concluded that Asia's differences from Mexico were greater than the similarities. Thus, while flows to Latin America fell, those to Asia increased after the Mexican crisis.

Korea's slowly moving peg multiplied the problem by slowing adjustment and giving market participants greater incentives to run for the exits before the *won* depreciated further, but the peg was not the basic cause of the crisis in Korea. Although we tend to refer to the currency crisis as resulting from speculative attacks on the currency, it was in reality much more the result of efforts to limit prospective losses than of overt speculation for gain.

It is interesting that the initial contagion from the Thai crisis created only relatively mild ripple effects on Korea. The initial wake-ups were primarily by borrowers and investors from Thailand's more immediate neighbors in Southeast Asia. Some market participants had begun to reallocate their positions, but there did not seem to be an immediate need for Korea to change its exchange rate policy. The wake-up call hit Korea with full force in October when its Northeast Asian neighbor Taiwan devalued. This stimulated a major run on Hong Kong, which the market judged to have a number of characteristics similar to Taiwan. This run in turn stimulated the beginning of large outflows from Korea. Korea initially attempted to ride out the storm with only quite limited daily depreciations of the *won*, but this quickly proved to be unworkable, and the government wisely and relatively promptly abandoned its policy of pegging.

Role of IMF in First Crisis

The role of the IMF in the Asian crisis has been widely criticized and with some justification. In Indonesia the IMF program contained far too many conditions—over a hundred—although many of these were put in at the request of Indonesian officials rather than the IMF. The program with Korea was more focused but was still deeply unpopular. Indeed, in Korea it is common to refer to the crisis as the IMF crisis. This negative view of the IMF has lingered, and it is reported that this led to the Korean government to rebuff IMF overtures during the current crisis for Korea to make use of the new IMF short-term lending facility for countries that have been following good economic policies.

Undoubtedly, some of the hostility toward the IMF in Korea was generated by the IMF's refusal to accept the view that Korea was an innocent victim in the 1997 crisis. And on this the IMF was right. But the current crisis is quite different. Today Korea and a large number of other emerging-market countries are much more the innocent victims.[52]

The continued resentment of the IMF in Korea is quite understandable, but a good case can be made for giving the IMF another chance. Its policy pro-

---

52. This is not true of all crisis-hit emerging-market economies; for example, political instability has been a major factor underlying the crisis in Ukraine.

grams in Korea were not nearly as bad as strong critics (Furman and Stiglitz 1998; Radelet and Sachs 1998) have maintained. A large part of their critique was based on the assumption that Korea's main problem was unjustified contagion. Were this correct, then the IMF program would have indeed been greatly flawed. But the problems in Korea's financial sector turned out to be real (defenders of the IMF include Boorman et al. 2000; Mishkin 2006).

One of the IMF's biggest problems was that its lending programs had not been sufficiently updated to deal with the new world of high capital mobility facing emerging-market economies (Bird 2003; Truman 2006; Willett 2006). The IMF's basic approach had been developed when capital mobility was low and crisis conditions developed over a much longer time period. As capital mobility grew, some revisions to the IMF's lending policies were made, but they were much too incremental. This left the IMF way behind the curve. Not only had the movement toward front-loading funding in the face of capital account crisis been much too modest, the amount of funding that the IMF had available had not kept up with the rapid growth of international trade and especially investment. In retrospect it is clear that, had the IMF been able to make much greater funding available quickly, much of the substantial overshooting of depreciation of the crisis-hit Asian currencies could have been avoided. In the absence of such funding the IMF's strategy was to advocate monetary tightening to limit the extent of currency depreciation.

Critics such as Joseph Stiglitz (Furman and Stiglitz 1998) argued that this was essentially wrongheaded because in a financial crisis tightening monetary policy would increase bankruptcies and worsen the crisis. There is of course some truth to this criticism. The standard textbook recommendation during a currency crisis is to tighten monetary policy; but for a financial crisis, the standard prescription is to loosen monetary policy. Because the IMF's traditional focus has been much more on currency than on financial crisis, it is not surprising that the institution went for the tight-money prescription. There is a genuine dilemma here for policy in a highly open economy, however. With large, unhedged foreign debts, depreciation also increases bankruptcy problems, and for some economies this may be a more powerful effect than would follow from the tight money needed to reduce the amount of depreciation. The best trade-off will vary substantially from one economy to another.

As long as a country has been following generally prudent monetary and fiscal policies, the best solution to this dilemma is to use heavy official purchases in the foreign exchange market to limit the amount of overdepreciation of the currency and hence allow easier domestic monetary policy. Such a strategy is unlikely to be successful when it is taken to the extreme of attempting to defend a fixed parity. The track record of IMF loans to try to maintain such pegs is quite poor (Bird and Willett 2007). Attempting to maintain a peg increases the costs of exit and can greatly increase the amount of capital flowing out during a crisis. However, substantial intervention to limit large overdepreciation in the short run once a peg has been abandoned is a quite different matter.

In the 1997–98 crisis, Korea's effective reserves were near zero, the current account deficit was substantial, and help on this front from the IMF was quite insufficient.[53] Today the situation is quite different. There is no large current account deficit requiring net capital inflows to be financed, and Korea has a high level of owned reserves. In addition, along with several other leading emerging-market countries, Korea now has a $30 billion swap line with the Federal Reserve and has also negotiated substantial swap lines with China and Japan.

---

53. Despite the large headline figures for the size of the IMF program, the amount of funding that could be used to defend the currency was actually quite small.

10

Crisis Hits Korea

Korea's Position Was Stronger Than Many Realized

It is interesting to note that, although the global dimensions of the current crisis came to dominate economic and financial developments in Korea by the later part of 2008, there had been considerable independence of financial behavior in Korea in the several preceding years. Consistent with the decoupling hypothesis, Korea's stock market boomed through late 2007 while the U.S. markets fluctuated horizontally, and the Korean stock market index (KOSPI) began to fall well before there was general recognition that emerging markets would take a hard hit from the fallout from the subprime crisis. The fall of the *won* also started well before the crisis went global and seems to have been associated with the newly elected Korean government.

Figure 10-1 shows that the turnaround in the *won* began before strong global effects of the U.S. subprime crisis began to be felt in emerging-market countries. The new government clearly felt that the strength of the *won* was inconsistent with its policy objective of accelerating growth and began an effort to talk down the *won*. Although such jawboning is often ineffective, sometimes it is too effective, and this was the case with the *won*. The market began to lose confidence in the new government's economic policies, and sentiment in the foreign exchange market did an about-face. The *won* began depreciating more rapidly than the government wanted to see and, as was discussed in Chapter 2, the general trend in official intervention in the foreign exchange market went from selling to buying the *won*.

Figure 10-1: **Won-Dollar Exchange Rates, Standard & Poor's 500 Index, and the Korean Stock Market Index (KOSPI) January 2004–June 2009**

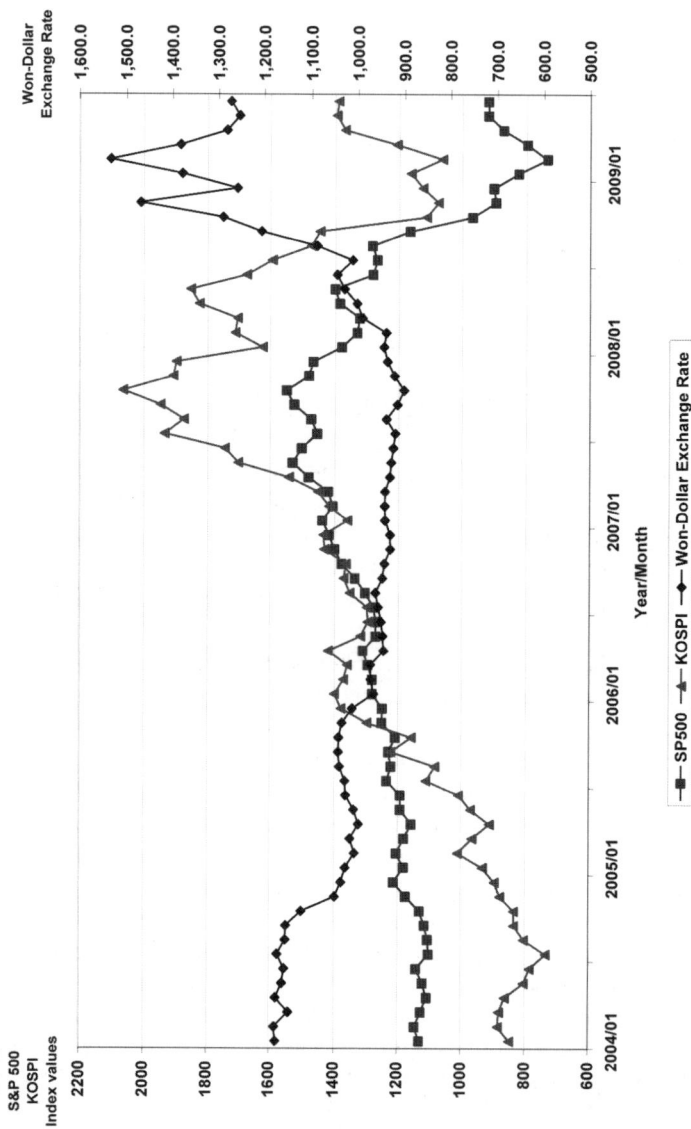

Source: Standard & Poor's and KOSPI.

The reversal in the *won* may have contributed to the perception that Korea was the Asian country most vulnerable to financial contagion. Other factors contributing to this perception were the recent large expansion of short-term foreign bank debt, the high proportion of potentially reversible foreign ownership of portfolio equity, and the relatively high reliance of the Korean banking system on wholesale as opposed to deposit funding.

Indeed, one could draw some powerful and disturbing parallels between Korea and the United States. In both there had been falling rates of personal savings, increasing consumer debt, and rapidly rising housing prices. These analogies could be misleading, however, since the bubble elements in the Korean housing market were much weaker than in the United States and were not accompanied by the disastrous types of financing that developed in the United States (Cargill and Guerrero 2007; Cargill 2009). Especially important was that the Korean financial system was much sounder than in 1997 and had seen relatively little involvement in the exotic new types of instruments that wreaked such havoc in the United States and Europe.

Derivatives and the KIKO Problem
Yoonmin Kim is coauthor of this section.

The markets for forward transactions in the foreign exchange market have grown greatly. Although these are primarily of the plain vanilla variety that have caused relatively little complaint in the United States and Europe, they can be used to speculate as well as to hedge foreign exchange risk; some have expressed concern that the market for nondeliverable forwards has been a major source of pressure on the *won* during the current crisis (Kang 2009). As a part of the general international reevaluation of the oversight of derivatives, the markets for forward exchange in developing and emerging-market countries should not be overlooked. It will be important, however, not to forget the important benefits they can bring in helping to reduce international currency risks.

The recent pressures on the *won* have been due only to a minor extent to Korean investments in asset-backed securities that have turned toxic. There has been a good deal of controversy in Korea, however, about another type of newly developed financial derivatives—currency option contracts known as knock-in knock-out (KIKO; *Figure 10-2*)—that were sold by both the local and foreign banks in Korea to many small- to medium-sized Korean exporters as insurance to prevent losses from the depreciation of the U.S. dollar (J. K. Kim 2008).

The instrument basically works as a hedging device against volatile currency markets to protect against possible losses from depreciation of the U.S. dollar. The U.S. dollar has, however, appreciated way beyond expectations, and many companies that contracted to repay debt in U.S. dollars to the foreign banks in such cases suffered from a drought of funds to repay them according to their contract agreements. It has been estimated that 97 firms lost $1.3 billion as of August 2008, and they filed a class action against 13 major foreign and domestic banks in early November 2008, claiming (J. K. Kim 2008) that "the currency options they hold are unfair and should be nullified amid the huge losses caused by the Korean *won*'s steep fall."

Figure 10-2: **Example of Knock-In Knock-Out (KIKO)**

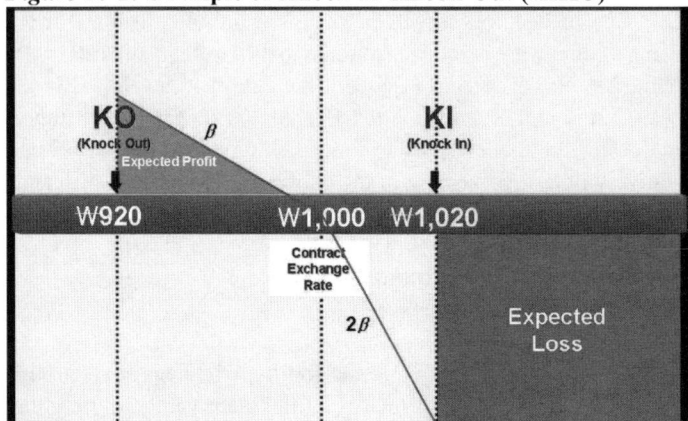

Source: Authors' concept

Analyzing Capital Outflows

As financial conditions tightened in the industrial countries, there was a widespread falling off and then a reversal of capital flows to emerging markets. The spread of the crisis generated a general flight from risk, and, because emerging markets are generally understood as falling into the risky category, a general pullback was to be expected. In addition, countries thought to be especially vulnerable because of a large current account deficit or heavily exposed financial sectors were especially hit. Iceland was perhaps the most dramatic case, to be replaced later by a number of central and eastern European countries.

Despite the widespread perception that Korea was especially vulnerable, a careful analysis suggests that it is not so obvious that this was true. Not only was Korea not running a large current account deficit (it was in surplus when the crisis started), it had amassed international reserves of some $260 billion, most of which were highly liquid. It had weathered the credit card crisis successfully and, unlike in 1997, its financial system was basically sound. While it was not unreasonable to conclude that Korea was the most vulnerable of the major emerging-market economies of Asia, on the basic facts it was not terribly vulnerable.

Perceptions are what count in market behavior, however, and many in the media and the markets seemed to focus much more on the negative aspects than the positive ones. Rumors that short-term debt will not be rolled over can quickly become self-fulfilling. It seems that almost any country that becomes heavily engaged with global financial markets can be subject to such problems. While I concur with Thomas Cargill (2009) that the claims of great vulnerability were themselves "greatly exaggerated," they can be self-fulfilling. In situations of considerable uncertainty, individuals and corporations tend to protect themselves by being quite risk averse. There is an asymmetric payoff function. The private cost of pulling money out in case of a false alarm is much less than the cost of keeping it in a situation and having things go bad. Thus, there is a disconnect between private and social costs and benefits: the risk-averse private sector behavior can turn a mild crisis into a highly damaging one. There is a classic collective action problem in such situations similar to the traditional problem of bank runs.

In the foreign exchange market this presents a strong case for considerable government intervention in the foreign exchange market to help offset or cushion the effects of such private sector behavior. This is one of the most important types of cases that economists who favor some type of international lender of last resort have in mind because this—unlike the situation with many financial institutions in the United States and Europe—seemed pretty clearly to be much more of a liquidity than a solvency type of crisis. Because Korea had already accumulated a high level of international reserves, the government did not really need to turn to international sources of liquidity although the swap lines provided by the Federal Reserve and the central banks of China and Japan provided an extremely helpful boost to market confidence.

It is not clear what proportion of the capital outflows from Korea during the crisis was due to such excessive fears. It is quite understandable that some highly diversified investors with little particular knowledge of Korea would be influenced by such concerns, while well-informed actors would be more skeptical. Considerable amounts of the pullbacks from emerging markets were due primarily to the need to use these funds to offset losses and meet margin calls. In this regard institutions will tend to sell off their most liquid assets first. As a consequence, the high liquidity of the Korean stock market was in this situation a source of vulnerability.

Lowe-Lee (2009) reports that "foreign investors . . . began to doubt the health of a nation's financial system" and "analysts began to doubt Korean banks' ability to acquire dollars to pay maturing external liabilities." Given Korea's huge foreign exchange reserves, the latter fear seems to have been quite far-fetched unless there had been a deep loss of confidence in the government's and the BOK's abilities to manage the crisis. In any event, such fears fortunately proved to be misplaced. In the wake of the dramatic intensification of the financial-market disruptions following the failure of Lehman Brothers, the U.S. government rescue of AIG, and the other events of September 2008, the government moved quite forcefully to help stabilize Korean markets. A $130 billion rescue package was announced, $100 billion of which was to guarantee up to $100 billion of foreign debt insured by Korean banks between 20 October 2008 and 30 June 2009. With its large foreign reserves, this guarantee was quite credible and greatly increased the ability of Korean banks to successfully roll over maturing borrowings. That many of the loans were from head offices to the Korean branches of large international banks was also important.

As shown in *Table 10-1*, at the end of 2008 foreign loans to Korea were still at more than $145 billion, falling by less than $20 billion from the peak end-of-the-year value of more than $160 billion in 2007 and still well above the end of 2006 figure of $123 billion. The total of the other investment category shows no decline, with the levels increasing mostly from $243 billion at the end of 2007 to $250 billion at the end of 2008, roughly double the $123 billion of 2005. These, however, were the unusual years, with the 2008 figures not being out of line with the annual figures between 1998 and 2005. Foreign holdings of debt securities also fell only modestly to $127 billion at the end of 2008, from $137 at the end of 2007 and still double the level of 2005.

Table 10-1: **Foreign Investment into Korea, 2001–08 in billions of U.S dollars**

Investments	2001	2002	2003	2004	2005	2006	2007	2008
Total volume	248.8	277.2	337.8	413.5	539.4	652.3	826.3	601.3
Foreign direct Investment	53.2	62.7	66.1	87.8	104.9	115.8	122.0	85.3
Portfolio investment	106.4	116.2	165.0	210.3	310.5	352.4	456.7	251.7
Equity securities (stocks)	70.0	75.7	116.8	156.4	249.5	276.4	320.1	124.7
Debt securities (bonds)	36.4	40.5	48.3	53.9	61.0	76.0	136.6	127.1
Financial derivatives	0.4	0.9	0.9	0.9	1.3	2.4	4.9	14.3
Other investment	88.8	97.4	105.8	114.5	122.8	181.7	242.8	250.0
Loans	67.3	73.2	73.8	74	75.6	122.8	162.9	145.8
Banks	34.2	41.3	46.1	47.0	51.2	96.2	135.4	115.0

Source: M. K. Kang, "Global Financial Crisis and Systemic Risks in the Korean Banking Sector," Academic Paper Series (Korea Economic Institute) 4, no. 5 (2009).

The dramatic drop was in the value of foreign stock market holdings. While considerable commentary has focused on the outflow of foreign funds from the Korean stock market as a major cause of the strong downward pressure on the *won*, the importance of these outflows has been greatly exaggerated. This has likely come largely from looking at the numbers for the dollar value of foreign holdings in the Korean stock market. These plummeted from $320 billion at end of 2007 to only $125 billion at end of 2008, but the majority of this decline reflected declines in the KOSPI and the *won*, resulting in a huge drop in the dollar value of the Korean stock market. Actual outflows, while far from trivial, were much smaller.

As seen in *Table 10-2,* the net outflow of portfolio investment in 2008 was a little over $15 billion, down from the levels of the two preceding years of over $20 billion net outflows apiece. The years 2006 and 2007 had been dominated by the huge increase in Korea's portfolio investments abroad (*Table 10-3*), stimulated in large part by the easing of restrictions. From end of 2005 to end of 2007, Korean holdings of foreign bonds rose from $38 billion to $54 billion, and stock holdings rose from $14 billion to $105 billion. After running consistent surpluses from 2002 through 2007, Table 10-2 shows that the total financial account of the BOP turned strongly negative, from a surplus of approximately $9.5 billion in 2007 to a deficit of $51 billion in 2008, a turnaround that was roughly matched by the use of international reserves. The net balance of other investments in the BOP for 2008 was –$10.6 billion, a relatively small deficit although quite a drop from the $40 billion plus surpluses of the two preceding years. In fact, in 2008 all of the categories turned negative, with the balance of financial derivatives also recording its first negative value since 2001, a substantial $14 billion. By the first quarter of 2009, although some outflows continued, the deficit in the overall financial account had fallen to less than $1 billion, so the worst of the financial part of the crisis appeared to be contained. For a variety of reasons discussed earlier, the outflows from Korea were especially large. Unlike the 1997 crisis, however, they were not large in relation to Korea's much stronger international reserve position. This allowed the Korean government to respond much more strongly to the crisis than it had in 1997 and as a result has been able to cushion the effects quite considerably (Cargill 2009).

The financing of international trade and of SMEs had been hit particularly hard around the globe, and the Korean economy's heavy reliance on both made it especially important to deal with the credit crunches in both of these areas. The BOK responded promptly to inject both *won* and dollar liquidity into the markets, and it continued to reduce interest rates. The government also took action to provide funding for measures to deal with distressed assets and needs for capital increases at financial institutions (Lall and Eskesen 2009).

Confidence was also boosted by the announcement of the creation of a $30 billion swap line with the Federal Reserve and subsequent arrangements with China and Japan. Given Korea's substantial reserve position, such measures should not have been needed, but, amid concerns by many that a repeat of 1997–98 might be in the offing, these had an important psychological impact.

Table 10-2: **Balance of Financial Account in Korea 1998–2009 (January–April), in billions of U.S dollars**

	1998	1999	2000	2001	2002	2003	2004	2005	2006	2007	2008	2009 (Jan.– Apr.)
Financial account total	-3.368	2.430	12.725	-2.660	7.338	15.308	9.352	7.097	21.098	9.516	-50.895	-0.738
Balance of foreign direct investment	0.673	5.136	4.285	1.108	-0.224	0.100	4.588	2.010	-4.540	-13.836	-10.595	-1.195
Balance of portfolio investment	-1.224	9.190	12.177	6.706	0.346	17.287	6.599	-3.518	-23.230	-26.058	-15.367	4.347
Balance of financial derivatives	-0.654	-0.513	-0.179	-0.123	0.362	0.619	2.020	1.790	0.484	5.445	-14.333	-4.894
Balance of other investment	-2.162	-11.382	-3.557	-10.351	6.854	-2.699	-3.856	6.815	48.384	43.965	-10.600	1.003
Loans from abroad	-1.508	-13.455	-4.858	-13.208	1.934	-5.032	-0.935	1.022	44.180	41.968	-19.582	-7.207

Source: Bank of Korea, Economic Statistics System, http://ecos.bok.or.kr/.

Table 10-3: **Korean Investment Abroad, Outstanding Claims of Residents, 2001–08, in billions of U.S dollars**

Foreign investment	2001	2002	2003	2004	2005	2006	2007	2008
Total volume	185.0	206.8	258.1	329.7	368.4	465.6	596.8	491.5
Direct investment abroad	20.0	20.7	25.0	32.2	38.7	49.2	74.8	95.5
Portfolio investment	7.9	11.6	19.6	33.1	52.1	97.8	158.6	75.4
Equity securities (stocks)	1.2	1.8	3.4	9.0	13.9	36.8	104.9	47.9
Debt securities (bonds)	6.8	9.8	16.1	24.1	38.2	60.1	53.8	27.5
Financial derivatives	0.4	0.9	0.8	1.1	1.0	1.4	2.3	9.1
Other investment	53.9	52.2	57.5	64.3	66.2	78.3	98.9	110.2
Loans	20.5	17.5	21.2	23.9	23.2	25.5	35.9	45.2
Banks	18.6	16.3	19.8	21.3	20.6	21.7	31.1	40.3

Source: Bank of Korea, Economic Statistics System, http://ecos.bok.or.kr/.

At the time this is written—July 2009—financial conditions are still far from normal in Korea, the United States, and around much of the globe, but there is a strong sense that the worst of the credit crunch is past. Risk spreads on a wide range of financial instruments, while still elevated, have fallen substantially from their heights in the last quarter of 2008, and the liquidity of many markets is increasing while volatility has fallen. Especially important for Korea is that the *won* appears to have turned the corner and in recent months has begun to recover some of its previous losses.

From Financial- to Trade-Based Contagion

Financial developments tend to affect the real economy with a lag. Korea and most other emerging markets' low levels of direct exposure to securities based on subprime loans led to initial expectations that these countries would be largely immune to the effects of the subprime crisis. This view has changed drastically, first as the credit crunch developed and then as effects on the real economy began to be felt. As a result of both the increased cost and reduced availability of trade financing and the recessions in the industrial countries, the exports of most Asian economies have taken major hits, and this has begun to spread to the broader economy. The current phase of global contagion is now operating most heavily for countries like Korea through the trade interdependence channel. As 2008 progressed, Korea's growth rate dropped quarter by quarter until in the fourth quarter it turned negative.

A strong case can be made, however, that by mid-2009 the worst of the downturn is past. Reflecting this view in early July, the IMF upgraded its forecast for the Korean economy. Its GDP growth projections were raised from –4 percent to –3 percent for 2009 and from +1.5 to +2.5 percent for 2010 (see also Lowe-Lee 2009). In Korea's 2009 Article IV review, the forecast for 2009 was raised further to –1.75 percent, reflecting expectations of a return to growth in the second half of the year (Lister 2009).

Strong Policy Responses

Projections for Korea's resumed growth are due in no small measure to the strong policy actions taken by the government and the BOK. The government's fiscal stimulus program has been substantial, approximately 2.1 percent of GDP, and the BOK has drastically cut interest rates. Such strong variations in the 1997 crisis would likely have led to massive capital flight, but the substantial improvements during the past decade in the soundness of Korea's financial system and its substantial reserve position allowed such stimulative policies to be undertaken without inducing unmanageable capital outflows.

Should More Reserves Have Been Used to Cushion the Crisis?

With hindsight, if one is looking for possible faults with generally quite successful policy actions amid the crisis, a leading candidate would be whether more international reserves should have been sold to better cushion the effects of the fourth quarter capital outflows and reduce the magnitude of the fall of the *won*. Substantial reserve sales were undertaken, on the order of $60 billion (see *Figure 10-3*), but this still left roughly $200 billion of reserves available.

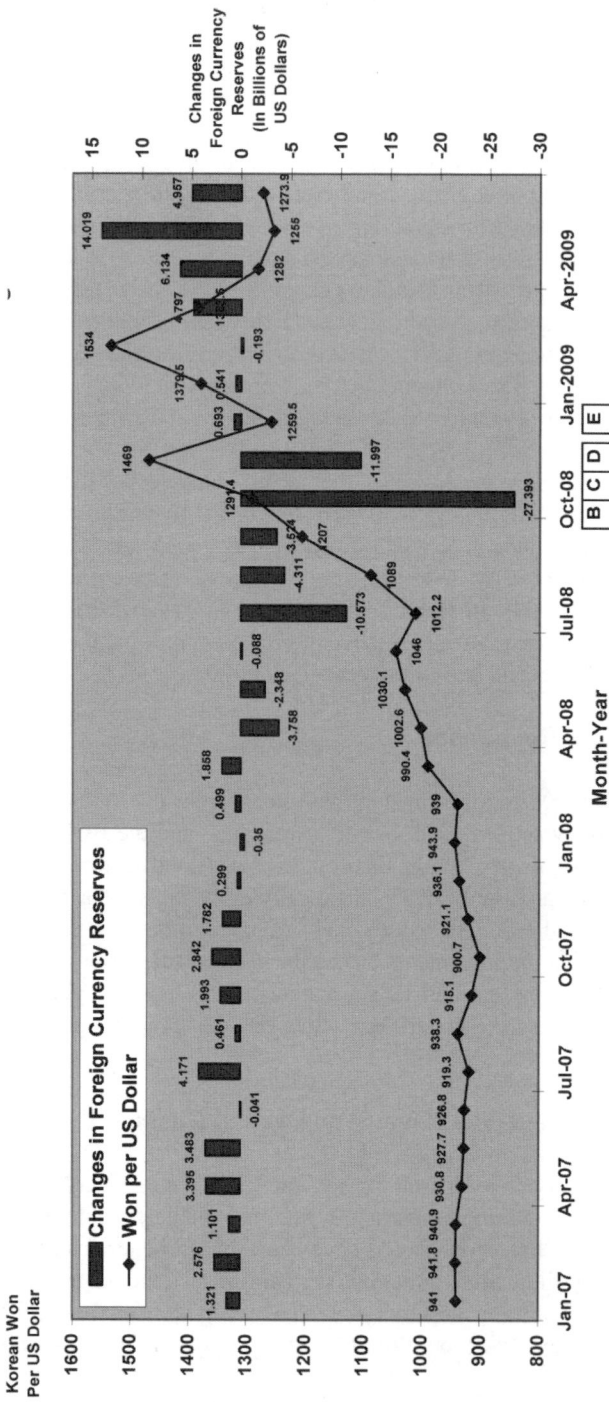

Figure 10-3: **Changes in Korea's Foreign Currency Reserves Compared with the Won-Dollar Exchange Rate January 2007–June 2009**

Source: International Financial Statistics database of the International Monetary Fund; author's calculations.
Timeline: B: Guarantees on the bank debt (Oct 19, 2008); C: US swap (October 30, 2008); D: Nov. 17, 2008 - trade financing; E: Dec 12, 2008 - China swap

If my argument is correct that a substantial portion of the international financial outflows from Korea during the crisis was due to the repercussions of the financial crisis abroad and to the views that overstated the vulnerability of Korea to the crisis, then this presents one of the few sets of conditions where very large scale sterilized intervention in the foreign exchange market is justified. In such a case even larger intervention could be appropriate. And under these conditions it would be likely to be effective if backed by strong government policies. The substantial appreciation of the *won* since February combined with a recoupment of more than $30 billion in reserves suggest that there is likely some truth in this analysis.

Legitimate questions can be raised about the effectiveness of sterilized interventions. They certainly have limited effectiveness for attempting to maintain a pegged rate in the face of large capital outflows. And among some of the major industrial countries international capital mobility may be so high that sterilized intervention will generally be ineffective except in the cases where internationally coordinated intervention can send policy signals that offset expectations if or when markets become temporarily thin and disorderly in the face of great uncertainty. For emerging-market economies with flexible rates, however, there should be scope for sterilized intervention to have effects in countering crisis situations, which bring uncertainty and rapid increases in risk aversion. How strong such effects are is the crucial question, and it is one that is exceptionally hard to investigate. In addition to the lack of publicly available information on intervention, our exchange rate models are far from precise enough to measure accurately the counterfactual of what would have happened in the absence of intervention.

Because much intervention is of the leaning-against-the-wind variety, intervention will only slow, not halt or reverse, exchange rate movements. Thus, when looking at the continued climb of the *won* in the early and middle parts of this decade despite substantial continued intervention, it is easy to have concern that the intervention was largely ineffective. The relevant question, however, is how much more would the *won* have appreciated in the absence of the intervention. We can estimate this with exchange rate models, but we would find a wide range of results using different models, just as there has been recent controversy about the equilibrium value of China's currency.

Furthermore, there are strong reasons to believe that exchange rate effects of a given sized intervention can vary greatly depending on the circumstances. Just as market commentators frequently point to perceived changes in the risk appetites of investors in stock markets, the effective short-run elasticities in foreign exchange markets are likely to vary greatly depending on such factors as the level of uncertainty in the market and the credibility of government and central bank officials. Although answers will not come easily, more attention to the study of the effectiveness of foreign exchange market intervention should be an important topic for researchers both within and outside central banks and governments.

Dealing with Variability of Capital Flows

The current crisis provides another vivid example that international capital flows can be highly variable and that the causes of seizing up do not always have to do with developments in the recipient countries. One possible response to this variability of capital flows is to impose tight controls, but this could impose substantial efficiency costs. Taxes or controls on large capital inflows are a more sensible approach, but many economists believe that strong prudential regulation is the best course of action (Eichengreen 1999). Traditional micro prudential rules have proven insufficient for controlling excessive expansion of credit and leverage. One desirable side effect of the current crisis has been its stimulus to the need for more attention to macro systemic risks rather than a focus on institution-by-institution analysis of balance sheets.

Financial institutions should certainly be required to maintain sufficient capital to guard against idiosyncratic shocks and the use of excessive leverage. But, if all institutions kept reserves sufficient to deal adequately with major systematic shocks, they would be able to engage in very little productive lending. There are tremendous economies of scale in using centralized reserves to deal with such major shocks, and the government is the natural collective entity to hold these reserves.[54]

A wise strategy is for governments to add to their international reserves a proportion of many types of capital inflows. Although sufficient analysis has not yet taken place to say just what this proportion should be and how it should vary across types of financial flows, this is an important topic for policy research, and ballpark estimates of reasonable proportions can be obtained from the type of analysis presented in Chapter 4. This reserve management approach by itself does not account for the social costs of reserve accumulation. Thus, just as there is a strong case for requiring banks to contribute to the cost of accumulating funds to provide deposit insurance, there is a case for imposing moderate fees on capital involved to cover the costs of holding additional reserves. Whether such an approach would be efficient in practice is at present an open question, but it is one that deserves consideration.

---

54. This argument extends to reserve pooling across countries as well; this is a function the IMF was designed to meet.

11

Conclusions and Policy Recommendations

Korea's Monetary Exchange Rate and Financial Strategies Are Basically Sound

Our analysis finds that the policies of inflation targeting and managed floating have served Korea well. Despite some susceptibility to the inflationary pressures that were sweeping Asia during the middle of this decade, Korea's overall inflation record since the 1997–98 crisis has been good. Exchange market pressures have at times complicated policymaking and justified official intervention, so Korea has been wise to follow a managed float rather than the free float that some officials misleadingly still claim Korea to be following.

With hindsight one can second-guess some of the specifics of postcrisis intervention policies. In my own judgment the BOK's leaning-against-the-wind intervention was too strong in the latter part of the period of *won* appreciation and should have been stronger during the period of sharp depreciation of the *won* during the current crisis, but these are issues over which it is difficult to reach definitive judgments, especially as the events are happening.

Korea is sometimes charged with practicing mercantilist policies, but such charges do not hold up to careful analysis. Although Korea may have leaned too hard against the winds of appreciation, this is a far cry from beggar-thy-neighbor policy; and, although it did have large reserve accumulations during most of this decade, these came much more from large capital inflows than from a huge current account surplus. Korea has certainly not been a major contributor to the problem of global current account balances. Overall exchange market intervention policy has been reasonable.

Beliefs that the complications generated by varying exchange market pressures would go away if Korea joined a common Asian currency are based on faulty analysis. Although some pressures would be eliminated, those that would remain could have much more damaging effects on the Korean economy, forcing it to adopt macroeconomic policies inappropriate for the needs of the economy. Of course, there would also be benefits from being in a large currency area. In aggregate countercyclical policies would be likely to be more powerful, and Korea would undoubtedly have faced less depreciation of the *won*. Given the widespread market perception that Korea was the Asian country most vulnerable to the crisis, however, this common external shock would have had asymmetric effects within Asia. Thus, Korea would have faced a combination of both a symmetric shock for which fixed exchange rates are particularly well suited and an asymmetric shock for which flexible rates are generally better. Overall, it is difficult to conclude whether during the crisis Korea would have been hurt less as a member of an Asian currency area or with its current managed float and independent monetary policy. What is incorrect is to argue that Korea would have been obviously better off during the crisis if it had been a member of a broad currency area. The substantial difficulties that have been facing many of the countries in the eurozone illustrate this point.[55]

Taking a longer-run perspective, several recent studies have concluded that on some criteria the benefits for Korea would be greater than the costs. Typically, however, such studies have failed to give sufficient attention to the full, broader range of considerations that affect the total costs and benefits of joining a currency area. When these are taken into account, our analysis indicates that the case that Korea would benefit from joining a common Asian currency is quite weak. We show that some of the most important considerations give conflicting signals. Although within Asia Korea trades most heavily with China and Japan, its general pattern of macroeconomic correlations with these countries is considerably lower than with many Southeast Asian countries. This common monetary policy would not work well for all currency area members. Geopolitical considerations also greatly reduce the likelihood that a common Asian currency would be politically feasible even it if were economically desirable. While the European experience with economic integration has led some to think that the creation of the euro was the logical outcome of the integration process, we argue that it was in fact a rather low-probability event generated by a particular set of geopolitical considerations

---

55. For opposing views on this issue in the European context, see Dougherty (2008, sec. B) and *Economist* (2008, 68).

that no longer obtain in Europe. Given the historical rivalry between China and Japan, there is little realistic prospect of their joining an Asian currency area within the next decade or two, and creating such an area without them would lack much of its rationale.

We should not let grand schemes of monetary union stand in the way of taking less dramatic but more practical steps to increase Asian economic, monetary, and financial cooperation. The European experience does suggest that economic integration can be a powerful force for overcoming historical distrust among nations. There are many reasons to promote greater economic integration and cooperation within Asia that need not rely on a goal of monetary union. It is particularly important to develop stronger institutions to help strengthen cooperation.

International capital flows can make life more difficult for policymakers trying to choose optimal policies, but we find that they have not seriously undermined the BOK's ability to implement effective monetary policy. Korea has made great strides since the 1997–98 crisis toward improving the soundness of its financial system, undertaking further liberalization in a more sensible manner, and strengthening prudential regulation and supervision. Much still needs to be done to continue to improve the efficiency of the operation of the financial system, especially in its international dimensions.[56]

Heavy engagement with the global economy imposes costs as well as benefits, but there is little reason to believe that on balance the benefits do not greatly exceed the costs. The outward-oriented development strategies of Korea and many other Asian countries have been proved clearly superior to the inward-oriented policies that were often followed by others, but this does not suggest that exports should be artificially stimulated at the expense of the rest of the economy. Just as it is essential that the United States act to curb its recent reliance on excessive consumption, Korea and a number of other Asian economies need to develop economies that are better balanced and that rely more strongly on domestic sources of growth.

Korea Is in a Much Stronger Position to Deal with the Current Crisis Than in 1997

In the 1997–98 crisis, the primary causes of the huge capital outflows were desires to reduce exposure to Korean financial assets and unhedged foreign currency liabilities and the inadequacy Korea's of international reserve position. This shortage of international reserves combined with a substantial

---

56. See the series of reports prepared by the researchers of the Korea Institute of Finance (KIF); a summary is given in Researchers of the KIF (2008) and K. S. Kim (2008). See also the suggestions by Kang (2009).

current account deficit sharply limited the government's ability to adopt expansionary policies and also resulted in substantial overdepreciation of the *won*, which in turn led to greater financial losses. While the current government's initial management of the turnaround in the *won* left a good deal to be desired, recent policy actions have been sound and applied with a steadier hand. A considerable part of the recent capital outflows are motivated not by concerns about Korea but by the needs of foreign investors to repatriate funds to cover margin calls and losses on other investments. It is true that the Korean stock market had become overvalued as a part of the global bubble and has subsequently tumbled dramatically, but so have markets around the globe. Korea suffered more foreign exchange market pressure than other Asian currencies in large part because of the higher proportion of foreign investment in its stock market before the crisis and concerns about the rapid expansion of its short-term foreign debt in recent years. The outflows were large in absolute terms but not relative to the high level of reserves that Korea had accumulated.

In the current crisis Korea has been in a much better position to respond than in the 1997 crisis. Its financial system is much stronger, and its international liquidity position was far superior. Although it can be argued that short-term foreign borrowing by Korean banks was allowed to expand too fast in 2006 and 2007, there were also reasons for having only limited concern about this development, especially given the very strong international reserve position that had been accumulated. While many standard types of calculations of reserve adequacy suggested that excessive international reserves had been accumulated by the middle of this decade, concerns about the high proportion of foreign ownership in the Korean stock market combined with this rapid buildup of short-term foreign debt and the large capital outflows by Korean residents stimulated by financial liberalization were sufficient to give rise to concerns among some market participants. These interacted with the poor execution of government policies to talk down the *won* to generate severe strains in the foreign exchange market before the effects of the U.S. subprime crisis began to spread to emerging markets. As a consequence of these factors, Korea became the most hard-hit country in Asia in terms of financial-market disturbances.

The pattern of capital outflows during this crisis has differed substantially from the 1997 crisis, with stock market outflows in the current crisis greatly exceeding those in 1997 while short-term bank flows have remained fairly stable, providing some justification for the authorities' relative lack of concern about their buildup. It is interesting that the substantial outflows of foreign holdings of Korean stocks appear to have had as much to do with the relatively high liquidity of the Korean market as with dire concerns about the Korean economy. With the huge financial losses generated in the industrial countries hit by the crisis, it is not surprising that those needing to repatriate capital would sell off their most liquid assets first. Thus, to some extent Korea was a victim of its very success in improving the liquidity of its financial markets.

On the bright side, the improved quality of Korea's financial system and its large holdings of international reserves have allowed Korea to respond to this crisis with expansionary rather than contractionary monetary and fiscal policies and to make use of its swap lines and sales of international reserves to help reduce the decline of the *won*. In the 1997 crisis none of these options was really available. Thus, despite being seen as especially vulnerable by many financial-market participants, Korea has been in a much better position to respond to this crisis than it was in 1997.

This does not mean that the Korean economy has escaped considerable damage, however. As with the other export-dependent Asian economies, the recessions in the industrial countries have hit Korean exporters quite hard, and this in turn affects the overall economy. In addition, the freezing up of credit markets generated sharp increases in the cost and declines in the availability of trade finance, which has also contributed to falling volumes of international trade and increased difficulties of operation for the SMEs that account for so much of the Korean economy. Fortunately, financial markets have generally begun to function again, and the cost and availability of credit, while not back to precrisis levels, have improved substantially. Thus, there are good reasons to believe that the worst of the global financial crisis is past. The fall of the *won* has ended, and upward pressures have been sufficiently strong for Korea to begin to recoup some of the reserves sold at the height of the crisis.

The effects of the crisis on the real economies are continuing, however. Although there are some grounds for optimism that as of midsummer 2009 many economies are beginning, or are at least close to beginning, to turn around and Korea's GDP has started to grow again, there is considerable danger that recoveries in many economies may be quite weak. A major source of concern is the lingering holes in the balance sheets of major financial institutions in the industrial countries. While there has been considerable successful raising of capital and the U.S. stress tests have pronounced that none of the major U.S. financial institutions deserves to be classified as insolvent, many independent experts are much more pessimistic, suggesting that expected future earnings will be far from sufficient to fill the true holes in many institutions' balance sheets. Japan in the 1990s and many other examples suggest that failures to fully clean up balance sheets lead to prolonged stagnation, and many experts are concerned that politics and "cognitive capture" have kept U.S. officials from facing up to the full costs of restoring the banking system to health.

The situation in Europe is even worse, with a far lower proportion of likely losses having been acknowledged on the books of the banks. Thus, despite some large emerging-market economies such as China and India showing strong signs of recovery, the general climate for the growth of international trade appears likely to remain weak for a considerable time. If correct, this further increases the case for Korea and other export-dependent economies to further strengthen efforts to rebalance their economies.

A number of commentators have argued that the crisis supports concerns that Korea had become too open to global financial markets and had allowed "excessive" foreign investment in the Korean stock market and a dangerous buildup of short-term foreign debt by the Korean branches of international banks. Considerable concern has also been expressed about the role played by speculation in the market for nondeliverable forward exchange. Such concerns deserve careful attention, but the best policy responses are not obvious. Large financial inflows do increase the risk of sudden stops and hence can impose an important systemic risk that would be difficult to capture by the standard prudential regulation of individual institutions.

This in principle can present a case for capital controls, but their well-known inefficiencies make it important to investigate whether better solutions can be found. In general there is a presumption in favor of tax rather than control measures to correct such negative externalities. While now abandoned, Chile's "tax" system of required zero interest deposits lengthened the maturities of capital inflows a good bit without having much discouraging effect on total capital inflows. Thus, depending on one's objectives, this experiment could be judged as a success or a failure. Whether or not direct measures are taken to discourage high levels of liquid financial inflows, it is clear that part of a sensible national risk management regime would be to use a portion of these inflows to increase international reserves. Obtaining better estimates of what such proportions should be is an important area for policy research. And, because such additional reserve accumulation is costly, a case can be made for imposing a fee on inflows to help cover these costs, but such an approach should not be adopted without careful study. Any such measures need to be taken within the context of a strong system of prudential oversight. Korea has made great strides in this area since the 1997 crisis, and its recent failures have been far less than those in the United States and Europe, but Korea has much to gain by being an active participant in the efforts now beginning to substantially reform financial regulation at the global level.

Reforming the Global Financial System

The current global crisis should put to rest any lingering beliefs that financial markets can always manage themselves. When doubts are raised about the solvency of important counterparts in financial networks, the microeconomic incentives facing individual market participants can greatly magnify shocks. Thus, a relatively low proportion of bad assets or credit risks in the system can lead broad segments of financial markets to seize up, engage in runs on particular institutions and securities, or both. This is a key reason why financial systems need lenders of last resort to reduce the danger that broad segments of the financial system can implode under stress.

The existence of such lenders of last resort (or guarantors of last resort) in turn generates moral hazard. As financial systems grow in complexity, a growing number of institutions may become too big or too interconnected to fail. This in turn tends to reduce their incentives for careful risk management. There is considerable disagreement about how important the various channels of moral-hazard influence have been in generating recent crises, but it is clear that the responses to the current global crisis will greatly increase the potential for moral hazard and contribute to future crises if adequate safeguards are not adopted. Such considerations provide a strong rationale for government regulations to limit excessive risk taking by institutions subject to such moral-hazard incentives. There is a clear need for a better system of resolution authority for large troubled financial institutions that allows temporary government takeovers and imposes costs on managers and investors without completely disrupting the operation of the financial system. This will definitely not be an easy task, either technically or politically, but we are currently seeing the huge costs of not having such an effective regime.

In thinking about future reforms for financial regulations, several key issues come to mind. One is that, although there is a clear case for good regulation, actual regulation has often worked poorly. While deregulation has frequently been blamed for the U.S. crisis, a high proportion of the most serious problems developed in sectors that were still regulated. While Alan Greenspan's degree of faith in the ability of the financial sector to police its own activities was clearly excessive, his skepticism about the effectiveness of traditional financial regulation was much better placed. We clearly need to adopt regulatory strategies where the regulators do not have to be much smarter than the private sector actors for regulations to work. This suggests placing greater reliance on crude but effective measures like capital and leverage ratios instead of on more sophisticated measures that can more easily be gamed. It is also important to recognize that the perverse incentive structures that led to the widespread nature of the current crisis were far more pervasive than just those generated by moral hazard from potential government bailouts.

We need a new approach to financial regulation. Considerably more emphasis should be placed on evaluating the incentive structures within important financial institutions than on accessing the details of their complicated risk management models. Where incentive structures are seriously out of balance, competitive pressures can make the situation worse rather than better, as investment managers and institutions feel compelled by their competitors to take on more risk to keep up current returns and market shares.[57] Because financial risks are so hard to measure ex ante, proposals that a sizable portion of compensation in the financial sector should be deferred for some time until a better appreciation of risks can be obtained have considerable merit. Introducing some degree of individual liability for damages generated by excessive risk taking may also be worth considering. The case for such liability is especially strong when government bailouts are required.

It is clear that prudential regulators need a great deal more information than has been available to them in the past. Some of the information about the positions of individual institutions should of course remain confidential, but considerably more transparency of public information is needed as well. Where to draw the balance on this issue will be an important issue for study. It is clear that in the United States and Europe both regulators and market discipline failed. We need to try to improve the operation of both—viewing them as complements not substitutes. The improvement of both will require better information as well as the provision of better incentives to make use of this information.

More attention clearly needs to be paid to the potential costs of financial innovations, and a better balance obtained between the benefits of the continued work for innovation and the danger that some innovations that provide substantial private benefits can also generate huge social costs. It is important to remember that the major cause of the global crisis was not financial liberalization per se, but the failure of governments and regulatory agencies to provide proper oversight of this liberalization. In part because of liberalization, the Korean financial system is far sounder today than before the crisis of 1997.

History makes clear that financial innovation, liberalization, and regulation can all be subject to substantial unintended consequences. These can never be entirely eliminated, but careful study prior to choosing and implementing policies can certainly reduce the incidence of such unintended consequences. Fortunately, for some time to come, too little rather than too much risk taking is likely to be the greater problem in most credit and financial markets. Thus, there is time to think through reforms carefully. But we must not let striving for perfection be the enemy of the good. If we do not begin to make progress now, the willingness of key actors in the political process to give the

---

57. Recent reports suggest that concerns with maintaining or increasing market share were major factors in the decisions of Citigroup and also Fannie Mae and Freddie Mac to adopt riskier investment strategies.

needed attention to these issues will begin to fade. This opportunity to substantially reform regulatory strategies should not be allowed to go to waste.

While the Group of 20 summit in November 2008 predictably failed to live up to the hype of a new Bretton Woods generated by some politicians, it was a worthwhile meeting. Perhaps its most important aspect was the choice of membership, with the inclusion of many important emerging-market nations rather than just the traditional industrial-country powers. The agreement that membership in the Financial Stability Board will be broadened to include countries such as Korea is an important accomplishment. Korea is well positioned to take a leading role in helping to chart new directions for global financial regulation. Also important in this respect will be helping to refocus attention more on macro prudential issues such as reducing the pro-cyclical nature of traditional capital adequacy regulations and dampening the contagion effects generated by standard value-at-risk models.

As was discussed, the traditional approaches to both private sector risk modeling and management and prudential regulation have focused primarily on individual institutions under the implicit assumption that at the macro level the financial system would continue to operate well and would not be substantially influenced by the developments in an individual institution. This independence assumption makes analysis much easier, but it fundamentally distorts reality. The new Basel II banking regulations, while making some improvements on Basel I, still fail to take such complex interdependence sufficiently into account. Recognition of this type of problem is increasing. It is imperative that prudential regulators and private sector risk managers pay greater attention to the lessons from the current crisis than they did from the crisis of 1997–98. Emerging-market countries such as Korea have demonstrated that they did learn a great deal from the earlier crises and adjusted policies accordingly. Therefore, they should be in a strong position to take leadership in this effort.

It is also worth another major effort at reforming the IMF to help bring it more fully into the age of financial globalization.[58] The IMF is a perplexing mix of typical bureaucratic inertia combined with an unusual ability to sometimes learn from past mistakes. In recent years, it had become largely sidelined as an important global actor—with some justification, given its track record. The global nature of the current crisis highlights the positive role that a well-functioning IMF could play. Its new Short-Term Liquidity Facility is a much-needed step toward increasing its capacity to play a role more closely approximating a genuine international lender of last resort and is designed

---

58. For discussions of the needs for IMF reform and some thoughtful proposals, see Truman (2009); for recent discussions of the IMF's role in global surveillance, see Bird and Willett (2007) and Goldstein and Lardy (2008).

much better than its ill-fated predecessor, the Contingent Credit Lines adopted after the Asian and Russian crises.

The IMF suffers, however, not only from bureaucratic problems but also from the heavy influence of major powers on its policies. Substantial reforms are needed to increase its legitimacy, and a key aspect of this is to give more effective power to emerging-market economies. Reports indicate that at the November 2008 summit many nations wanted to put the IMF more solidly in the center of the global financial system and provide it with the greater resources necessary to play such a role effectively, but the U.S. government was cool to these ideas. It is to be hoped that with a new administration in power in the United States such positions will be rethought.

Korea's Pivotal Position for Reform

Korea is well positioned to begin a more positive engagement with the IMF, using its experiences with the IMF during the Asian crisis as a basis for taking leadership in promoting reforms. Its upcoming position as chair of the Group of 20 gives it increased potential to play this role and makes it especially important to discard blanket negative views of the IMF and put forward constructive proposals for its improvement. Korea should also continue leadership in pushing for increased Asian monetary and financial cooperation. As was argued in Chapter 8, it should be recognized that this will be a long, slow process and is likely not to result in the dramatic developments like the creation of a common currency, but it can be highly valuable just the same. Korea should not let the grandeur of unrealistic discussion of Asian monetary union deflect attention from the slow process of developing institutional frameworks to help facilitate regional monetary and financial cooperation. Although the prospects for strengthening the Chiang Mai Initiative and bringing it into use are unclear, the development of a collectively financed Asian monetary and financial institute or secretariat that provides an independent staff to help support the work of ASEAN Plus Three in these areas should be a high priority. For advocates of increased Asian monetary and financial cooperation, there is a rich agenda to pursue.

Appendix A

Economic Estimates of Sterilization and Offset Coefficients for Korea

This appendix is coauthored with Alice Ouyang, who is the lead author.

Our estimates are based on Ouyang, Rajan, and Willett (2008); this model modifies the theoretical model developed by Brissimis, Gibson, and Tsakalotos (2002), which derives both the balance of payments and the monetary reaction functions from explicit minimization of a simple loss function of the monetary authority, subject to a number of constraints that reflect the working of the economy. The estimated simultaneous equations are simplified as follows:[59]

$$\Delta NFA_t^* = \alpha_0 - \sum_{i=0}^{n}\alpha_{1i}\Delta NDA_{t-i}^* + \sum_{i=0}^{n}\alpha_{2i}\Delta mm_{t-i} + \sum_{i=1}^{n}\alpha_{3i}\Delta p_{t-i} + \sum_{i=1}^{n}\alpha_{4i}y_{c,t-i} + \sum_{i=0}^{n}\alpha_{5i}G_{c,t-i}$$

$$(1a) \quad + \sum_{i=1}^{n}\alpha_{6i}\Delta REER_{t-i} + \sum_{i=0}^{n}\alpha_{7i}\Delta(r_{t-i}^* + E_t s_{t+1-i}) + \sum_{i=1}^{n}\alpha_{8i}(d_2 - 1)\sigma_{s,t-i} + \varepsilon_t$$

$$\Delta NDA_t^* = \beta_0 - \sum_{i=0}^{n}\beta_{1i}\Delta NFA_{t-i}^* + \sum_{i=0}^{n}\beta_{2i}\Delta mm_{t-i} + \sum_{i=1}^{n}\beta_{3i}\Delta p_{t-i} + \sum_{i=1}^{n}\beta_{4i}y_{c,t-i} + \sum_{i=0}^{n}\beta_{5i}G_{c,t-i}$$

$$(1b) \quad + \sum_{i=1}^{n}\beta_{6i}\Delta REER_{t-i} + \sum_{i=0}^{n}\beta_{7i}\Delta(r_{t-i}^* + E_t s_{t+1-i}) + \sum_{i=1}^{n}\beta_{8i}(d_1 - 1)\sigma_{r,t-i} + v_t$$

The **balance of payments function** (equation 1a) consists of seven control variables, incorporating both push and pull factors. Push factors motivate capital to leave creditor countries in search of better returns. Pull factors motivate capital flows into specific recipient countries. The rationales for the inclusion of variables are as follows: A rise in the money multiplier for M2

---

59. Please refer to Table B-1 in Appendix B for the definitions of the variables.

increases the domestic money and pushes the interest rate down, hence reducing capital inflows. Higher inflation heightens concerns about currency depreciation, causing a reduction in capital inflows.[60] Higher lagged real output could worsen the current account (owing to the income effect), reducing foreign reserve accumulation. An expansionary fiscal policy (higher government expenditure) will raise cyclical income and once again worsen the current account.[61] Foreign reserves will be decumulated because of a decrease in the current account if the real effective exchange rate (REER) is overvalued (price effect). A rise in either the change in foreign interest rates or in the expected exchange rate depreciation can also lead to capital withdrawals from the country. Finally, to limit exchange rate volatility, the central bank tends to buy or sell foreign reserves (that is, foreign exchange market intervention) when there is an excess supply of or demand for foreign currency, respectively. The more volatile the exchange rate, the more heavily the central bank will intervene. Therefore, the expected sign for the interaction term should be negative.

The **monetary policy function** (equation 1b) consists of seven control variables in the monetary reaction function in addition to the change of net foreign assets. These control variables are considered important factors influencing monetary policy actions. The theoretical model suggests that the expected signs for these explanatory variables are negative, indicating that monetary authorities generally implement a contractionary monetary policy to defend a country's currency and to adjust to a rise in inflation, the money multiplier, or the expected exchange rate depreciation. In addition, monetary authorities adopt an anticyclical monetary policy if they contract domestic credit when there is a rise in real GDP growth rate or fiscal deficit. However, we note that the expected sign for the fiscal spending should be positive if monetary authorities monetize a government's fiscal deficit. Also, both an overvalued REER and higher exchange rate–adjusted foreign interest rates can cause a deficit in the balance of payments. Monetary authorities tend to implement a policy of high interest rates (that is, a contractionary monetary policy) to attract more capital inflows to reach external balance. Finally, to keep domestic interest rates less volatile, the central bank will inject or withdraw funds from the market when the domestic money market is in deficit or in surplus, respectively. Again, the more volatile the domestic interest rate, the more

---

60. In addition, in practice, higher inflation could engender greater uncertainty, leading to reduced capital flows.

61. Three caveats should be noted. One, it is important to consider the context of expansionary fiscal policy. If adopted in response to an economic downturn, the impact may not be similar to that in response to output above trend. Two, the focus here is on short-term rates; in most circumstances one would expect higher budget deficits to cause a rise in long-term interest rates. Three, it is also important to consider the impact of market expectations. If higher government expenditure is viewed as a sign of fiscal profligacy, this could lead to a rise in country risk premium and consequent capital flight.

heavily the central bank will intervene. We also anticipated a negative sign for the interaction term.

Data and Definitions

The estimation is based on monthly data for the sample period from January 1985 to October 2008. We divide the whole sample period into two sub-samples: the precrisis period defined as January 1985 to June 1997 and the postcrisis period defined as July 1998 to October 2008. By comparing the different values of offset and sterilization coefficients in these two subsamples, we can ascertain how the extent of sterilization and degree of capital mobility for Korea have changed in the two periods. One of the difficulties in estimating the model is the development of proxies for exchange rate expectations, which are not directly observable.

There is no one best way to proxy these expectations, so we make use of several different methods that have been used in the literature. We are fortunate that our estimates are not terribly sensitive to which proxy is used. One common assumption in the literature is that economic agents have unbiased foresight of future exchange rates. Thus, the actual nominal exchange rate at the next period is used to proxy the expected exchange rate for the next period. The two other most common assumptions are static expectations of future exchange rate and the use of three-month *won*-dollar forward rate as a predictor of the future spot rate. In other words, the current spot rate is used as the predictor of the future rate, as would occur if the exchange rate followed a random walk.

Table B-1 in Appendix B summarizes the definitions and sources of the various data used in the estimating equations. The relevant variables, such as the change in the "adjusted" ΔNFA_t^* and ΔNDA_t^* (where * denotes adjustments that are discussed in next section), are scaled by monetary base. To check for stationarity, we applied the standard unit root test using the Augmented Dickey Fuller (ADF) to each of the variables and found them all to be stationary at the 10 percent level of significance for both the precrisis and postcrisis periods, except the exchange rate–adjusted foreign interest rates with forward-looking expectations (see *Table B-2* in Appendix B).[62] We used the Hodrick-Prescott (HP) method to measure the trend of real output, government expenditure, and inflation. In addition, we used the standard deviation of the within monthly change in the daily U.S. dollar bilateral exchange rate and short-term uncollateralized call rates to proxy the volatility of exchange rate and volatility of domestic interest rate, respectively.

---

62. Siklos (2000) pointed out a similar problem with the Hungarian-German interest rate differential and has argued that interest rates should not be difference stationary.

Adjusting the Net Foreign Asset and Net Domestic Asset Figures

Since the changes of net foreign assets (NFAs) and net domestic assets (NDAs) are taken from monetary authorities' balance sheets, we must be careful of how monetary authorities report the revaluation effects derived from exchange rate fluctuations, interest earnings earned from foreign reserves accumulation, and loans from international organizations (such as International Monetary Fund and the World Bank). It could cause a severe bias if we used the book values of NFAs and NDAs to conduct empirical research.

To correctly measure the change in NFAs and NDAs, we have to exclude the revaluation effect and interest earnings from the net foreign assets (that is, foreign assets minus foreign liabilities). Because the BOK's investment portfolio is unknown and interest earnings are not usually considered as significant as the revaluation effect, we assume that the interest earnings are not substantial and can be ignored for now. In addition, foreign assets include monetary gold and foreign exchange. To exclude monetary gold from the foreign assets, we use the product of foreign reserves denominated in the U.S. dollar and exchange rates (domestic currency divided by the U.S. dollar) to proxy foreign assets. The net foreign assets without monetary gold are as follows:

$$NFA_t = R_t \times s_t - FL_t$$

where R_t is the foreign reserves denominated in the U.S. dollar; and S_t is the exchange rate against the U.S. dollar.

Because the revaluation effect is the change of NFAs caused by exchange rate fluctuations, we measure the revaluation effect as follows:

$$\text{Revaluation effect} = NFA_{t-1}(\frac{s_t}{s_{t-1}} - 1)$$

Therefore, the revised change of net foreign assets = $\Delta NFA_t^* = NFA_t - NFA_{t-1}(\frac{s_t}{s_{t-1}})$

Since the revaluation effect can affect not only ΔNFA_t^* but also ΔNDA_t^*, we have to exclude the revaluation effect from ΔNDA_t^* as well. Therefore, the new ΔNDA_t^* is

$$\Delta NDA_t^* = \Delta NDA_t + \Delta NOA_t - \Delta K_t + \text{Revaluation effect}$$

$$= \Delta NDA_t + \Delta NOA_t - \Delta K_t + NFA_{t-1}(\frac{s_t}{s_{t-1}} - 1)$$

ΔNFA_t^* and ΔNDA_t^* will be used as the dependent variables in equations (1a) and (1b), respectively.

Empirical Results for Korea

The two-stage least square method was used to estimate the simultaneous equation. Because of data limitations, the empirical results for the forward rate expectations are available for only the postcrisis period. The empirical results are presented in *Table B-3* in Appendix B. The estimated precrisis offset coefficient is around 0.5, while the estimated sterilization coefficients range from 0.63 to 0.65.[63] This suggests that Korea had a moderate degree of capital mobility before the crisis, and the BOK also undertook fairly substantial high sterilization operations. After the crisis, while the estimated offset coefficient increased modestly to 0.68, the estimated sterilization coefficient increased substantially to around 1 under all the assumptions for proxying exchange rate expectations.

The estimated coefficients for the change in the money multiplier are consistently negative and significant in both periods. Increases in inflation and real output above trend have consistently negative effects in both equations but are significant only before the crisis. The estimated coefficients for the government expenditure deviations from the trend are positive before the crisis, but turn negative after the crisis, indicating that the BOK tended to monetize the government expenditure before the crisis. However, they are insignificant for all the cases. The volatility term has the correct sign for the exchange rate and interest rate before the crisis but is statistically insignificant or turns positive in the postcrisis period. The other variables are statistically insignificant in both periods with inconsistent signs, except for the lagged change in the REER and the exchange rate–adjusted foreign interest rate in the monetary reaction function before the crisis.

In summary, Korea is estimated to have had a moderate degree of capital mobility in the precrises period, which increases moderately afterward. This is consistent with the impression that Korea has been gradually opening up its capital market in recent years, but that this has been partially offset on capital mobility by the dampening effect of greater exchange rate volatility. In addition, the empirical results show that Korea sterilized around 65 percent of capital inflows before the crisis, but it tended to aggressively sterilize the large amount of reserve accumulation during the postcrisis period.

Our empirical results are broadly consistent with the previous empirical studies of the topic. Kim (1990) and Joyce (1991) use ordinary least squares to estimate BOK's monetary reaction function and find that Korea sterilized

---

63. We describe the estimated offset and sterilization coefficients in absolute value terms.

approximately 63–76 percent of capital inflows during the 1960s and 1970s. Cavoli and Rajan (2006) apply this methodology and find that Korea fully sterilized capital inflows from 1990 to mid-1997. Moreno (1996), Takagi and Esaka (1999), Kim, Kim, and Wang (2004), and Oh (2005) use value-at-risk models to examine the extent of sterilization for Korea from the 1980s to the early 2000s. They all find that the BOK heavily sterilized the reserve accumulations during this period. Finally, G. Kim (1995) and Fry (1996) use simultaneous equations to estimate both offset and sterilization coefficients for Korea. G. Kim (1995) finds that the estimated offset coefficient is 0.35, indicating that Korea had relatively low capital mobility during the sample period from 1980 to 1994. Meanwhile, sterilization was around 0.76, suggesting heavy sterilization. Fry (1996) used annual data from 1960 to 1991 and found estimated offset and sterilization coefficients of 0.25 and 0.24, respectively, implying that Korea had relatively low capital mobility and sterilization during this period.

Overall these results are consistent with the view that, as Korea reduced its controls on capital flows, its international financial integration grew more generally over time. Korea has faced substantial international capital mobility, but this has not been sufficiently great to undermine the ability of the BOK to sterilize capital flows efficiently when it desires.

Appendix B

Tables in Support of Appendix A

Table B-1: **Definitions and Measurement of the Variables Used in Empirical Study**

Variables	Definitions	Measured as	Source of data
NFA_t^*	Foreign reserves denominated in domestic currency minus foreign liabilities	Reserve $(\$) \times s_t$ – foreign liabilities	CEIC
ΔNFA_t^*	The annual change in NFA_t^* without revaluation effect scaled by the monetary base (MB)	$[\, NFA_t^* - NFA_{t-12}^*(\frac{s_t}{s_{t-12}})\,]/MB_t$	CEIC
ΔNDA_t^*	The annual change in (net domestic assets + net other assets – capital item) + revaluation effect scaled by the monetary base	$[\Delta_{12}NDA_t + \Delta_{12}NOA_t - \Delta_{12}K_t + NFA_{t-12}^*(\frac{s_t}{s_{t-12}} - 1)\,]/ MB_t$	CEIC
mm_t	Money multiplier for M2	$M2/MB_t$	CEIC
Δmm_t	The change in money multiplier for M2	$Log(mm_t) - Log(mm_{t-12})$	Author's calculation
Δp_t	Inflation rate deviated from the trend	$[\,\pi_t$ – HP filter trend] / HP filter trend	CEIC
$y_{c,t}$	Cyclical income; the real output deviated from its trend scaled by the trend; the trend is measured by Hodrick-Prescott (HP) filter	[Real industrial production – HP filter trend] / HP filter trend	CEIC
$G_{c,t}$	Cyclical government spending; the government spending deviated from its trend scaled by the trend	$[G_t$ – HP filter trend] / HP filter trend	CEIC
$\Delta(r_t^* + E_t s_{t+1})$	The annual change in exchange adjusted foreign interest rate; the foreign interest rate is the interest rate for U.S. three-month treasury bill. $F_{3\text{-}month}$ is the three-month *won* deliverable forward rate	$\Delta_{12}[r_t^* + \ln(s_{t+1})]$ if perfect foresight. $\Delta_{12}[r_t^* + \ln(F_{3\text{-}month})]$ if forward-looking $\Delta_{12}[r_t^* + \ln(s_t)]$ if static expectations	CEIC
$\Delta REER_t$	The annual change in real effective exchange rate (REER)	$Log(REER_t) - Log(REER_{t-12})$	BIS
σ_s	Volatility of exchange rate	The standard deviation of the within monthly change in the daily spot exchange rate	BOK
σ_r	Volatility of domestic interest rate	The standard deviation of the within monthly change in the daily domestic interest rate (uncollateralized call rates rate)	BOK
d_1	Dummy variable for $\Delta NDA < 0$	$d_1=2$ if $\Delta NDA < 0$; 0 otherwise	Author's calculation
d_2	Dummy variable for $\Delta NFA_t < 0$	$d_2=2$ if $\Delta NFA_t < 0$; 0 otherwise	Author's calculation

Notes: BIS = Bank for International Settlements; BOK = Bank of Korea; CEIC = CEIC data.

Table B-2: **Augmented Dickey Fuller (ADF) Unit Roots Test for Korea: Precrisis and Postcrisis Periods**

Variables	Precrisis period (January 1985–June 1997)		Postcrisis period July 1998–October 2008	
	Type of test	ADF statistic (P-value)	Type of test	ADF statistic (P-value)
ΔNDA_t^*	Intercept	−3.009** (0.036)	Intercept and trend	−3.946** (0.013)
ΔNFA_t^*	Intercept	−2.985** (0.039)	Intercept and trend	−3.555** (0.038)
Δmm_t	Intercept	−3.227** (0.020)	none	−3.388*** (0.001)
Δp_t	Intercept and trend	−4.060*** (0.009)	none	−3.516*** (0.001)
$y_{c,t}$	Intercept	−3.059** (0.032)	none	−3.466*** (0.001)
$G_{c,t}$	Intercept	−2.883** (0.050)	none	−5.436*** (0.000)
$\Delta(r_t^* + E_t s_{t+1})$ (perfect foresight)	none	−2.225** (0.026)	none	−2.358** (0.018)
$\Delta(r_t^* + E_t s_{t+1})$ (forward-looking expectations)	—	—	none	−1.034 (0.270)
$\Delta(r_t^* + E_t s_{t+1})$ (static expectations)	none	−2.175** (0.030)	none	−3.026*** (0.003)
$\Delta REER_t$	none	−2.341** (0.020)	none	−3.683*** (0.000)
$(d_2 - 1)\sigma_s$	Intercept	−8.266*** (0.000)	Intercept and trend	−4.381*** (0.003)
$(d_1 - 1)\sigma_r$	none	−4.797*** (0.000)	Intercept	−9.833*** (0.000)

Source: Author's estimations.

Notes: * = significant at more than 10 percent; ** = significant at more than 5 percent; *** = significant at more than 1 percent. The null hypothesis of ADF test is that H_0: variable has a unit root.

Table B-3: Estimated Simultaneous Equations for Korea January 1985–June 1997 and July 1998–October 2008

	Three types of expectations											
	Perfect foresight: $E_t s_{t+1} = \ln(s_{t+1})$				Forward exchange rate: $E_t s_{t+1} = \ln(F_{3M,t})$				Static expectation: $E_t s_{t+1} = \ln(s_t)$			
	Jan. 1985–June 1997		July 1998–Oct. 2008		Jan. 1985–June 1997		July 1998–Oct. 2008		Jan. 1985–June 1997		July 1998–Oct. 2008	
Variables	ΔNFA_t^*	ΔNDA_t^*	ΔNFA_t^*	ΔNDA_t^*	ΔNFA_t^*	ΔNDA_t^*	ΔNFA_t^*	ΔNDA_t^*	ΔNFA_t^*	ΔNDA_t^*	ΔNFA_t^*	ΔNDA_t^*
Intercept	0.125*** (0.011)	0.087*** (0.018)	0.190*** (0.042)	0.061 (0.058)	—	—	0.179*** (0.045)	0.013 (0.058)	0.124*** (0.011)	0.090*** (0.018)	0.186*** (0.042)	0.076 (0.057)
ΔNDA_t^*	-0.509*** (0.067)	—	-0.668*** (0.057)	—	—	—	-0.660*** (0.063)	—	-0.489*** (0.066)	—	-0.680*** (0.055)	—
ΔNFA_t^*	—	-0.629*** (0.095)	—	-1.089*** (0.086)	—	—	—	-1.014*** (0.088)	—	-0.648*** (0.098)	—	-1.115*** (0.084)
Δmm_t	0.550*** (0.113)	-0.892*** (0.104)	1.157*** (0.215)	-1.176*** (0.277)	—	—	1.140*** (0.274)	-0.731** (0.338)	0.516*** (0.111)	0.867*** (0.107)	1.137*** (0.214)	1.246*** (0.271)
Δp_{t-1}	-0.072* (0.037)	0.167*** (0.037)	-0.110 (0.076)	-0.094 (0.090)	—	—	-0.099 (0.086)	-0.096 (0.098)	-0.068* (0.037)	0.166*** (0.039)	-0.105 (0.077)	-0.092 (0.092)
$y_{c,t-1}$	0.579*** (0.196)	-0.289 (0.216)	-0.569 (0.411)	-0.525 (0.465)	—	—	-0.657 (0.452)	-0.751 (0.499)	0.599*** (0.196)	-0.351 (0.222)	-0.539 (0.412)	-0.577 (0.469)
$G_{c,t}$	0.012 (0.026)	0.005 (0.028)	-0.017 (0.076)	-0.043 (0.092)	—	—	-0.040 (0.082)	-0.035 (0.094)	0.013 (0.026)	0.009 (0.028)	-0.013 (0.076)	-0.041 (0.093)
$\Delta(r_t^* + E_t s_{t+1})$	0.141 (0.238)	1.590*** (0.206)	-0.392 (0.264)	0.187 (0.325)	—	—	-0.457 (0.411)	0.227 (0.477)	0.031 (0.246)	1.560*** (0.226)	-0.454 (0.357)	-0.002 (0.412)
$\Delta REER_{t-1}$	0.138 (0.124)	0.359*** (0.130)	-0.136 (0.294)	-0.191 (0.343)	—	—	-0.065 (0.410)	-0.249 (0.473)	0.144 (0.124)	-0.248* (0.136)	-0.274 (0.360)	-0.267 (0.432)
$(d_2-1)\sigma_{s,t-1}$	0.013*** (0.004)	—	-0.003 (0.002)	—	—	—	-0.005 (0.003)	—	0.013*** (0.004)	—	-0.003 (0.002)	—
$(d_1-1)\sigma_{r,t-1}$	—	0.031*** (0.012)	—	0.259* (0.152)	—	—	—	0.719 (0.460)	—	-0.030** (0.012)	—	0.236 (0.150)
R-square	0.653	0.741	0.778	0.725	—	—	0.727	0.687	0.651	0.725	0.777	0.719
Adj. R-square	0.634	0.726	0.762	0.706	—	—	0.706	0.663	0.631	0.709	0.761	0.700

Source: Author's estimations.

Notes: * = significant at more than 10 percent; ** = significant at more than 5 percent; *** = significant at more than 1 percent. The simultaneous equations are estimated by two-stage least squares (2SLS).

References

Agenor, P. R., et al., eds. 1999. *The Asian Financial Crisis: Causes, Contagion and Consequences.* New York: Cambridge University Press.

Ahn, B. C. 2008. "Capital Flows and Effects on Financial Markets in Korea: Developments and Policy Responses." Paper no. 44. Basel: Bank for International Settlements.

Ahn, C., H. Kim, and D. Chang. 2006. "Is East Asia Fit for an Optimum Currency Area? An Assessment of the Economic Feasibility of a Higher Degree of Monetary Cooperation in East Asia." *Developing Economies* 44: 288–305.

Aizenman, J., and J. Lee. 2007. "International Reserves." *Open Economies Review* 18: 191–214.

Andrews, D. 2008. "The Political Geography of German Monetary Leadership." Paper presented at workshop on European integration, Scripps College, Claremont, California.

Andrews, D., and T. D. Willett. 1997. "Financial Interdependence and the State." *International Organization* (Summer): 479–511.

Angkinand, P., E. Chiu, and T. D. Willett. 2009. "Testing the Unstable Middle and Two Corners Hypotheses about Exchange Rate Regimes." *Open Economies Review* 20: 61–83.

Asia and Pacific Department. 2008. "Korea Adapts to Changing Landscape." *IMF Survey,* January.

Auerbach, N. N. 2001. *States, Banks, and Markets: Mexico's Path to Financial Liberalization in Comparative Perspective.* Boulder, Colo.: Westview.

Baek, S., and C. Song. 2001. "Is Currency Union a Feasible Option in East Asia?" In *Currency Union in East Asia,* ed. H. G. Choo and Y.

Wang, 107–45. Seoul: Korea Institute for International Economic Policy.

Bayoumi, T., and B. Eichengreen. 1994. "One Money or Many? Analyzing the Prospects for Monetary Unification in Various Parts of the World." *Princeton Studies in International Finance,* no. 76.

Bekaert, G., and C. R. Harvey. 2004. "A Chronology of Important Financial, Economic and Political Events in Emerging Markets—Korea." Country Risk Analysis, Fuqua School of Business, Duke University, Durham, N.C. http://www.duke.edu/~charvey/Country_risk/chronology/korea.htm.

Bird, G. 2003. *The IMF and the Future: Issues and Options Facing the Fund.* London: Routledge.

Bird, G., and T. D. Willett. 2007. "Multilateral Surveillance: Is the IMF Shooting for the Stars?" *World Economy* 8 (October–December): 167–89.

Boorman, J., T. Lane, M. Schulze-Ghattas, A. Bulíy, and A. R. Ghosh. 2000. "Managing Financial Crises: The Experience in East Asia." Working Paper no. 00/107. Washington, D.C.: International Monetary Fund.

Brissimis, S., H. Gibson, and E. Tsakalotos. 2002. "A Unifying Framework for Analyzing Offsetting Capital Flows and Sterilization: Germany and the ERM." *International Journal of Finance and Economics* 7: 63–78.

Bubula, A., and I. Ötker-Robe. 2003. "Are Pegged and Intermediate Exchange Rate Regimes More Crisis-prone?" Working Paper no. WP/03/223. Washington, D.C.: International Monetary Fund.

Burdekin, R. C. K., A. T. Denzau, M. W. Keil, T. Sitthiyot, T. D. Willett. 2004. "When Does Inflation Hurt Economic Growth? Different Nonlinearities for Different Economies." *Journal of Macroeconomics* 26: 519–32.

Burdekin, R. C. K., and P. Siklos. 2004. "Fears of Deflation and the Role of Monetary Policy: Some Lessons and an Overview." In *Deflation: Current and Historical Perspectives,* ed. R. C. K. Burdekin and P. Siklos, 1–27. New York: Cambridge University Press.

Bussiere, M. 1999. "External Vulnerability in Emerging Market Economies: How High Liquidity Can Offset Weak Fundamentals and the Effects of Contagion." Working Paper no. 99/88. Washington, D.C.: International Monetary Fund.

Calvo, G. A., A. Izquierdo, and L. F. Mejía. 2008. "Systemic Sudden Stops: The Relevance of Balance-Sheet Effects and Financial Integration." Working Paper no. 14026. Cambridge, Mass.: National Bureau of Economic Research.

Calvo, G. A., and C. Reinhart. 2002. "Fear of Floating." *Quarterly Journal of Economics* 117: 379–409.

Cargill, T. 2009. "The Impact of U.S. Financial and Economic Distress on South Korea." *Korea's Economy 2009* 25: 15–24.

Cargill, T., and F. Guerrero. 2007. "Bank of Korea Policy and the Asset Bubble Problem." *Korea's Economy 2007* 23: 8–18.

Cavoli, T., and R. S. Rajan 2006. "The Capital Inflows Problem in Selected Asian Economies in the 1990s Revisited: The Role of Monetary Sterilization." *Asian Economic Journal* 20: 409–23.

Chang, H. J., H. J. Park, and C. G. Yoo. 1998. "Interpreting the Korean Crisis: Financial Liberalization, Industrial Policy, and Corporate Governance." *Cambridge Journal of Economics* 22: 735–46.

Chinn, M., and H. Ito. 2006. "What Matters for Financial Development? Capital Controls, Institutions, and Interactions." *Journal of Development Economics* 81: 163–92.

Choi, G. 2007. "Toward an Exchange Rate Mechanism for Emerging Asia." In *Toward an East Asian Exchange Rate Regime,* ed. D. K. Chung and B. Eichengreen. Washington, D.C.: Brookings Institution Press.

Chosun Ilbo. 2008. "Spent Tens of Billions of Dollars to Learn That Touching 'Exchange Rates' Leads to Ill Results [editorial, in Korean]." 23 November. http://news.chosun.com/site/data/html_dir/2008/11/23/2008112300724.html

Chung, T. S. 2007. "2007 National Audit—Post-Exchange Rate Crises Fifty Trillion Won Loss Just from Exchange Rate Defense [in

Korean]." eDaily, 17 October. http://news.empas.com/show.tsp/
cp_ed/20071017n07089/.

Cohen, B. 1996. "Phoenix Risen: The Resurrection of Global Finance."
World Politics 48: 268–96.

De Grauwe, P. 2003. *Economics of Monetary Union.* New York: Oxford
University Press.

De Grauwe, P., and F. P. Mongelli. 2005. "Endogeneities of Optimum
Currency Areas: What Brings Countries Sharing a Single Currency
Closer Together?" Working Paper no. 468. Frankfurt: European
Central Bank.

Dekle, R., and A. Ubide. 1998. "Korea: Financial Sector Development and
Reform," Unpublished manuscript, International Monetary Fund,
Washington, D.C.

Demetriades, P., and B. Fattouh. 1999. "The South Korean Financial
Crisis: Competing Explanations and Policy Lessons for Financial
Liberalization." *International Affairs* 75: 779–92.

Desai, P. 2003. *Financial Crisis, Contagion, and Containment: From Asia
to Argentina.* Princeton: Princeton University Press.

Dooley, M., R. Dornbusch, and Y. C. Park. 2002. "A Framework for
Exchange Rate Policy in Korea," in *Korean Crisis and Recovery,*
ed. David T. Coe and Se-Jik Kim. Washington, D.C.: International
Monetary Fund; Seoul: Korea Institute for International Economic
Policy.

Dooley, M., and J. Frankel, eds. 2003. *Managing Currency Crises in
Emerging Markets.* Chicago: University of Chicago Press.

Dooley, M., and I. Shin. 2000. "Private Inflows When Crises Are
Anticipated: A Case Study of Korea." Working Paper no. 7992.
Cambridge, Mass.: National Bureau of Economic Research.

Dougherty, C. 2008. "Some Nations That Spurned the Euro Reconsider."
New York Times, 2 December.

Dwor-Frécaut, D. 2008. "Korea's Money Market." *Korea's Economy 2008*
24: 21–30.

Economist. 2008. "No Room in the Ark: The Euro May Not Be Quite as a Safe Haven as Enthusiasts are Claiming." *Economist,* 15 November.

Edwards, S., and J. A. Frankel, eds. 2002. *Preventing Currency Crises in Emerging Markets.* Chicago: University of Chicago Press.

Eichengreen, B. 1999. *Toward A New International Financial Architecture: A Practical Post-Asia Agenda.* Washington, D.C.: Institute for International Economics.

———. 2002. *Financial Crises and What to Do about Them.* New York: Oxford University Press.

———. 2004. "Monetary and Exchange Rate Policy in Korea: Assessments and Policy Issues." Discussion Paper no. 4676. Washington, D.C.: Center for Economic and Policy Research.

———. 2007a. "European Integration: What Lessons for Asia?" Paper prepared for Asian Development Bank project on Asian regionalism and presented to project workshop in Bangkok, July.

———. 2007b. "The Breakup of the Euro Area." Presentation to the NBER Summer Institute Preconference for the Project on the Euro, 12 July.

Fischer, S. 1999. "On the Need for an International Lender of Last Resort." *Journal of Economic Perspectives* 13 (4): 85–104.

Frankel, J. 2004. "Experience of and Lessons from Exchange Rate Regimes in Emerging Economies." In *Monetary and Financial Integration in East Asia: The Way Ahead,* vol. 2, part 1, ed. Asian Development Bank. New York: Palgrave Macmillan.

Friedman, M. 1953. "The Case for Flexible Exchange Rates." In *Essays in Positive Economics,* 157–203. Chicago: University of Chicago Press.

Fry, M. J. 1996. "Inflation and Monetary Policy in Pacific Basin Developing Economies." Unpublished manuscript.

Furman, J., and J. E. Stiglitz. 1998. "Economic Crises: Evidence and Insights from East Asia." *Brookings Papers on Economic Activity—2* 29: 1–114.

Genberg, H., and D. He. 2007. "Monetary and Financial Cooperation among Central Banks in East Asia and the Pacific." Paper presented at Claremont-Bologna-SCAPE Policy Forum on Capital Flows, Financial Markets, and Economic Integration in Asia, National University of Singapore, 30–31 July.

Goldstein, M. 2002. "Managed Floating Plus." *Policy Analyses in International Economics.* London: Routledge for Institute for International Economics.

Goldstein, M., and N. Lardy, eds. 2008. *Debating China's Exchange Rate Policy.* Washington, D.C.: Peterson Institute for International Economics.

Goodman, J., and L. Pauly. 1993. "The Obsolescence of Capital Controls? Economic Management in an Age of Global Markets." *World Politics* 46: 50–82.

Grieco, J. 1997. "Systemic Sources of Variation in Regional Institutionalization in Western Europe, East Asia, and the Americas." In *The Political Economy of Regionalism,* ed. E. D. Mansfield and H. V. Milner. New York: Columbia University Press.

Gros, D., and N. Thygensen. 1998. *European Monetary Integration.* New York: St. Martin's Press.

Haas, E. B. 1958. *The Uniting of Europe: Political, Social, and Economic Forces,* 1950–57. Stanford, Calif.: Stanford University Press.

Haggard, S. 2000. *The Political Economy of the Asian Financial Crisis.* Washington D.C.: Institute for International Economics.

Haggard, S., and J. Mo. 2000. "The Political Economy of the Korean Financial Crisis." *Review of International Political Economy* 7: 197–218.

Han, P. 2009. "Is East Asia an Optimum Currency Area? Evidence from the Application of Various OCA Criteria." Ph.D. dissertation, Claremont Graduate University, Claremont, California.

Hernández, L., and P. J. Montiel. 2003. "Post-Crisis Exchange Rate Policy in Five Asian Countries: Filling in the 'Hollow Middle'?" *Journal of the Japanese and International Economics* 17: 336–69.

Horowitz, S., and U. Heo, eds. 2001. *The Political Economy of International Financial Crisis: Interest Groups, Ideologies and Institutions.* Lanham, Md.: Rowman and Littlefield.

IEO (Independent Evaluation Office). 2005. "The IMF's Approach to Capital Account Liberalization." Washington, D.C.: International Monetary Fund.

————. 2007. "IMF Exchange Rate Policy Advice." Washington, D.C.: International Monetary Fund.

Ilzetzki, E. O., C. M. Reinhart, and K. S. Rogoff. 2008. "Exchange Rate Arrangements into the 21st Century: Will the Anchor Currency Hold?" Working paper.

Ito, T., and Y. C. Park. 2004. "Exchange Rate Regimes in East Asia." In *Monetary and Financial Integration in East Asia: The Way Ahead,* vol. 1, ed. Asian Development Bank. New York: Palgrave Macmillan.

Jadresic, E. 2007. "The Cost-Benefit Approach to Reserve Adequacy: The Case of Chile." In *Central Bank Reserve Management: New Trends, from Liquidity to Return,* ed. Age F. P. Bakker and Ingmar R. Y. van Herpt. Northampton, Mass.: Edward Elgar.

Jeanne, O., and R. Ranciere. 2006. "The Optimal Level of International Reserves for Emerging Market Countries: Formulas and Applications." Working Paper no. 06/229. Washington, D.C.: International Monetary Fund.

Joyce, J. 1991. "An Examination of the Objectives of Monetary Policy in Four Developing Economies." *World Development* 19: 705–9.

Kang, M. K. 2009. "Global Financial Crisis and Systemic Risks in the Korean Banking Sector." Academic Paper Series 4, no. 5. Washington, D.C.: Korea Economic Institute.

Katz, S. 1999. "The Asian Crisis, the IMF and the Critics." *Eastern Economic Journal* 25: 421–39.

Kawai, M. 2007. "Dollar, Yen, or Renminbi Bloc?" In *Toward an East Asian Exchange Rate Regime,* ed. D. Chung and B. Eichengreen, 90–119. Washington, D.C.: Brookings Institution Press.

Keil, M., A. Phalapleewan, R. S. Rajan, and T. D. Willett. 2004. "Estimating Interest Rate Interdependence in East Asia." In proceedings of conference, Monetary and Exchange Rate Arrangements in East Asia, ed. Y. Oh, D. R. Yoon, and T. D. Willett, Korea Institute of International Economic Policy, Seoul.

Keil, M., R. S. Rajan, and T. D. Willett. 2009. "Financial Interdependence, Capital Mobility and Monetary and Exchange Rate Cooperation in Asia." Paper presented at conference on Asian economic integration, Bangkok, November 2008; and Asia-Pacific Economic Association, Santa Cruz, California, June 2009. Undergoing revision.

Kim, G. 1995. "Exchange Rate Constraints and Money Control in Korea." Working Paper no. 1995-011A. St. Louis: Federal Reserve Bank of St. Louis.

Kim, J. B. 2008. "Improving Transparency in Financial Market." Korea Times, 9 May. http://news.naver.com/main/read.nhn?mode=LSD&mid=sec&sid1=001&oid=044&aid=0000073462&.

Kim, J. I. 2002. "Comments on 'A Framework for Exchange Rate Policy in Korea.'" in Korean Crisis and Recovery, ed. D. T. Coe and S. J. Kim. Washington, D.C.: IMF and Korea Institute for International Economic Policy.

Kim, J. K. 2008. "Banks Face Lawsuits for Overseas Fund Loss." Korea Times, 5 November. www.koreatimes.co.kr/www/news/biz/2008/11/123_33923.html.

Kim, J. S. 1990. "The Behavior of Korean Exchange Rate and Monetary Policy." Ph.D. dissertation, Claremont Graduate University, Claremont, California.

Kim, J. S., J. Li, R. Rajan, O. Sula, and T. D. Willett. 2004. "Reserve Adequacy in Asia." In proceedings of conference, Monetary and Exchange Rate Arrangements in East Asia, ed. Y. Oh, D. R. Yoon, and T. D. Willett, Korea Institute of International Economic Policy, Seoul.

Kim, K. S. 2008. "Opening Up to Capital Flows Poses Challenges." Korea Times, 31 December. http://news.naver.com/main/read.nhn?mode=LSD&mid=sec&sid1=001&oid=044&aid=0000079529&.

Kim, K., B. K. Kim, and Y. K. Suh. 2009. "Opening to Capital Flows and Implication for Korea." Working Paper no. 363. Seoul: Bank of Korea, Institute for Monetary and Economic Research.

Kim, S., S. H. Kim, and Y. Wang. 2004. "Macroeconomic Effects of Capital Account Liberalization: The Case of Korea." *Review of Development Economics* 8: 624–39.

Kim, S., and W. Kim. 1999. "Recent Developments in Monetary Policy Operating Procedures: the Korean Case." Policy Papers. Basel: Bank for International Settlements.

Kim, S., and D. Y. Yang. 2008. "Managing Capital Flows: The Case of the Republic of Korea." Discussion Paper no. 88. Tokyo: Asian Development Bank Institute.

Krueger, A. 2002. "Comments on 'A Framework for Exchange Rate Policy in Korea.'" in *Korean Crisis and Recovery,* ed. D. T. Coe and S. J. Kim. Washington, D.C.: IMF and Korea Institute for International Economic Policy.

Krueger, A., and J. Yoo. 2002. "Chaebol Capitalism and the Currency Crisis in Korea." In *Preventing Currency Crises in Emerging Markets,* ed. S. Edwards and J. A. Frankel. Chicago: University of Chicago Press.

Lall, S., and L. L. Eskesen. 2009. "Korea's Near-Term Economic Prospects and Challenges." *Korea's Economy 2009* 25: 1–7.

Lee, C., K. Lee, and K. Lee. 2000. "Chaebol, Financial Liberalization, and Economic Crisis: Transformation of Quasi-Internal Organization in Korea." Unpublished manuscript, University of Hawaii at Manoa, Department of Economics.

Lee, J. Y. 2008. "Korea's Way Out of Financial Crisis," *Korea Times,* 4 April. http://news.naver.com/main/read.nhn?mode=LSD&mid=sec&sid1=001&oi d=044&aid=0000072416&.

Lee, S. K. 2006. "The Year's Top Ten News in Seoul Foreign Exchange Market [in Korean]." eInfoMax, 18 December. www.einfomax.com/Smart/SmartHome/main.aspx.

Levchenko, A., and P. Mauro. 2007. "Do Some Forms of Financial Flows Help Protect against 'Sudden Stops'?" *World Bank Economic Review* 21: 389–411.

Levy-Yeyati, E., and F. Sturzenegger. 2005. "Classifying Exchange Rate Regimes: Deeds vs. Words." *European Economic Review* 49 (August): 1603–35.

Li, J., O. Sula, and T. D. Willett. 2008. "Exchange Rate Regimes and Optimal Reserve Holdings in a World of Capital Account Crises." In *China and Asia: Economic and Financial Interactions,* ed. Y. W. Cheung and K. Y. Wong. New York: Routledge.

Lister, J. 2009. "IMF's Annual Assessment of Korea's Economy: Praise—with Some Suggestions." *Korea Insight,* 1 September.

Loayza, N., H. Lopez, and A. Ubide. 2001. "Comovements and Sectoral Interdependence: Evidence for Latin America, East Asia, and Europe." *IMF Staff Papers* 48: 367–96.

Lowe-Lee, F. 2009. "Economy: U Shape or W Shape Recovery?" *Korea Insight,* 1 May.

Mansfield, E. D., and H. V. Milner, eds. 1997. *The Political Economy of Regionalism.* New York: Columbia University Press.

Marsh, D. 2009. The Euro: *The Politics of the New Global Currency.* New Haven: Yale University Press.

Martin, P., J. Westbrook, and T. D. Willett. 1999. "Exchange Rate Based Stabilization in Latin America." In *Exchange-Rate Policies for Emerging Market Economies,* ed. R. Sweeney, C. Wihlborg, and T. D. Willett. Boulder, Colo.: Westview.

McCauley, R. N. 2007. "Assessing the Benefits and Costs of Official Foreign Exchange Reserves." In *Central Bank Reserve Management: New Trends, from Liquidity to Return,* ed. Age F. P. Bakker and Ingmar R. Y. van Herpt. Northampton, Mass.: Edward Elgar.

McKibbin, W. J., J. W. Lee, and Y. C. Park. 2004. "The Transpacific Imbalance: An East Asian Perspective." Paper presented at session on global imbalances and East Asia's exchange rate policy, Western Economic Association International conference, Vancouver, B.C.

McKinnon, R. 1982. "Currency Substitution and Instability in the World Dollar Standard." *American Economic Review* 3: 320–33.

———. 2005. *Exchange Rates under the East Asian Dollar Standard: Living with Conflicted Virtue.* Cambridge: MIT Press.

McKinnon, R., and G. Schnabl. 2004. "The East Asian Dollar Standard, Fear of Floating, and Original Sin." *Review of Development Economics* 8: 331–60.

McNamara, K. 1998. *The Currency of Ideas: Monetary Politics in the European Union.* Ithaca, N.Y.: Cornell University Press.

Mishkin, F. S. 2006. *The Next Great Globalization: How Disadvantaged Nations Can Harness Their Financial Systems to Get Rich.* Princeton: Princeton University Press.

Moreno, R. 1996. "Intervention, Sterilization and Monetary Control in Korea and Taiwan." *FRBSF Economic Review* 3: 23–33.

Mundell, R. 2003. "Prospects for an Asian Currency Area." *Journal of Asian Economics* 14: 1–10.

Noble, G. W., and J. Ravenhill, eds. 2000. *The Asian Financial Crisis and the Architecture of Global Finance.* New York: Cambridge University Press.

Noland, M. 2005. "South Korea's Experience with International Capital Flows." Working Paper no. 11381. Cambridge, Mass.: National Bureau of Economic Research.

Oh, J. 2005. "Sterilized Intervention and Effectiveness of Monetary Policy in a Small Open Emerging Economy: The Korean Experience." Paper presented at Western Economic Association International conference, San Francisco, 9–13 July.

Ouyang, A. Y., R. S. Rajan, and T. D. Willett. 2008. "Managing the Monetary Consequences of Reserve Accumulation in Emerging Asia." *Global Economic Review* 37 (June): 171–99.

Park, Y. C., C. S. Chung, and Y. Wang. 2001. "Fear of Floating: Korea's Exchange Rate Policy after the Crisis." *Journal of the Japanese and International Economies* 15 (June): 225–51.

Parsley, D., and II. Popper. 2009. "Evaluating Exchange Rate Objectives in Monetary Policy Rules: An Application to Korea." Presentation at 2009 annual meetings of Asia Pacific Economic Association and Western Economic Association International.

Pempel, T. J., ed. 1999. *The Politics of the Asian Economic Crisis.* Ithaca, N.Y.: Cornell University Press.

Permpoon, O. 2008. "Essay in OCA Analysis: An OCA in East Asia." Ph.D. dissertation, Claremont Graduate University, Claremont, California.

Pontines, V., and R. S. Rajan. 2008. "The Asian Currency Unit (ACU): Exploring Alternative Currency Weights." *Macroeconomics and Finance in Emerging Market Economies* 1: 269–78.

Posner, R. A. 2009. *A Failure of Capitalism: The Crisis of '08 and the Descent into Depression.* Cambridge: Harvard University Press.

Potchamanawong, P. 2007. "A New Measurement of Capital Controls and Its Relation to Currency Crises." Ph.D. dissertation, Claremont Graduate University, Claremont, California.

Potchamanawong, P., A. Denzau, S. Rongala, J. Walton, and T. D. Willett. 2008. "Capital Controls." In *The Design and Use of Political Economy Indicators: Challenges of Definition, Aggregation, and Application,* ed. K. Banaian and B. Roberts. New York: Palgrave Macmillan.

Radelet, S., and J. D. Sachs. 1998. "The East Asian Financial Crisis: Diagnosis, Remedies, Prospects." *Brookings Papers on Economic Activity—1* 28: 1–74.

Rakshit, M. 2002. *The East Asian Currency Crisis.* Oxford: Oxford University Press.

Reinhart, C. M., and V. R. Reinhart. 2008. "Capital Flow Bonanzas: An Encompassing View of the Past and Present." Working Paper no. 14321. Cambridge, Mass.: National Bureau of Economic Research.

Reinhart, C. M., and K. S. Rogoff. 2004. "The Modern History of Exchange Rate Arrangements: A Reinterpretation." *Quarterly Journal of Economics* 119: 1–48.

Researchers of the KIF (Korea Institute of Finance). 2008. "Post-Crisis Vision of Korea's Financial Industry." *Korea Herald,* 18 June. http://news.naver.com/main/read.nhn?mode=LSD&mid=sec&sid1=001&oid=044&aid=0000074684&.

Rhee, G. J., and E. M. Lee. 2005. "Foreign Exchange Intervention and Foreign Exchange Market Development in Korea." In *Foreign Exchange Market Intervention in Emerging Markets: Motives, Techniques and Implications,* 24: 196–208. Basel: Bank for International Settlements.

Rhee, J. C. 1994. *The State and Industry in South Korea: The Limits of the Authoritarian State.* New York: Routledge.

Ruiz-Arranz, M., and M. Zavadjil. 2008. "Are Emerging Asia's Reserves Really Too High?" Working Paper no. WP/08/192. Washington, D.C.: International Monetary Fund.

Sandholtz, W., and A. S. Sweet. 1998. *European Integration and Supranational Governance.* New York: Oxford University Press.

Schaechter, A., M. Stone, and M. Zeimer. 2000. "Adopting Inflation Targeting: Practical Issues for Emerging Market Economies." Occasional Paper no. 202. Washington, D.C.: International Monetary Fund.

Schindler, M. 2009. "Measuring Financial Integration: A New Data Set," *IMF Staff Papers* 56: 222–38.

Schmitter, P. 2004. "Neofunctionalism." In *European Integration Theory,* ed. A. Wiener and T. Diez. New York: Oxford University Press.

Siklos, P. 2000. "Capital Flows in a Transitional Economy and the Sterilization Dilemma: The Hungarian Experience, 1992–97." *Journal of Policy Reform* 3: 413–38.

Sompornserm, T. 2009. "Financial Liberalization and International Capital Flows." Paper presented at 84th annual conference, Western Economic Association International, 29 June–3 July 2009, Vancouver, B.C.

Song, J. E. 2008. "Currency Market Needs Full-Blown Liberalization." *Korea Times,* 2 May. http://news. naver.com/main/read.nhn?mode=LSD&mid=sec&sid =001&oid=044&aid=0000073240&.

Srisorn, L., and T. D. Willett. 2009. "Neofunctionalist Spillover Theory and Endogenous OCA Analysis: Lessons from Europe for Asia." Paper presented at the European Union Studies Association international conference, Los Angeles, 23–25 April.

Suh, C. B., and J. H. Koo. 2008. "Recipe for Success of Financial Conglomerates." *Korea Times,* 7 May. http://news.naver.com/ main/read.nhn?mode=LSD&mid=sec&sid1=001&oid=044&ai d=0000073383&.

Sula, O., and T. D. Willett. 2009. "The Reversibility of Different Types of Capital Flows to Emerging Markets." *Emerging Markets Review.*

Takagi, S., and T. Esaka. 1999. "Sterilization and the Capital Inflow Problem in East Asia, 1987–97." Discussion Paper no. 86. Economic Planning Agency, Economic Research Institute, Tokyo.

Tan, A. C., and C. Schneider. Forthcoming. "Pluralization of Politics, Win-sets, and Perverse Financial Liberalization: The Case of Taiwan." In *Governance in a New Democracy: The Case of Taiwan,* ed. John F. S. Hsieh. Armonk, N.Y.: M. E. Sharpe.

Truman, E. M. 2004. *Inflation Targeting in the World Economy.* Washington, D.C.: Institute for International Economics.

———. 2006. "A Strategy for IMF Reform." *Policy Analyses in International Economics* no. 77. Washington, D.C.: Institute for International Economics.

———. 2009. "The IMF and the Global Crisis: Role and Reform." Remarks to the Tulsa Committee on Foreign Relations, 22 January; and to the Dallas Committee on Foreign Relations, 23 January.

Ungerer, H. 1997. *A Concise History of European Monetary Integration: From EPU to EMU.* Westport, Conn.: Quorum Books.

Watanabe, S., and M. Ogura. 2006. "How Far Apart Are Two ACUs from Each Other? Asian Currency Unit and Asian Currency Union." Working Paper no. 06-E-20. Tokyo: Bank of Japan.

Westbrook, J., and T. D. Willett. 1999. "Exchange Rates as Nominal Anchors." In *Exchange-Rate Policies for Emerging Market Economies,* ed. R. Sweeney, C. Wihlborg, and T. D. Willett. Boulder, Colo.: Westview.

Wihlborg, C., T. D. Willett, and N. Zhang. 2009. "Real Exchange Rate Movements and Endogenous OCA Analysis." Paper presented at the European Union Studies Association international conference, Los Angeles, 23–25 April.

Wijnholds, J. O., and A. Kapteyn. 2001. "Reserve Adequacy in Emerging Market Economies." Working Paper no. WP/01/143. Washington, D.C.: International Monetary Fund.

Willett, T. D. 1977. *Floating Exchange Rates and International Monetary Reform.* Washington, D.C.: American Enterprise Institute.

———, ed. 1988. *Political Business Cycles: The Political Economy of Money, Inflation, and Unemployment.* Durham, N.C.: Duke University Press.

———. 2000. "International Financial Markets as Sources of Crisis or Discipline: The Too Much, Too Late Hypothesis." *Princeton Essays in International Finance,* no. 218 (May).

———. 2002. "Crying for Argentina." *Milken Institute Review* (2nd qtr.): 50–59.

———. 2003a. "Fear of Floating Needn't Imply Fixed Rates: An OCA Approach to the Operation of Stable Intermediate Currency Regimes." *Open Economies Review* 14: 71–91.

———. 2003b. "The OCA Approach to Exchange Rate Regimes: A Perspective on Recent Development." In *The Dollarization Debate,* ed. D. Salvatore, J. W. Dean, and T. D. Willett. New York: Oxford University Press.

———. 2006. "The IMF and Capital Account Crisis: The Case for a Separate Lender of Last Resort and Conditionality Functions." In *Globalization and the Nation State: The Impact of the IMF and the World Bank,* ed. G. Ranis, J. R. Vreeland, and S. Kosak, 351–71. New York: Routledge.

————. 2007. "Why the Middle Is Unstable: The Political Economy of Exchange Rate Regimes and Currency Crises." *World Economy* 30 (May): 709–32.

Willett, T. D., M. Keil, and Y. S. Ahn. 2002. "Capital Mobility for Developing Countries May Not Be So High." *Journal of Development Economics* 68: 421–34.

Willett, T. D., and Y. Kim. 2006. "Korea's Postcrisis Exchange Rate Policy." *Korea's Economy 2006* 22: 5–15.

Willett, T. D., E. Nitithanprapas, I. Nitithanprapas, and S. Rongala. 2005. "The Asian Crises Re-Examined." *Asian Economic Papers* 3: 32–87.

Willett, T. D., I. Nitithanprapas, and Y. Kim. 2008. "Taking Seriously the Concept of Exchange Market Pressure for Classifying Exchange Rate Regimes: A Two-Parameter Approach." Working paper, Claremont Graduate University, Claremont, California.

Willett, T. D., O. Permpoon, and L. Srisorn. Forthcoming. "Asian Monetary Cooperation: Perspectives from the Optimum Currency Area Analysis." *Singapore Economic Review.*

Willett, T. D., O. Permpoon, and C. Wihlborg. 2008. "Endogenous OCA Analysis and the Early Euro Experience." Working paper, Claremont Graduate University, Claremont, California.

Williamson, John. 2000. *Exchange Rate Regimes for Emerging Markets: Reviving the Intermediate Option.* Washington, D.C.: Institute for International Economics.

Wolf, M. 2009. "Central Banks Must Target More Than Just Inflation." *Financial Times,* 5 May.

Wyplosz, C. 2001. "A Monetary Union in Asia? Some European Lessons." Paper prepared for conference, "Future Directions for Monetary Policy in East Asia," Reserve Bank of Australia, 24 July.

About the Author

Thomas Willett is the Horton Professor Economics and Director of the Claremont Institute for Economic Studies in the Department of Economics, Claremont Graduate University and Claremont McKenna College. Areas of specialization include international and monetary economics, political economy, and economic policy, international financial crises and public choice or political economy analysis of national and international economic policies. A major facet of his professional activity has been to improve the dialogue between economists and political scientists. He is the Director of the Claremont Institute for Economic Policy Studies, and former head of the International Research Department at the U.S. Treasury. He earned his Ph.D in Economics at the University of Virginia.